THE LAST LIBERAL
&
OTHER ESSAYS

ALSO BY RAMACHANDRA GUHA

The Unquiet Woods: Ecological Change and Peasant Resistance in the Himalaya

Wickets in the East

Spin and Other Turns

Savaging the Civilized: Verrier Elwin, His Tribals, and India

Environmentalism: A Global History

The Use and Abuse of Nature (with Madhav Gadgil)

An Anthropologist among the Marxists and Other Essays

The Picador Book of Cricket (edited)

A Corner of a Foreign Field: The Indian History of a British Sport

THE LAST LIBERAL
&
OTHER ESSAYS

Ramachandra Guha

permanent black

Published by
PERMANENT BLACK
D-28 Oxford Apartments, 11, I.P. Extension,
Delhi 110092

In association with
RAVI DAYAL PUBLISHER
E-51, Sujan Singh Park,
New Delhi 110003

Distributed by
ORIENT LONGMAN PRIVATE LTD
Bangalore Bhopal Bhubaneshwar Chandigarh
Chennai Ernakulam Guwahati Hyderabad Jaipur
Kolkata Lucknow Mumbai New Delhi Patna

ISBN 81-7824-073-4

Typeset in Adobe Garamond
by Guru Typograph Technology, Dwarka, New Delhi 110045
Printed by Pauls Press, New Delhi 110020
Binding by Saku

For Keshav Desiraju and Gopal Gandhi
the most *civilized* of civil servants

Contents

Acknowledgements

Behind every published writer are some risk-taking editors. The essays printed in these pages were first commissioned by Kanak Mani Dixit at *Himal*; Krishna Raj at the *Economic and Political Weekly*; Subhashree Krishnaswamy at the *Indian Review of Books*; Ayesha Kagal at the *Times of India*; Rudrangshu Mukherjee at *The Telegraph*; John Ryle at the *Times Literary Supplement*; and, above all, Nirmala Lakshman at *The Hindu*. Most essays do not appear here as originally published; they have been substantially revised and expanded for the book. Yet without these kindly editors they would never have been written at all.

I owe a very large debt to Rukun Advani, who, fifteen years ago, published my first book, and has now published this one. In between, he has encouraged and chastised me, and run his red pen over texts of all sizes and tones.

A little above Rukun in the hierarchy of my creditors is my wife, Sujata. My thinking and my prose owe much to her deeply developed sense of discrimination. She has made an excitable extremist into some kind of moderate: though it has taken her twenty years.

'When the facts change I change my mind. And what do you do, sir?'—John Maynard Keynes, to an unnamed dogmatist

Introduction:
Nehruvian Indians

I call myself a Nehruvian Indian. How else would you describe a Tamil whose family has been domiciled for four generations in Karnataka, but who was born in Dehra Dun, educated in Delhi and Calcutta, and who, from the sound of his name, could be taken for a Bengali? The identity of most Indians is determined by their language, caste, religion, and native village. But I witnessed my first sunset two thousand miles north of where my forefathers come from. My grandfather called himself a Brahmin and wore a thread; my father didn't, while I detest caste. The languages I speak are English and Hindi (in that order). And while I do not disown my ancestral faith, what I make of Hinduism seems rather different from what its modern votaries claim it stands for.

I like to think that the term 'Nehruvian Indian' captures more than my own c.v. Take this incident from the life of a professor of history named A.R. Khan. He teaches in Shimla, but much of his family lives in Pakistan. His brother in Karachi invited him to his daughter's wedding and had persuaded him to stay on for a whole month after the ceremony. However, a week after he left India Professor Khan phoned a friend in Delhi: he was coming back in two days, could he please be picked up at the airport? The friend went to Palam airport to meet him and asked why he had come back so soon. '*Wahan sab saalé Mus-sulman hain*', said Professor Khan—everyone is a bloody Muslim ·there. '*Na koi Tripathi, na koi Sengupta ya Chavan, na koi Ahluwalia aur na koi Menezes. Main ek hafte mein bore ho gaya.*' The social homo-geneity of Pakistan was killing. Its people all spoke the same language, and subscribed to the same faith.

I heard this story, years ago, from the friend of the professor who picked him up at the airport. I recently found it repeated by the columnist Saeed Naqvi, who put his brother Shanné where I have put A.R. Khan: as the Indian Muslim who visits Pakistan to see his relat-ives but returns early, disappointed by the dreary dulness of the Pro-mised Land. This re-telling is testimony perhaps not only to the story's worth, but also to its truth. India is not, or at least not yet, a Hindu Pakistan. For that we have to thank plenty of men and women, but most of all our first and long-serving prime minister, Jawaharlal Nehru.

In his book *The Good Boatman*, Rajmohan Gandhi asks the ques-tion: why did Mahatma Gandhi anoint Nehru his heir? The choice is (or was) puzzling, for in many respects the two men spoke a differ-ent language. One was religious while the other was not. One was abstemious but the other was not. One looked backwards to a pre-industrial past while the other wanted to claim a modern factory future. One was a proto-anarchist who turned his back on public ins-titutions, the other worked from the commanding heights of the state. Why, given these fundamental differences in personality and ideology, did Gandhi designate Nehru his successor?

To answer this puzzle Rajmohan Gandhi takes us back to the summer of 1947. In this, the last weeks of a united India, Mahatma Gandhi referred to himself as a Sindhi and a Punjabi, as a lover of all socialists and a father to young communists. These multiple identi-ties, says Rajmohan, show how the Mahatma strove strenuously to 'include all India in his family.' So, all his political life, did Jawaharlal Nehru. This cannot be said with the same certainty of other members of Gandhi's inner circle. Thus, Vallabhbhai Patel and C. Rajagopala-chari must both also have been on the very short list from which the

Mahatma chose his successor. However, while Patel was as deeply committed to inter-communal harmony, and Rajagopalachari was a religious pluralist who also worked to abolish 'untouchability', neither was wholly able to escape the mark of his parish. Patel was seen by many Indians as a Gujarati Hindu, Rajaji as a Tamil Iyengar. Likewise, other candidates for the succession were, rightly or wrongly, typecast in the popular mind by their social origins. Azad was viewed as a Muslim, albeit a nationalist Muslim; Rajendra Prasad as a Bihari Hindu, and a rather traditional one at that.

It was Jawaharlal Nehru who, of those who followed or came after Gandhi, best upheld his inclusive patriotism. Like the Mahatma, in his person and in his faith he transcended the divisions of race and religion, caste and class, gender and geography. He was a Hindu who was befriended by Muslims, a Brahmin who did not observe the rules of caste, a North Indian who would not impose Hindi on the South, a man who could be trusted and respected by women. After Gandhi, Nehru was the most non-parochial of Indians.

In 1993 the sociologist André Béteille was approached by the newly established Rajiv Gandhi Foundation to recommend candidates for fellowships they planned to endow. He asked me whether he could suggest my name and got a sermon in exchange. 'I am happy to be a Fellow of the Nehru Memorial Museum', I said, 'but I would never accept anything named after Indira Gandhi or Rajiv Gandhi.' I then listed a series of political crimes and errors committed by the two. I spoke of how they were autocrats while Nehru was a democrat; cynical manipulators where he was decent and idealistic. Professor Béteille listened to me with amused tolerance. Three or four years later he rang to tell me he had just been offered a fellowship by the Rajiv Gandhi Foundation. 'I have also turned it down', he said. Then he added, wickedly: 'Not, like you, for political reasons, but for aesthetic ones.'

To be a Nehruvian Indian means one must rigorously separate Jawaharlal on the one side from Indira and Rajiv and Sonia on the other. It also means that one must re-unite him with Mahatma Gandhi. For too long now, Indian intellectuals have been made to choose between the two. One was either a 'Gandhi man' (or woman), or a 'Nehru man' (or woman). Thus, if one was a cultural theorist or a scholar of popular protest, one tended to celebrate Gandhi and debunk Nehru. If one was a theoretical scientist or economic planner it was usually the other way round. But, looking at the country crumbling around us, it is past time that we underlined what Nehru shared with Gandhi: an inclusive vision of India, a disregard for the particularities of region, religion, caste, and language; a commitment to dialogue and democracy, and to decency and transparency in public life.

About ten years ago, I read an essay by the doyen of Sovietologists, Robert Conquest, which referred to a comment made in the early 1970s by the critic Cyril Connolly. Connolly had claimed that Lenin would, in terms of political relevance, 'age' much better than Gandhi. Writing after the fall of the Berlin Wall, Conquest remarked on how wildly off the mark that judgement was. When I wrote him a note of congratulation, Conquest replied that in his view, among the differences between Lenin and Gandhi was that the Mahatma was *civilized*. So he was, and so was his sometimes errant disciple, Jawaharlal Nehru.

II

Contemporary India, with its large and small corruptions, its hatreds and its violence, is not a pretty sight. When asked what he thought about Western civilization, Mahatma Gandhi is reported to have said: 'I think it would be a good idea.' Recalling this remark, the anthropologist Shiv Visvanathan suggests that, were the Mahatma to be reborn now, and were he to be asked what he thought of Indian civilization, he would answer: 'That also would be a good idea.'

God knows, there is much to criticize. But, there is something (and sometimes someone) to praise as well. One of the more admirable individuals in contemporary India is the present chief election commissioner, who has disregarded the slurs hurled at him by high-ranking politicians, and gone about his job with minimal fuss and much efficiency. I am myself very partial to intelligent and honest public officials: indeed, two such are the dedicatees of this book. But I also keep an eye out for those who do good things outside government.

Asked by an interviewer how he chose his themes, Michael Frayn answered: 'Ideas adopt you, like a lost dog on a walk.' This might be so for novelists and playwrights. However, historians are more likely to be chosen by people than by ideas. This book profiles some of the characters who have adopted me in my twenty years as a practising historian. The people I have written about here include writers, scholars, scientists, activists, and statesmen. Some were world famous, others celebrated only in a tiny little circle; all, however, intrigued and interested me. Often, they carried out multiple careers, as politicians who were also writers, or as novelists who were also social reformers. In some cases I have chosen to write more about their work and writings; in others, of their character and personality. I have also included portraits of foreign radicals, remarkable in their own right, and whose lives are an example or warning to us in India. Other essays deal with more general themes, such as the arts of biography and autobiography, and the enchantment of second-hand bookshops.

I like to think that these essays somewhat reflect the attributes of the legendary editor William Maxwell, as described by John Updike: 'He had a gift for affection, and another—or was it the same gift?— for paying attention.' More specifically, I hope these essays display affection and attention towards my homeland. Relevant here is the story of the return to Russia, after fifty years in exile, of the composer Igor Stravinsky. He detested the Soviet regime and what it stood for, which is why he had stayed away so long. Speaking at a banquet in his honour, held at the Metropole Hotel in Moscow, Stravinsky said:

A man has one birthplace, one fatherland, one country—he can only have one country—and the place of his birth is the most important factor in his life . . . I did not leave Russia of my own will, even though I disliked much in my Russia and in Russia generally. Yet the right to criticise Russia is mine because Russia is mine and because I love it, and I do not give any foreigner that right.

I feel like this about India, except that I also assume the right to praise
it in ways that a foreigner cannot comprehend.

A man can have only one homeland, yes, but my homeland has
many varieties of peoples and cultures. Being a 'Nehruvian Indian' is
to deny that there is any single essence to Indian civilization, to reject
the idea that one can list some core attributes of what it takes to be
an Indian. This, of course, is true of some other people's homelands
too. In 1907, James Joyce gave a lecture in Trieste, titled 'Ireland:
Island of Saints and Sages'. Attacking the idea that Ireland belongs
only to the authentically Irish, Joyce remarked: 'Our civilization is an
immense woven fabric in which very different elements are mixed . . .
In such a fabric it is pointless searching for a thread that has remained
pure, virgin and uninfluenced by other threads nearby.' This was a
warning against Irish Catholic nationalism, against a kind of cultural
chauvinism which reduced national identity to a religion and a language. The warning applies with great force to contemporary India.
One should quote Joyce to Hindutva-*vadis*, or, better still, acquaint
them with these remarks of the Kannada writer Shivarama Karanth,
one of the Indian radicals honoured in this book. How is it possible,
remarked Karanth,

> to talk of 'Indian culture' as if it is a monolithic object? . . . Our scholars
> say 'this is Aryan culture'. But do they realise what transformations this
> 'Aryan culture' has undergone after reaching India? . . .
>
> Indian culture today is so varied as to be called 'cultures'. The roots
> of this culture go back to ancient times: and it has developed through con-
> tact with many races and peoples. Hence, among its many ingredients,
> it is impossible to say surely what is native and what is alien, what is bor-
> rowed out of love and what has been imposed by force. If we view Indian
> culture thus, we realise that there is no place for chauvinism.

Shivarama Karanth was a one-time Congressman who, in Nehru's
lifetime, left the party and even stood against it in elections. However,
to be a Nehruvian Indian does not mean that one must agree with all
that Nehru said or did. (I myself think his economic policy moderately flawed, his neglect of primary education shocking, his dismissal

of the Communist government in Kerala unfortunate, and his under-estimation of China and the Chinese tragic.) It means only that in some key respects—social tolerance, respect for diversity and for democratic procedure, the refusal to reduce India or 'Indian-ness' to a dominant religious or linguistic ethos—one stands where Nehru did. In these respects Karanth was certainly a Nehruvian Indian. So was that great critic of Nehru's economic and foreign policies, C. Rajagopalachari. In the ways that now most matter to us, Rajaji and Nehru—who had both been raised in the same political stable, Gandhi's Congress—were against the common enemy. Consider thus Rajaji's remarks on the Jana Sangh, a party which, he pointed out, 'has quite a few good leaders . . . What is needed however is a broadmindedness that not just practices toleration but looks upon Mussulmans, Christians, Parsis and others as politically and cultur-ally as good as Hindus.'

These remarks apply more directly still to the Jana Sangh's suc-cessor, the Bharatiya Janata Party. Indeed, to be a Nehruvian Indian requires one to decisively reject the politico-religious creed that goes by the name of 'Hindutva'. This by no means implies an aversion to Hinduism. Rajaji was a practising Hindu: no one knew more about the faith than he, no one did more to bring its stories and teachings to a modern public. Nor, contrary to current propaganda, was Nehru hostile to Hinduism. His Last Will and Testament reveals a mystical feel for the rivers and mountains that are sacred to us. His *Discovery of India* was even attacked by socialists as being too sentimental in its treatment of Hindu philosophy and aesthetics.

Speaking for myself, I am a Nehruvian Indian who is happy also to be described as a Hindu. I have given my children classical names, straight out of our pantheon. I deeply admire the architecture and music that my religion has inspired. But I cannot abide the move-ment to make a united political community of 'eight hundred million Hindus', which will then terrorize Indians of other faiths as well as those of no faith at all.

Like some other writers who make it their business to comment on

current affairs, I am a regular recipient of hate mail from Hindutva-
vadis. This message, from an anonymous mailer, in response to a piece
I published on the rhetoric of the Sangh Parivar, is representative:

> Why don't u think about all the atrocities muslims all over the world per-
> petrate on all other religions . . . u pseudo secular, spineless, english speak-
> ing rascal.

Fortunately, there are also other kinds of readers. One such wrote to
The Hindu in response to an essay (reprinted here) on the great
Chipko leader Chandi Prasad Bhatt. His letter said:

> It was nice that an environmental writer is writing about the man who
> devoted all his life to mountain people and the environment. For us young
> social workers and activists, Chandi Prasad Bhatt will always be a source
> of inspiration. Thanks to [*The Hindu*] for breaking the regional, linguis-
> tic, mountain–coastal and north–south barriers in a true environmental
> sense.

The correspondent's name was Jayprakash Pawar, and he wrote from
my old home town, Dehra Dun. That other ethnic *pahari*, Jawaharlal
Nehru, would have been proud of him. And so should we. So long as
there are Indians who seek to break down barriers, there is hope for
our land.

People and Places

766 Kilometres
from Somewhere: Sevagram

For the well-heeled Indian, the level crossing provides an irregular but not unwelcome taste of the flavours of Bharat. This is where he stops, involuntarily, his progress from one city to the next interrupted by the accidental intersection of road and railway track. Waiting for the train to pass, he steps down from his car, answers the call of nature, and experimentally buys the local food and drink sold by an opportunistic vendor.

The two level crossings I myself know best are in the far north and the deep south. One is at a village named Sakhotitanda, on the Delhi–Dehradun highway, the crossing a hundred yards from a railway station of the same name. The place has its own eponymous sweet—*Sakhoti ka laddoo*—a lump of *besan* mixed with jaggery made in mills which squeeze the sugarcane that grows on fields along the road. The sweet is sticky and the air hot, a bare breeze swaying the cane stalks watered by canals long diverted from the Jumna by British engineers. As one sucks the *laddoo* and contemplates the landscape, a train slowly bumps its way into Sakhoti station and a shriek of bus horns commands the signalman to open the gate.

The other crossing lies just past the ancient temple town of Paschimavahini in southern Karnataka. Drive from Bangalore on the Mysore road, turn right after Srirangapatnam, climb an incline and stop dead as you meet the railway track. This road leads to the bird sanctuary of Ranganthitoo, and beyond it, to Coorg. On weekdays, at least, it is a road bereft of traffic except for the odd bus and farmer's tractor and planter's Sumo. The refreshment here is *yeleneer* or coconut water, grown on land made bountiful by canals built by the legendary engineer Mokshagundam Visvesvarayya. The train in this place whizzes past—it might be the Shatabdi Express to Chennai—and the views are altogether more pleasant. Down the slope lie decrepit but still exquisite shrines; up and forward, a little to the right, one can see the Kaveri turn west for the only time in its seaward journey.

Sakhoti and Paschimavahini are places I know well, their arrival a sign that one is already far advanced on a road to or from a place one might call home. But I cannot say I was on the look-out for the level crossing that I encountered while travelling in a taxi from Nagpur to Sevagram, a sixty-kilometre journey that starts on the Hyderabad highway and continues on a series of progressively narrower and more rural roads. I was on my first visit to a village sacred in the historical geography of modern India. I had been reading Gandhi, and reading about Gandhi, for thirty years. I followed with anticipation the decreasing numbers on the milestones—Sevagram *panch*, Sevagram *char*. Before I reached the three-kilometre marker my vehicle was interrupted by a metal barrier.

The land here was arid, without irrigation, the rainfall less than twenty inches a year. No *laddoos* or *yeleneer* were on sale. I took a walk. It was late afternoon and the heat of the day was slowly dissipating. I went past a clump of acacia towards the railway track. In the guard's house two men were talking; in the distance, a grey partridge was calling. Then, adjacent to the track, I saw a white stone, square at the bottom but nicely curved at the top, and with a single number printed on it: 766. We were three kilometres from Sevagram, but seven hundred and sixty-six from some place else. It could have been Bombay, or Madras, or Calcutta, or Delhi, for this part of the track was common to the great north–south and east–west grids of the Indian Railway.

Gandhi's own journey to Sevagram had more than one interruption. In September 1933 he moved from Ahmedabad to the town of Wardha, at the invitation of his great disciple and benefactor, Jamnalal Bajaj. On twenty acres of orange orchards gifted by Bajaj, the Gandhians had started an ashram, named Maganwadi after the Mahatma's nephew Maganlal, who had been with him in South Africa and was subsequently the first manager of the ashram at Sabarmati. In Maganwadi were begun experiments for the 'revival, encouragement and improvement of village industries and the moral and physical advancement of the villages of India.'

The change of scene thus denoted a change of profession. The politician and agitator, the initiator of the Dandi March and the participant at the Round Table Conference, was now turning full time to social work. In November 1933 Gandhi commenced an all-India campaign against untouchability. In one of his first public meetings he remarked that 'it is good fortune for me that my tour begins at Wardha, which is the geographical centre of India. I want it also to be the centre of this movement.'

The work on khadi and such like was placed in the safe hands of the brilliant, truculent Tamil economist J.C. Kumarappa. Gandhi, meanwhile, proceeded on his tour to throw open the temples, speaking at villages and towns throughout the land, followed everywhere by a group of nasty Sanatanist Hindus who shouted slogans against him and attempted, with varying degrees of success, to disrupt his meetings. A year later Gandhi returned to Wardha, announced his resignation from the Congress, and said he would devote himself exclusively to village work.

Gandhi was initially based at Maganwadi, but in the summer of 1936 moved to a plot of land in the village of Segaon, five miles away. This site was also owned by Bajaj, and deemed suitable for her master's new home by his most selfless—and most selflessly fanatic—devotee, Mira Behn. It was Mira who had the land cleared and a cottage built for Gandhi, just 'one big room thirty feet long and fifteen feet broad, with a good plinth and open verandahs.'

This cottage, later named 'Adi Niwas', is where Gandhi lived for the next eighteen months. But the large hall was used continuously for meetings, and to escape the noise he moved in 1938 to a hut across the courtyard, originally meant for Mira Behn. It was in this hut, the famous 'Bapu Kuti', that Gandhi stayed until he went to jail in 1942. After his release he was advised by his doctors to move to a house built by Jamnalal Bajaj for his own use, which had a higher plinth and stone floor, and more effectively kept out the damp. This house also had an east-facing verandah, where Gandhi would have his morning massage, in the sun. He stayed here for less than a year, leaving on the 25th of July 1946 for the riot-torn villages of Noakhali, never to return.

Soon after Gandhi moved there, the village changed its name to 'Sevagram', to distinguish itself from a larger village which was also named 'Segaon'. (It is said that the change was urged by the post office, which anticipated a sudden surge of activity and wanted its men to be clear about where which letters were to be sent). In Sevagram Gandhi had gathered around him his closest followers. There were his secretaries, Mahadev Desai and Pyarelal Nayar; Jayaprakash Narayan's wife Prabhavati and Pyarelal's sister Sushila; two remarkable ladies from the Punjab, Amtus Salam and Rajkumari Amrit Kaur; and the tall Ceylonese teacher E. Aryanayakam and his Bengali wife, Asha Devi. These people were inclined towards a life of service, not politics. They were 'ashramites' rather than Congressmen.

To move his base to the heart of India was a decision Gandhi took with care. Some of his old followers, as well as his political associates, wanted him to remain in Gujarat, a state well equipped with what then passed for modern communication, and only a few hours from Bombay. Gandhi, however, liked the idea of living in an isolated hamlet in the heart of India. True, the railway passed not far from the village, but it took days and days to get to the centres of political power. The number 766 I had seen by the track, I later discovered, denoted the distance in kilometres from Bombay. Delhi lay nearly twelve hundred kilometres to the north, Calcutta twelve hundred to the east. Madras was almost exactly a thousand kilometres to the south.

Sevagram was in the middle of nowhere. No sooner had Gandhi shifted there than it became the centre of everything. For, as Mira Behn remarks, 'although Bapu had left the Congress officially, yet the Congress had not left him. They wanted to go their own way, but whenever they got into difficulties they wanted Bapu to help them.' Nehru, Kripalani, Patel, Rajaji, Maulana Azad, Sarojini Naidu, Badshah Khan and Rajendra Prasad—all made the obligatory trek to Sevagram, taking the train to Wardha and then a bullock cart to their leader's doorstep. Eventually, Gandhi was drawn back into politics. It was in Sevagram that the decision was taken to launch the Quit India movement in August 1942.

The history and meanings of Sevagram are most conveniently explored through a small illustrated pamphlet prepared by Rambhau Mahaskar. This provides details of the place's discovery, its preparation for the arrival of the leader, the colleagues who followed him there, and the powerful men who came to visit. We are reminded that when Bapu first saw Segaon, on the morning of 30th April 1936, he was already sixty-six years old. We are told that while building his hut Mira was instructed not to spend more than five hundred rupees, and to use materials locally available (such as palm leaves, bamboo, stone and, most abundantly, mud). In an appendix tucked away at the end, Rambhau provides the results of a little statistical exercise he set himself. All told, Gandhi lived 2,141 days at Sabarmati, or with that ashram as his base. The corresponding figure for Sevagram/Wardha is 2,488 days. Curiously, the tally for the third of his Indian homes— the various dispersed branches of His Majesty's Hotel—is close enough to the others, at 2,111 days.

A delightful description of Sevagram in its pomp is contained in Bhisham Sahni's memoir of his brother Balraj. Before he became an actor in Bombay, Balraj was an ardent nationalist, spending time in Tagore's Santiniketan before joining the Basic Education movement started by Gandhi in 1937. When Bhisham visited him at Sevagram the following year, he found his brother aglow with the charm radiated by Gandhi but just a little put off by the rules regarding diet and personal conduct. In the tonga from the station he smoked through a packet of *bidis*, a commodity totally forbidden inside the ashram walls. His wife warned the visiting brother that he would get no meat, only rice and daal, to be eaten with the right hand only (Punjabis like to break their bread with both hands). They washed their plates and clothes and cleaned their lavatories. There were no tea shops outside, nor flower beds, observed Bhisham; still, 'the extensive landscape looks green and fresh, with palm and date trees dotting the horizon . . . The fields are very tidily demarcated giving the look of a government farm.'

Bhisham Sahni writes of an aspect of Gandhi's non-violence that seems to have escaped historians and political theorists. He was invited to join the pre-dawn walk at which visitors or followers spoke to Gandhi about personal or political matters. 'Anyone can join in', Balraj told him, 'there is a dark-skinned fellow, an "Ashramite", who accompanies Gandhiji every day. He smells awfully. Whenever he finds anyone sticking too long to Gandhiji, he quietly starts walking by his side and the fellow falls back within seconds. This is Gandhiji's non-violent method of regulating interviews.'

Four years after Bhisham Sahni, the American journalist Louis Fischer came to Sevagram. His stay is described in *A Week with Gandhi*, a book published in 1943 which is prefatory to and independent of the mammoth life that Fischer was to eventually publish. Fischer wrote mostly of political subjects, of questions asked and answers elicited about fascism, non-violence, and the Hindu–Muslim problem. He stayed in 'Sevagram's guest house—a one-room mudhut with earthen floor and bamboo roof.' At his first meal he was offered a 'vegetable mess'; however, 'with a liberal use of salt, the food was not untasty.' By mid week he had changed his mind. 'At lunch Gandhi said, "Fischer, give me your bowl and I will give you some vegetables." I told him that I had eaten the mess of squash and spinach four times in two days and had no desire for more.'

Fischer has left a vivid account of how Gandhi wrote—sitting upright on a hard bed, legs crossed scissors-fashion, one fountain pen in his hand and three others at attention in stands nearby—and of

Mahadev Desai spinning—'bald and paunchy, dressed only in a loin cloth', squatting on a floor mat turning out his five hundred yards a day. As he spun, Mahadev explained the methods of a man he knew like no other. The secret of Gandhi's influence, he said, was his controlled passion, that sublimated 'sex and anger and personal ambition. Gandhi can admit that he is wrong. He can chastise himself and take the blame for the mistakes of others, as when he called off a civil disobedience movement because it became violent. Gandhi is under his own complete control. That generates tremendous energy and passion within him.'

By contrast with Fischer's previous interviewees—Roosevelt, Stalin and Churchill—Gandhi came across as conspicuously open-minded. 'I am essentially a man of compromise', the Indian leader told the visitor, 'because I am never sure that I am right.' Gandhi, wrote Fischer, 'never hesitates to admit error, and by preference he does so publicly.' (The implied contrast is with other world leaders, but it could also be made with some lesser and later Gandhians, who do not seem to have ever made a mistake.) The transparency of his thinking, remarks the American journalist, was of a piece with the transparency of his life. 'Part of the pleasure of intimate intellectual contact with Gandhi is that he really opens his mind and allows the interviewer to see how the machine inside works. When most people talk they try to bring their ideas out in final perfect form so that they are least exposed to attack. Not so with Gandhi. He gives immediate expression to each step in his thinking.'

Fischer visited Sevagram in the month of June. The temperature was in excess of 110° Fahrenheit. He had no choice, for a war was on, and he had to catch Gandhi before Gandhi called for satyagraha and disappeared into jail.

For my own first visit to Sevagram I had sensibly chosen the month of December. And whereas the American sat 'twenty-seven hours in the hot, dusty express train' to get to Nagpur, I could fly there. The friend who met me at the airport suggested that I begin my historical sightseeing that very evening. He took me to Diksha Bhoomi, the site where B.R. Ambedkar and his followers converted to Buddhism in October 1956. It was past ten when we got there. The gate was locked, but we got a fair sight of the memorial built by the Maharashtra government, a white spherical structure that had an austere and pure grandeur when viewed against the night sky.

The next day, after lunch, I called at Diksha Bhoomi once more. The purity of the night vision was now complicated by the chipped steps leading in and the metal rods hanging out, denoting a task unfinished (or under-funded). To the left of the memorial there was a bronze bust of Ambedkar, with fresh flowers strewn around it. To the right was the tree under which he had converted, now enclosed by a tasteful wrought-iron railing. Outside the gate there were pavement stalls busily selling Ambedkar's books and photographs, cassettes with songs celebrating his life, assorted Buddhist literature, and stories of other rebels against the Establishment: Lenin, Engels, Marx and Ravidas. In this centre of adversarial social radicalism, one book caught my eye: the Marathi edition of *What Congress and Gandhi have done to the Untouchables*.

The author of that book had visited Sevagram, once. In April 1936, writes D.G. Tendulkar in his monumental life of Gandhi, 'the Harijan question was in the fore and Dr Ambedkar had gone to see him at Segaon.' He does not seem to have gone there again. The talks were inconclusive; for ever afterwards, Ambedkar viewed the Mahatma as an adversary. But an Indian born after the deaths of Ambedkar and Gandhi can be permitted to count both men as heroes.

At any rate, I proceeded with a clean conscience from Diksha Bhoomi to Sevagram. I reached the ashram just in time for evening prayers. These were held in the courtyard between Adi Niwas and Bapu Kuti. We sat on thin mats placed on gravel, facing a large and leafy tree, other trees throwing dark shadows around us. The only illumination came from a tubelight somewhere in the middle distance. It was magical.

The prayers were led by an elderly man playing a simple stringed lute. He sang tunefully and so did his mates—a surprise to one whose book knowledge suggested that Gandhians did not appreciate fine art or good music. After the songs were chanted some verses from the Gita, and then some pages were read by lantern light from Sushila Nayar's account of her time in jail with Gandhi. The excerpt was chosen to illustrate the sacrifice of the patriot. It described how the prisoners celebrated what was then called Independence Day, 26th January 1943.

I returned to Sevagram at nine the next morning. The place was as lovely by day, quiet and contemplative, its two dozen tiled huts interspersed with tall trees. The tree to which we had prayed the previous night was a *pipal,* planted by Gandhi in 1936. There were *neem* and mango trees, too, planted by Vinoba and Kasturba and other such characters from the great modern mytho-historical epic that is Gandhi's life. So far as my untrained eye could tell, all the trees were indigenous. They would have been mere saplings while the Mahatma lived there.

I walked into Adi Niwas and sat down on the floor. The place was wonderfully cool because of the many doors and windows and the mud beneath me. After half an hour of an unnatural silence I went over to Bapu Kuti. This was more compact: not a single hall but with alcoves set aside for prayer, sleep, and work. Against one wall lay a small glass cabinet with Gandhi's possessions. Above the cabinet its contents were scrupulously enumerated and specified. The list of 'articles used by Bapu' read:

1. Wooden Paper-Weight
2. Country Stone
3. Japanese Holy Cloth
4. Cup for Tooth Set
5. Ink-Stand
6. Spittoon
7. Bottle for Boiled Drinking Water
8. Pen and Pencil-Stand
9. Pins and Tags Container
10. Three Idol Monkeys

11. Rosary
12. Wooden Bowl
13. Sandle-wood [*sic*] First-Aid Box
14. Folding Spinning-Wheel

In this single, skimpy list we can find Gandhi the health faddist; Gandhi the writer, editor and correspondent; Gandhi the craftsman and rural economist; above all, Gandhi the religious ecumenist. In her book *Bapu Kuti*, Rajni Bakshi speaks of how this hut still serves as a source of nourishment for Indians who never saw Gandhi, but who have been moved by his example to lead exemplary lives of their own. The cast of characters celebrated by Bakshi includes scientists who design low-cost and eco-friendly technologies, activists who fight for the right to information, and doctors who provide appropriate health care for rural communities—different people doing different things, their work united only by a spirit of service that they share with Mohandas K. Gandhi.

I came out of Bapu Kuti and sat on a bench facing it. A man passed by, clad in a khadi kurta-pyjama. We got talking. He was a teacher who had lived in the ashram for twenty years, taking the principles of Basic Education to the villages around. He told me that, soon after Gandhi moved to Sevagram, Mira shifted to another village four miles distant. Every morning, said the teacher, Bapu and Kasturba walked towards Mira's home. Ba would stop after a mile and sit down under a tree. Gandhi would proceed further, allow Mira to take her daily darshan, and pick up his wife on the return journey. The teacher suggested that the walk was too long for Ba, but I suspect that she might not have wanted to see her husband's adopted daughter anyway. (Indeed, the letters published in Mira's memoir, *A Spirit's Pilgrimage*, suggest that she had to move from Sevagram as she was perceived to be too possessive of Bapu.)

A little later another ashramite passed my way. He was a young Scotsman, no more than twenty-five, who had been here the past three months, and would one day return to start an organic farm in his homeland. The next man I stopped was Rambhau Mahaskar, the author of the booklet about Sevagram. Like the schoolteacher, Rambhau was lean and superbly fit, fit in the Gandhian rather than gymnasium sense of the term. He was a Kannadiga who had spent the past fifty-seven years in this place. I asked if we could speak, but he said he had work elsewhere. But when he heard I was a historian he asked whether I knew Dharampal. When I said I did, he told me that Dharampal was living in the ashram, and directed me to the hut where he stayed.

Dharampal is a man in his late seventies whose whole life has been shaped by signals coming from Sevagram. In 1942 he left his college in Lahore to go to prison during the Quit India movement. After he came out of jail he joined Mira Behn in an ashram she had set up in the lower Himalaya, just beyond Rishikesh. Later, he worked with Jayaprakash Narayan on *panchayati raj* and rural development. But then he married an Englishwoman and moved to her country. He stayed there almost twenty years, spending his days looking through old records in the India Office Library. After his wife died he returned to India and began publishing the fruits of his researches. His books include a study of eighteenth-century Indian science, a study of the traditional roots of Gandhian satyagraha, and a study of indigenous education in pre-British India. His method is to write an introduction and then let the documents speak for themselves. The first book, in particular, has had a considerable influence, spurring younger scholars to begin serious work on the history of Indian science and technology.

Through the 1980s Dharampal lived with a group of his admirers in Madras. We met there, and sometimes in Delhi, talking of the past rather than the present. Over the years Dharampal had put me on the trail of archival collections that I had no idea about. In our talks we deliberately stayed clear of politics, for Dharampal's search for the soul of India has on occasion led him very close to the Sangh Parivar. I had too much respect for him to make this aspect central to our own conversations.

Now, when we met in Sevagram, it was Dharampal who began a

disagreement. 'I read your book on Verrier Elwin', he said, and, 'he was a very bad man who sought to fragment our society' (*wo bahut kharab admi tha, jo hamare samaj ka batwara karna chahta tha*). I sensed the drift of his thought—that Elwin emphasized what separates *adivasi* culture from classical Hinduism—and directed the conversation to a subject we could both respect. As ever, he gave me some insightful tips, on where to search for letters written to, rather than by, Gandhi. As for himself, he now lived in Sevagram and spent less and less time away from it. This man, I thought, would approach Gandhi very differently from an academic historian. His interest was personal, emotional, spiritual: not, like mine, merely professional.

Later that day I caught a glimpse of Dharampal once more. After lunch in a Madrasi *dhaba* I had entered my taxi when I saw the old Gandhian walking away from me, eyes straight ahead of him. Though not tall, he is of a robust build, with a round and strong head. From the back he looked like a Roman senator, dressed in white, a red *toga* draped around his shoulder. A *jhola* was slung across one side; the other arm held an umbrella, a sun-shade doubling up as walking stick. He had evidently come to the market, and, having bought the essentials—a bar of soap and some writing paper perhaps—was returning to the ashram. I contemplated offering him a ride home. But it seemed more dignified to allow him to walk, in the manner to which he was accustomed, in keeping with the quiet simplicity of the life he had chosen to uphold. I watched his retreating figure for a while before asking the driver to head back to Nagpur.

Coming to Sevagram, I had eyes only for milestones. Going away, I was more relaxed and could take in other signs. Just after the level crossing I saw a sign for a Dr J.C. Kumarappa Ashram. I stopped the taxi and walked inside, but the office was shut, it being Saturday. A poster painted on the wall informed me that the ashram was started in 1992 to commemorate Kumarappa's birth centenary. There was a lady in the premises, who taught tailoring to village girls. From her I learnt of the ashram's other activities, such as carpentry and bee-keeping.

I got into the car and hit the road again. In ten minutes I crossed a river, a straggly stream of water with acres of sand on either side. Just past the river lay Paunar Ashram. I had actually seen the sign on the way in, but ignored it, for the ashram's founder, Vinoba Bhave, has long been my least favourite Gandhian. But now my historian's conscience called, and I went in. What I saw confirmed an already strong distaste. It was built next to a temple washed in green lime, a North Indian temple, typically undistinguished in appearance. The ashram was a higgledy piggledy collection of buildings, with stone paths rather than gravel, and lots of cement but few trees. Vinoba's room had a tablet made of polished green marble, with 'Gitaye; Ram Hari' written on it, in Devanagari. There were statues outside, one of a Nandi Bull, another of Parvati, also a *shivaling*. Most characteristic were the four paths around the courtyard, named (one feels certain) by the sanctimonious Vinoba himself: *Tyag path*, *Karm path*, *Samya path*, and *Gyan path*.

Vinoba lived in Paunar from 1938 to 1951, intermittently in his Bhoodan and anti-cowslaughter days, and again from 1970 to 1982. (It was here that Indira Gandhi came to successfully seek his blessings during the Emergency). The ashram lacks charm, beauty, austerity and integrity. It is all that Sevagram is not. Its exhibitionist Hinduism is in sharp contrast to the non-denominational but deeply felt spirituality which fills Gandhi's place. Perhaps its inmates read and prayed, but it is difficult to believe that they ever argued or laughed.

A Gandhian in Garhwal:
Chandi Prasad Bhatt

In the first week of June 1982 I began a secular pilgrimage deep into the Alakananda valley. My destination was Gopeshwar, a town that clings to a hill somewhat short of Badrinath, and the living deity I wished to pay tribute to was Chandi Prasad Bhatt, founder of the Chipko movement.

From Dehradun, where I lived, I took an early morning bus to Rishikesh and then another to Gopeshwar. The route was redolent with mythology and history, and the landscape diverse: pine forests on one hill, skilfully cut terraces on another, bare and exposed soil on a third. The bus stayed on the left bank of the Ganga until Devprayag, after which we crossed the now divided river to follow the Alakananda. Around noon we reached Srinagar, the ancient capital of Garhwal. This lay in a low valley and was hot and dusty and altogether unappealing (such decent buildings as it ever had had disappeared in a flood, in 1894). I had lunch in a bazaar that was home to a million flies, and got back into the bus. Except that it wouldn't start. I got out once more. After a brief subterranean inspection the driver gave his verdict: the radiator had burst and the passengers had now better look out for themselves.

With three or four others I got into a white taxi. We passed a series of hamlets situated on the union of sundry lesser rivers that fed the mighty Alakananda. After one such *sangam*, at Sonprayag, we turned a corner and saw a shepherd boy approach us, driving his flock. He wore a tightly buttoned-up tunic and had a felt cap on his head. In his right hand was a stick to discipline his sheep. As we passed he flung out his (previously unengaged) left hand at the taxi and yelled: 'H.N. Bahuguna!'

I can still see, as I write this, the boy and his vivid gesture. But at this distance in time I should perhaps explain it. That summer, after decades of self-imposed exile, the veteran politician Hemavati Nandan Bahuguna had returned to his native Garhwal to fight a by-election against his former party, the Congress. He spoke, he said, for the victimized hill folk against the fat cats of the plains. One cannot be sure he spoke for himself—Bahuguna was a notorious opportunist who had made his own career in the plains—but he certainly did speak for his constituents—as for instance that little shepherd. For, in those pre-liberalization days, a private taxi represented almost the apex of consumer society, and anyone who sat in a taxi was certifiably from the plains. Had the bus not broken down, had we passed the sheep and its tender in that bus, no hand would have been flung accusingly at us, there would have been no invocation by name of a born-again rebel-politician.

One hopes that the shepherd boy had also heard of Chandi Prasad Bhatt, for Bhatt was a man born in the hills who had chosen to stay: to stay there and serve. To him, Garhwal and the Garhwalis were not an exploitable resource, to be turned to when one's political career was in the doldrums. Bhatt's life-work had been to make his people self-reliant: self-reliant economically, socially, ecologically. But the relevance of his work was by no means restricted to the Himalaya. The movement he started and the ideas it generated were to exercise a powerful appeal for the people of the Indian plains—indeed, for rural people everywhere.

Chandi Prasad Bhatt was born on the 23rd of June 1934, in a family of priests who tended the temple of Rudranath, which nestles in a forest at 13,000 feet. Rudranath is part of the 'Panch Kedar', the five

Himalayan temples dedicated to Shiva, the most venerated of which is Kedarnath. As a boy, Chandi Prasad went up often to the family shrine, the journey also alerting him to local traditions of folk ecology. When he walked through the *bugiyal*—the alpine pasture—he had to take off his shoes so as not to harm flowers. In one four-kilometre stretch above the Amrit Ganga, there was a ban on spitting, coughing and pissing: on anything at all that might cause pollution in the river below. There were taboos on plucking plants before the festival of Nandasthmi, in September, after which the restraint was removed so that the plucking of the now ripened flowers also released their seeds.

Once, on the walk to Rudranath, Chandi Prasad met a shepherd burning the flowers of the sacred and beautiful *brahmakamal*. He asked why, it being the week of Nandasthmi, and the shepherd answered that he wouldn't have, normally, except his stomach ached horribly and the extract of the flower would cure him. But, the offender quickly added, he had broken off the plant with his mouth, like a sheep, so that the deity would think that it was nature's natural order rather than the hand of man at work.

While acquiring such informal education in ecology, Chandi Prasad studied in schools in Rudraprayag and Pauri, stopping short of taking a degree. To support his mother—his father had died when Chandi Prasad was a baby—he taught art to children for a year before joining the Garhwal Motor Owners Union (GMOU) as a booking clerk. With the GMOU he was posted up and down the Alakananda, in large villages with names as lovely as Pipalkoti and Karanprayag. His years selling bus tickets, he says, alerted him to the social diversity of India, for many of his customers were pilgrims from different parts of the country, practising various trades and professions.

How did an obscure transport clerk become an influential social worker? In Bhatt's telling, the transformation started with his attending a public meeting in Badrinath in 1956. The star speaker here was the great Jayaprakash Narayan, popularly known as JP, another speaker was the local Sarvodaya leader Man Singh Rawat. The young

man was deeply impressed by both. Now, he would seek out news of
JP or Vinoba and their Sarvodaya movement. When the time came
to take his annual holiday, he spent it with Man Singh Rawat in the
interior villages of Uttarakhand. Man Singh's brother owned three
buses of the GMOU. If this rich man (by local standards) can abjure
his inheritance for Sarvodaya, thought Chandi Prasad, why not me?

Between 1956 and 1960 Chandi Prasad spent his leave learning
about Sarvodaya from Man Singh and his wife Sashi Behn, who had
been trained by the legendary Sarla Behn at the Laxmi Ashram in
Kausani. There were educative treks with the Rawats and also one, in
1959, with Vinoba Bhave. China was now making menacing moves
on the Indian frontier. The other Asian giant's challenge, said JP, was
not merely military, but also ideological. A call for more volunteers
was answered by Bhatt, who, in 1960, made his *jeevan daan* to the
Sarvodaya movement. It was a considerable sacrifice, for he was now
married and had a child.

With a few friends, Bhatt first ran a labour co-operative that helped
repair houses and build roads, its members sharing the work and
wages equally. Then, in 1964, was founded the Dashauli Gram Seva
Sangh, which has justly been called the 'mother organization of the
Chipko movement'. That movement of course lay a decade in the
future. Still, it is worth noting that the foundation stone of the DGSS
was laid by a woman—Sucheta Kripalani, chief minister of Uttar Pradesh—while the land was donated by another woman, Shyama Devi.

My account of Bhatt's early years and initiation into Sarvodaya
comes from an extended interview he recently granted me: the first
time, I believe, that this reticent and consistently self-effacing man
has chosen to speak to an outsider about such things. With the founding of the DGSS, however, we enter the domain of the public man,
'Bhatt' rather than 'Chandi Prasad'. The DGSS's emphasis was on
local employment generation through the promotion of weaving,
bee-keeping, herb collection, and cottage industries that would sus-
tainably use forest produce. In 1968 JP and his wife Prabhavati visited

Gopeshwar: seeing the work of Bhatt and his fellows, they said they were reminded of the spirit of sacrificial heroism had that marked Gandhi's movement.

The activities of the DGSS occasionally brought it into conflict with the government. The clashes were usually minor and usually resolved, till, in 1973, the Forest Department refused to allot the DGSS a batch of hornbeam trees from which to make agricultural implements. To their dismay, these same trees were then auctioned off to a sports goods company in distant Allahabad. The DGSS's feelings were echoed more strongly by the residents of Mandal, a village that lay adjacent to the disputed trees. At Bhatt's suggestion, the villagers threatened to hug the trees rather than allow the loggers in. As Chipko's first historian, Anupam Mishra, notes, the term originally used by Bhatt was the Garhwali 'angalwaltha', or embrace, a word more resonant of local feelings than the Hindi word 'chipko', i.e. 'to stick'.

The protest at Mandal was followed by several such actions against commercial forestry in the villages of the Alakananda valley. One such protest, at Reni in the spring of 1974, was the work wholly of women led by the remarkable Gaura Devi. Meanwhile, the other great Gandhian of Garhwal, Sunderlal Bahuguna, broke off a trek through Uttarakhand to be with and celebrate the protesters. What he saw was conveyed in articles he wrote in the respected nationalist weekly of Dehradun, *Yugvani*. Bahuguna hailed Chandi Prasad Bhatt as the 'chief organizer' (*mukhya sanchalak*) of the Chipko Andolan. This, he added, was not an economic movement that would subside once its demands were met: on the contrary, its main aim was the fostering of love towards trees in the hearts of humans. For Chipko, observed Bahuguna, safeguarding the hill forests was but the first step towards transforming the relationship between humans and nature.

Chipko was born in the Alakananda valley; its midwives were Bhatt and his co-workers in the DGSS. Later, it moved eastwards to Kumaon, where protests against commercial forestry were co-ordinated by left-wing students of the Uttarakhand Sangharsh Vahini; as well as westwards, to the Bhagirathi valley, where the movement was led by Sunderlal Bahuguna and his associates.

Within its original home the movement had entered its second phase: that of reconstruction. Under Bhatt's leadership the DGSS organized dozens of tree-plantation and protection programmes, motivating women (especially) to re-vegetate the barren hillsides that surrounded them. Within a decade, this work had begun to show results. A study by S.N. Prasad of the Indian Institute of Science showed that the survival rate of saplings in DGSS plantations was in excess of 70 per cent, whereas the figure for Forest Department plantations lay between 20 per cent and 50 per cent.

In the early 1980s the DGSS became the DGSM, with 'Mandal' replacing 'Sangh'. By any name, it remains an exemplary organization. Its work has been lovingly described in a booklet written by the journalist Ramesh Pahari and published in 1997 by the Peoples Science Institute in Dehradun. Pahari, who has known Bhatt for three decades, writes of his 'simplicity and modesty, but [also his] firmness of ideas and decisions.' He quotes a Dalit member of the DGSM committee, Murari Lal, to the effect that 'Bhattji has fought bigger battles for removal of social inequities, than for environmental protection.' It was in Murari Lal's village that the first tree-plantation programme was organized. This one-time construction worker has been aninseparable associate of Bhatt for thirty-five years. Their relationship is based on mutual respect, the only irritant being the Gandhian's objection to Murari Lal's love of tobacco.

Chandi Prasad Bhatt has little time for writing, but when he has put pen to paper his words convey both understanding and wisdom. Twenty years ago, in the journal *Pahar*, he wrote a soberly argued critique of large dams, later published in English under the title *The Future of Large Projects in the Himalaya* (Nainital, 1992). He has also written insightfully on forest conservation, urging a creative synthesis between the 'practical knowledge' of peasants and the 'latest scientific knowledge' of the state.

Chandi Prasad Bhatt is a great pioneering environmentalist, an actor and thinker of remarkable range and achievement who, by virtue of his innate modesty and lack of fluent English, remains much less known and honoured than he should be. He has no trumpet, nor any trumpeteers. One really has to go to Garhwal to know the measure of his work, and that of his colleagues. To me, these words of Ramesh Pahari seem almost exactly right: 'a variety of issues being discussed all over the world today—the advancement of women and Dalit groups and their participation in decision-making, ecology, environment, traditional rights of people, the indigenous knowledge of people, basing development processes on successful experiences and self-reliant economics—have first been worked on by DGSM thirty-odd years ago; and without any fanfare'. I think one can repeat that last clause: *without any fanfare.*

II

Let me return to that bus and taxi journey of twenty years ago, where we met the shepherd boy who spoke, or rather shouted, for H.N. Bahuguna. Later that same evening I reached Gopeshwar. After depositing my bags in a *sarkari* guest house I made for the office of the Dashauli Gram Swarajya Mandal. I had just begun work on a social history of the Himalayan forests, a project in which Bhatt's work would naturally figure rather heavily. I hoped over the course of the next few days to interview him at length about Chipko and, with luck, to scrutinize the files of the DGSM as well.

That evening, however, someone else had got there before me. This was a doctoral student from the University of Roorkee who had come to consult Bhatt about *his* project. He wished to choose twenty villages, ten located more or less on a motor road, the other ten more than five kilometres off the road. In these villages he would adminster a questionnaire on the availability of various goods and services to test his hypothesis that access to roads was crucial for rural uplift.

This Roorkee economist wanted to survey twenty villages in all: but which twenty? He had never been to Garhwal before, and no reliable maps juxtaposing villages and roads existed. Thus, his sample came to be constituted by Chandi Prasad Bhatt. Bhatt spoke in chaste Hindi, accented here and there by his native tongue (soft s's, as in '*pasupalan*', and the occasional substitution of vowels, as in '*kohte hain*' for '*kehte hain*'). From the storehouse of his memory he drew out the names of twenty villages; ten right by the road, ten distant from it. But that was not enough: he had also to provide the economist directions and useful contacts. So he would say, for example:

> Take the bus to Chopta. Get down at Hanumangarhi. Walk on for a kilometre, past an oak forest, and then take the path leading up the hill to the left. This leads to the village of Bemru, which I am sure is more than five kilometres from the road-head. Ask for the school-master: his name is Pran Nath. Tell him I have sent you. He will help you with the questionnaire.

It was a command performance, extending over an hour, and conducted for an audience of two. This fellow, I thought, must have trekked across every hill and every valley in upper Garhwal, and very nearly talked to every man, woman and child too. As I walked back to my room that night I was reminded of an episode from the *Mahabharata*. Bhatt, I felt, was Krishna, and the Roorkee boy and I Duryodhana and Arjuna, respectively. I would have to wait until the next day to get what I wanted from him: his work with forests and Chipko. I trusted I would put that to more creative use, for, as I saw it, my rival's project seemed rather to trivialize Bhatt's awesome knowledge of the geography of Garhwal.

Over the next week, with the economist safely away in his villages, I talked at length to Bhatt and went over the documents he showed me. These I later juxtaposed with interviews conducted and documents read elsewhere in the hills. What I finally learnt about Chandi Prasad Bhatt the Chipko leader is narrated in my book *The Unquiet Woods*. But here, let me stick with the man. He was, and indeed still is, very handsome: of medium height, but erect and beautifully proportioned, an oval face clothed in a neat beard, dark bright eyes looking directly at you. In his native heath he exudes a quiet confidence and dignity; not, however, always outside it. Thus, in October 1983 I saw him in the Kumaon town of Pithoragarh, releasing the first issue of a research annual on the Himalaya. Inside a fairly large conference room this pioneer of Chipko could not comfortably face the crowd. He clutched the microphone hard with both hands for assurance, when a practiced speaker would have stood away from it. The next day, however, he spoke more naturally in the open, at the village of Chandak-Sikhrana—at the time badly battered by magnesite mining.

In September 2001 I heard Chandi Prasad Bhatt speak in Mussoorie, in honour of P. Srinivas, the brave forest officer who was killed searching for Veerappan. He still spoke softly, and with shy sincerity, but he seemed more at ease now with the appurtenances of modern technology: with the mike, and with slides and a slide projector. With their aid he took an audience of aspiring civil servants through a magisterial ecological history of the Himalaya: the glaciers, the rivers, the forests, the fields. The slides came from his own travels, and the language he used to gloss them was exquisitely clear: as clear, indeed, as his description of a free-flowing hill river; '*shishe jaise chamakta hua jal*': water as shiningly transparent as a pane of glass. He documented the degradation caused by humans, but also their potential for ameliorative action. Responsible environmentalism, he said, could be of the P. Srinivas kind, or of the Chipko kind. It could come from upright officials or from concerned citizens; or, better still, by the two in combination.

The first question from the audience dealt not with the Himalaya but the Narmada Bachao Andolan (NBA). The questioner claimed that the NBA was motivated by foreign agents who wished to hold up India's development. Bhatt gently reminded him of the historical experience of displaced people in India. As he said, '*doob shetra wale log ko chinti ké bhi neeché samjha jata hai*': the oustees of dams are treated worse than ants. Characteristically, he moved on from criticism to construction. An estimated 47,000 hectares were to be irrigated by the Sardar Sarovar dam. Why shouldn't 10 per cent of this be alloted to those displaced by the project? He had spoken of this when he visited Gujarat after the earthquake of January 2001, and thought also that this was a solution the NBA could fruitfully pursue.

Those who know Chandi Prasad Bhatt and his work have long felt that—from the English language press at any rate—he has never got his just deserts. The Chipko movement that he and his colleagues started was a definitive moment in the history of environmentalism. Before Chipko, it was thought that the poor were too poor to be green. After Chipko, indeed through Chipko, it was demonstrated that peasants and tribals had a greater stake in the responsible management of nature than did supposedly sophisticated city-dwellers. Then again, it was Bhatt who first taught Indian environmentalists that it was not enough just to protest against destruction: they must also set about the process of reconstruction. Seeking always to improve the lives of the poor, Bhatt has sought to humanize modern science rather than reject it, to democratize bureaucracy rather than demonize it.

I have memories of talking with Chandi Prasad Bhatt and of listening to him talk. But let me end with a memory of, as it were, simply passing him on the road. One evening in Delhi I was driving past a row of truly high-voltage institutions: the India International Centre, the World Wildlife Fund, the Ford Foundation, the World Bank and the United Nations Development Programme. There, on this road, I passed two middle-aged men clad in khadi, talking. I turned into a side lane and watched them for a while. They were Bhatt and Anupam Mishra—the early chronicler of Chipko I mentioned, a man of integrity and achievement and the author of masterly surveys of water management in Rajasthan. They continued talking till a bus came along; they hopped into it, and were lost to me.

Then, and now, I speculated as to where the two men were coming from. From a meeting at the WWF perhaps? In that case, there should have been other people around. Or else, perhaps some of these *other* people had gone to the IIC for a drink, still others to the World Bank pool for a swim. Even had they the necessary memberships, I cannot imagine Chandi Prasad Bhatt or Anupam Mishra exercising either option. In them lives a spirit of quiet service which once existed freely in our politics and our activism, a spirit that has been excised from the one sphere, and is gravely threatened in the other.

The Wisest Man in India:
Aspects of C. Rajagopalachari

I. A Life's High Points

The first and, as it happens, last time I wept at the death of a political leader was on the 26th of December 1972. I was already distraught, for the previous day I had watched the last day of my first Test match, and India had lost. The morning after, the cricket news was not even on the front page. This was taken over, for the most part, by the death of Chakravarti Rajagopalachari, lawyer, scholar, philosopher and statesman, the man whom Mahatma Gandhi had called 'the keeper of my conscience'.

Gandhi died before I was born, and Nehru died when I was only six. Rajaji was the one man left over from an age when the profession of politics still drew in men of character and integrity. Being a sentimental sort of fellow, I suppose I would have wept anyway, but the tears flowed more freely because the leader who had just died came from my own community of Tamil Brahmins. My father subscribed to *Swarajya*, the Swatantra Party weekly where Rajaji spoke out in opposition to the socialist heresies of Indira Gandhi. My mother had bought Rajaji's translations of the *Ramayana* and the *Mahabharata*, which I read and re-read both for the lucid language and the extravagant colourfulness of their contents.

For the modernizing Tamil Brahmin of those days, Rajaji was *sui generis*. This was a man who had been the first Indian governor-general, sitting where Robert Clive and Warren Hastings had once sat. This was the man who was related by marriage to Mahatma Gandhi, a man who had followed his Master in opposing Untouchability and promoting Hindu–Muslim harmony. What made these progressive views more palatable to families such as mine was that Rajaji was no left-wing atheist but a deeply believing Hindu. Rajaji further endeared himself to us by his superb understanding of the language of professional advancement, English.

Like Gandhi, Rajaji was a committed Hindu who yet had an abiding love for Christ and Christian values. He would not have minded dying on Christmas Day, but would not, I think, have wanted to so comprehensively push a Test match result off the front page. For unlike the Mahatma he liked outdoor sports. His own boyhood hero was a cricketer, B. Jayaram, his fellow student at Central College, Bangalore. Jayaram was a greatly gifted left-handed all-rounder, of whom his British principal wrote: 'Had he the same opportunities as W.G. Grace he would have been as great, for he had an eye as quick and a wrist as supple as the Doctor's.' (This was an opinion possibly shared by W.G., for, while studying geology in London, Jayaram was chosen to play for the Doctor's crack team, London County.)

I recently came across the full-page spread run on Boxing Day, 1972, by Rajagopalachari's hometown newspaper, *The Hindu*. This extended obituary was embellished by as many as seven pictures. The pictures were: (1) Rajaji leading a group of Congress volunteers in 1930, en route to breaking the salt laws in Vedaranyam; (2) Rajaji opening a TB sanatorium in 1939, while serving as Prime Minister of Madras; (3) Jawaharlal Nehru introducing his cabinet colleagues to Rajaji when the latter took over as the first Indian governor general in 1948; (4) Rajaji with his cabinet colleagues while chief minister of Madras, in 1953; (5) Rajaji, again as chief minister of Madras, wishing Andhras good luck on the formation of their state in 1953; (6) Rajaji receiving the Bharat Ratna from the president of India in

1954; (7) Rajaji with John F. Kennedy at the White House in 1962, where he had gone as the head of a Gandhian peace delegation.

This was a heroic attempt at illustrating the high points of Rajaji's political career. But, perhaps out of respect or deference, it omitted the low points. These included the last-minute denial to him of the office of president of India in 1950; and his unceremonious exit, at his own party's command, from the office of chief minister of Madras in 1954. Apparently, when Rajagopalachari's parents had had his horoscope cast, the astrologer told them that their baby's future would include 'the fortunes of a king, of an exile, of a guru, and of an outcaste. The people will worship him; they will also reject him. He will sit on an emperor's throne; he will live in a poor man's hut.'

I don't know whether Rajaji himself believed in astrology. I somehow doubt it. But he had an uncanny knack of being wise before the event, and paying for it. In 1941–2 he proposed to the Congress that they work out an accommodation with the Muslim League. He was vilified for this: had he been listened to, perhaps we might have been spared the bloodletting of Partition. Then he opposed the Quit India movement, saying that the need rather was for constructive engagement with the British. The Congress big shots didn't listen—and indeed forced him to leave the party—but in retrospect he was proved right. By calling for a militant rebellion when the British were fighting a desperate battle for survival against Hitler and company, the Congress forfeited their trust. By sitting out the bulk of the war in prison, they allowed the Muslim League to go from strength to strength.

In 1951, as home minister in Nehru's cabinet, Rajaji warned the prime minister of the expansionist designs of Communist China. He wrote to Nehru that he felt 'hurt whenever Pannikar [the Indian ambassador in Beijing] tells us with extreme satisfaction that China is very friendly to us yet has no territorial ambitions. We do not want any patrons now, do we?' Eleven years later, by which time Rajaji and Nehru were in opposing political parties, India was invaded by China.

Those three acts cannot be undone, but in some other cases we might still take advantage of Rajaji's prescience. He was always in favour of better relations with Pakistan, and for allowing the people of Kashmir to live with dignity and honour. And he was an early advocate of market-based economics, a critic of what he memorably called the 'licence-permit-quota-raj', a phrase which ranks with the 'Hindu rate of growth' in describing an entire epoch of India's economic history, but which no one now remembers as originating in Rajaji's mind.

It seems to me that Rajaji's political career was characterized above all by a desire for reconciliation. Reconciliation between Hindu and Muslim, India and Pakistan, India and England, North India and South India, low caste and high caste: these were the recurrent themes of his public life. In a society marked by the deliberate encouragement of conflict and antagonism, his was a rocky road indeed. As he once wrote to a Quaker friend, 'those who are born to reconcile seem to have an unending task in this world.'

There was more to this life than politics. Thus Rajaji was, at various times, a successful lawyer and municipal administrator, a gifted short story writer (in Tamil), and a superbly effective popularizer of our epics. Rajaji liked to claim that 'the best service I have rendered to my people is the re-telling of the *Ramayana* and the *Mahabharata*.' These stories he told with a telling simplicity and directness, and without any theoretical gloss. For, as he said, 'the *Ramayana* is mother's milk for India. It should be left to itself and not philosophized. Mother's milk should not be sent to the chemical analyst!'

Once, while asked to give a speech in memory of Gandhi by the Mysore Assembly, Rajaji warned the organizers that he had 'a partiality for restraint in eulogy'. This eulogy of Rajaji has not been restrained, but it must at least make an attempt to be rounded. I thus take note of his sometimes acid tongue, and, more seriously, of his consistent unwillingness to face the electorate. In 1952, much against Nehru's wishes, he set the unfortunate precedent of choosing nomination to the Upper House in order to become chief minister of his state. Then again, Rajaji had a somewhat conservative attitude towards women. He saw them as home-makers and carriers of our culture, but not really as independent in their own right. As Paula

Richman points out, this attitude informs the depictions in his *Rama-yana* of Shurpanakha, and of Sita. Rajaji also abhorred the idea of women working. When a lady with small children approached him for a job, he remarked: 'I wonder how a woman with children can be wanting work! Alas for civilization and the pernicious habit of en-trusting the education of children to professional men and ourselves seeking odd work to fill our time!'

Like his mentor Gandhi, Rajaji cannot be easily pigeon-holed into the convenient labels—liberal, socialist, or conservative—of modern political thought. Forced to choose, one would, very reluctantly, have to call him a 'conservative'(lower case): but still, a rather special kind of conservative. A man who knew him well, the Australian diplomat Walter Crocker, provides this brilliant capsule summary of his per-sonality:

> Endowed with an exceptionally strong and quick mind, Rajaji was in spirit harmonious and without volatility or anything partaking of the theatrical. Vanity was excluded from his nature. Although he had so much affinity for traditional India, he knew the lore of the West, having a good acquaintance with the Bible and Plato and the English classics as well as with Jurisprudence and Economics; and he knew the case for economic development. Although he was religious, and conservative, he was not conformist. He had the true conservative's trait of combining scepticism about what man-made systems can do for human nature with the personal kindliness to individuals which socialists, dealing with human beings as statistical groups and abstractions, sometimes lack. And he had wit, that life-renewing gift.

Rajaji was not safe from human frailty or blindness. Still, seeing his life and career in the round, one might agree with the judgement of R.G. Casey, the bluff Australian who served as Governor of Bengal, that he 'was the wisest man in India'. At any rate, the wisest politician, and perhaps the best-read one, too. In April 1956, a journalist nam-ed N.S. Muthana went to meet Rajaji at his house. He was struck by two things: the lack of distinction of this former governor-general's abode—'a modest single-storied structure which looks like any other building on that road'; and the range of his reading. Stacked on a desk in front of Rajaji were G.K. Chesterton's Father Brown stories; two books on modern biology; Lewis Mumford's *Conduct of Life*; Valmiki's *Ramayana* (in Sanskrit); and a few Tamil works. These would be read over the next few weeks: waiting, in a book-case along the wall, were twelve volumes of the speeches of Edmund Burke, and an edition of Shakespeare.

II. Rajaji and Gandhi

As a young lawyer in Salem, Rajaji stumbled upon the works of Henry David Thoreau: his book, *Walden*, as well as his classic essay on civil disobedience. Then he read of an Indian lawyer who was putting these ideas into practice in South Africa. In 1913 he reprinted, at his own expense, a pamphlet describing Gandhi's jail experiences. After Gandhi's return to India in January 1915, he followed his activities with increasing fascination. However, he had to wait four years to meet him, their first encounter being in Madras in March 1919, in a house owned by the proprietor of *The Hindu*, Kasturiranga Iyengar.

When the two men met, Gandhi was planning his satyagraha against the Rowlatt Act. Rajaji energetically joined in, following the path of non-cooperation with the fervour of a convert. He went to jail in December 1921 and, after he came out a few months later, started an ashram of his own in Tiruchengode, to promote the Gandhian programme of khadi, prohibition, Hindu–Muslim harmony, and the abolition of untouchability. By now his law practice was a thing of the past. Then, when Gandhi announced a fresh round of satyagraha in 1930, he chose Rajaji to be the first to break the salt laws in South India.

Rajmohan Gandhi writes that, in all these campaigns, 'the Mahatma received C.R.'s instant understanding and wholehearted loyalty'. Another knowledgeable historian, Antony Copley, has called Rajaji 'Gandhi's Southern Commander'. Or, as the collector of Tanjore at the time of the Salt Satyagraha put it, he was 'probably the ablest and certainly one of the most intransigent' of Gandhi's followers.

On two separate occasions Rajaji was Gandhi's front man in beat-
ing off a challenge from Bengal, the province that had been in the
vanguard of the freedom struggle before the Mahatma's rise. In the
Nagpur Congress of 1922 he made the decisive speech that turned
the hall against Chittaranjan Das's promotion of council-entry and
in favour of Mahatma Gandhi's more militant programme of non-
violent non-cooperation. Seventeen years later, he made another
sharp speech, at the Tripuri Congress, held on the banks of the river
Narmada. Rajaji's barbs were aimed again at the Bengal party, but he
spoke this time from the side of caution, rather than radicalism. For
the office of president, the Gandhians had put up Pattabhi Sitaramayya
to oppose the incumbent seeking re-election, Subhas Chandra Bose.
Rajaji's intervention was marked by the sarcasm for which he was
notorious:

> There are two boats on the river. One is an old boat but a big boat, piloted
> by Mahatma Gandhi. Another man has a new boat, attractively painted
> and beflagged. Mahatma Gandhi is a tried boatman who can safely trans-
> port you. If you get into the other boat, which I know is leaky, all will
> go down, and the river Narmada is indeed deep.

As a disciple of Gandhi, Rajaji was mostly loyal but never subservient.
He could speak to him with a clarity and directness beyond the reach
of most other followers. When, in 1924, the Mahatma threatened to
abandon politics for social work, C.R. told him that would leave the
'national organisation [the Congress] to vacillation and drift'; indeed,
it would have 'the worst consequences' for the future of the freedom
movement. Ten years later, the Mahatma moved to retire again, a decision with which even Patel and Rajendra Prasad seem to have ac-
quiesced. This time Rajaji was even more forceful in his dissent. 'Your
retirement from the Congress will be a suicidal step', he told Gandhi:
'An intense and irrevocable feeling of defeatism will spread over the
whole nation, and kill political hope and enterprise . . . If you think
you can retire from the Congress now and keep it and yourself both
or either politically important, I think you will be sorely disappointed.'

Rajaji could tell Gandhi that he was being irresponsible, and he could also tell him that he was wrong: never more bravely than in the summer of 1942, when he went completely against the grain of nationalist opinion in opposing the Quit India movement. Rajaji thought a fresh satyagraha foolish when the situation demanded dialogue and reconciliation with both the British and the Muslims. As he bravely (and as it turned out correctly) put it: 'There is no reality in the fond expectation that Britain will leave the country in simple response to a Congress slogan.' Besides, by asking the British to leave, the Congress was issuing an open invitation to a colonizing power more brutal by far, than the Japanese. Fortunately, said Rajaji, Britain 'cannot add to her crimes the crowning offence of leaving the country in chaos to become a certain prey to foreign ambition.'

This opposition made ordinary Congressmen abuse and even—at a meeting in Bombay—throw black tar at Rajaji. The Mahatma, characteristically, would not allow political disagreement to come in the way of personal friendship. Their ties had been strengthened by the marriage, back in 1933, of Gandhi's son Devadas to C.R.'s daughter Lakshmi. I found a lovely little note of 1935, written from Rajaji's ashram in Tiruchengode. 'Lakshmi and babies are doing well in this climate. Specially Tara enjoys the open space and dustless, motor-less, grounds available for her tiny wanderings.' As the years went by, Rajaji's manifest interest in their grandchildren allowed Gandhi to develop, almost for the first time, a love for little babies who were descended directly from him.

Rajaji could disagree with Gandhi—and disagree sharply—but on some fundamental issues he was completely with a man whom he variously addressed in letters as 'My dearest Master', 'My dear Mahatmaji', and 'My dear Bapu'. One such issue was the abolition of untouchability, whose centrality to the Gandhian struggle Rajaji recognized earlier than any member of Gandhi's inner circle. A second was Hindu–Muslim harmony, a cause to which he was as devoted as the Mahatma himself. A third concerned the dignity of labour. Spinning, cleaning toilets, cleaning one's shoes—all these came easily to him, although they were scorned by his fellow Iyengar Brahmins and by the fashionably left-wing nationalists with whom he was also obliged to consort.

When Gandhi was assassinated on 30th January 1948, Rajaji was serving as the first Indian Governor of Bengal. He flew to Delhi to attend the cremation and came back with a portion of the ashes. The ceremony in the Hooghly has been described in a memoir by the governor's military secretary, Bimanesh Chatterjee. A motor launch took the party to the middle of the river, and the governor was handed over the urn containing the ashes for immersion. As he took the urn 'he became so overwhelmed that . . . he perilously swayed forward, and a couple of us had to hold him back. . . . When Rajaji finally sat down, he appeared exhausted. As the boat was speeding towards the bank, Rajaji said, "The ashes were pulling me".'

Two letters to Rajaji illustrate what united him with Gandhi, and what divided them both from some other kinds of Indians. The first, written in October 1946 by a lawyer living in Sandur, chastised Rajaji for prescribing non-violence. This man sarcastically asked whether 'because Gandhijee sings praises of non-violence in season and out of season, you too (being his relative) feel like delivering your sermon?' The lawyer disapproved of the sermon, and seemed to think there were less and less people willing to hear it. 'Consciousness has dawned upon the minds of the Hindus (even Congressite Hindus) that consolidation as Hindus would alone save them from political extinction. To-day's Hindu nation does not recognise "M.K.'s" and "C.R.'s"! It needs Savarkars and Mookerjees!'

The second letter was written to Rajaji on 12 February 1948 by a Muslim living in Sevagram:

Dear Brother,
    Sitting in the busy little cottage of the Mahatma—busy with the crowds coming in to look at his vacant seat . . .—I am turning to you in sad contemplation.
    We need prophets. I am convinced that we are left without a prophet now.

India will be lost if the opportunity to serve the world with his message and teachings is lost. You are I believe the fittest one to lead India in the Mahatma way. Muslims should be made to realize that the Mahatma way is the Quranic way.

A yearning and sad soul cries to you from near the humble seat of the great man . . . , to lead India to fulfil the Mahatma's message of Ahimsa, Truth, Casteless and Classless society.

In 2004, as in 1948, the future of India seems to hinge crucially on the relationship that the dominant community of Hindus is able to negotiate with members of other religious groupings—to beat them into submission, or to work co-operatively with them. These were the alternatives once offered to Gandhi and Rajaji; and these are the alternatives now offered to us.

Would that we choose as wisely as they.

III. Rajaji and Nehru

In the course of the past year or two, I have spent many absorbing days looking at the Rajaji papers, housed at the Nehru Memorial Museum and Library in Delhi. This vast collection contains original letters from world statesmen as well as by unknown Indians. Sometimes the latter are as interesting and insightful as the former. Consider a letter to Rajaji written in 1953 by a mofussil Tamil named Anantharaman. This offers the view that Rajaji, Nehru and Patel were, respectively, the 'head, heart and hands of Gandhiji'.

This is most appositely put. For Rajaji was unquestionably the most intelligent of Gandhi's close disciples, Nehru arguably the most humane, and Patel the most disciplined and practical. The pity is that they could never function together except for a very brief while. The relationship between Nehru and Patel has attracted much attention. Here I focus on the no less intriguing relationship between Nehru and Rajaji.

During the freedom movement, Nehru and Rajaji were comrades rather than companions. They were separated by upbringing; one was an aristocrat educated at Harrow and Cambridge, the other a self-made man from small-town South India. They were separated also by a thousand miles of peninsula. In terms of ideology too there were differences: Nehru was more inclined to militant socialist views, Rajaji more oriented towards accommodation with the adversary. But they were united by a shared ideal—the freedom of India—and a shared devotion to the Mahatma. (It was Rajaji whom Gandhi first designated as his successor, later changing his mind in favour of Nehru.) They met at Congress meetings, but did not seem to have been especially intimate. Still, the Tamilian had impressed Nehru enough to have him write in his autobiography of how Rajaji's 'brilliant intellect, selfless character, and penetrating powers of analysis have been a tremendous asset to our cause.'

It was from 1946 that the two men began to work more closely together. In the next eight years, while Nehru was prime minister in New Delhi, Rajaji was, successively, a minister in the Interim Government, governor of Bengal, governor-general of India, minister in the central government, and chief minister of Madras State. In all these jobs he had direct and regular dealings with Nehru.

Official business drew them closer at the personal level as well. The two men shared a cultivated interest in literature and the arts: it was only to Rajaji, and to no other Congressman, that Nehru could write recommending a recent book on the British character by the anthropologist Geoffrey Gorer; or praise the beauty of the folk traditions of India. After a visit to the north-east, the prime minister wrote to his southern colleague about the 'most lovely handloom weaving' he had seen there. He confessed to being 'astonished at the artistry of these so-called tribal people. I think it will be disastrous from many points of view to allow such an industry to fade away.' 'Altogether my visit to these north-eastern areas has been most exhilarating', wrote Nehru to Rajaji, 'I wish they were better known by our people elsewhere in India. We could profit much by that contact.'

Reading the correspondence between these two men, I was deeply moved by the nobility of their vision for a free India. In different ways, they both took heed of the Mahatma's message, working to reconcile competing points of views and alternative cultural or religious traditions. Particularly memorable was a handwritten letter of Nehru's that I came across. It was dated 30 July 1947, and it read:

> My dear Rajaji,
>   This is to remind you that you have to approach Shanmukham Chetty—this must be done soon.
>   I have seen Ambedkar and he has agreed . . .
>
> Yours
Jawaharlal.

This brief note requires some explanation. R.K. Shanmukham Chetty was a businessman in the South widely admired as being one of the best financial minds in India. Ambedkar, the Dalit leader, was a brilliant legal scholar. But both had been lifelong enemies of the Congress. Now, a mere two weeks before the political freedom Rajaji and Nehru had spent years in prison for, they were approaching these old adversaries to join the first cabinet of free India. It was a gesture remarkable in its wisdom and generosity. In the event, but only after overcoming the hostility of the other Congressmen, Chetty became finance minister; Ambedkar, minister for law.

In 1950 Nehru hoped to be able to make Rajaji the first president of the Republic, but Patel and the Congress Old Guard thwarted him. Later in the year Rajaji joined the cabinet, as minister without portfolio. After Patel's death in December 1950 he was asked to take over the crucial job of home minister. Not long afterwards, Rajaji left the cabinet and returned to Madras. The ostensible reason was tiredness, but he seems also to have felt that he was not being consulted enough. Anyway, his leaving Delhi was a tragedy, for Jawaharlal Nehru as well as for India. For, as Walter Crocker perceptively remarks in his study of Nehru, after Patel's death the prime minister 'needed the support of an equal. He needed, too, the criticism of an equal.' Now, Rajaji was as close to Gandhi, had sacrificed as much in the freedom movement, and was a man of conspicuous integrity besides. He was indeed 'the intellectual and moral equal of Nehru'. Had a way been found to retain Rajaji in Delhi, this would have, says Crocker, 'ended the situation prevailing in which no one could, or would, stand up to the Prime Minister; the situation whereby he was surrounded by men all of whom owed to him their jobs, whether as Cabinet Ministers or as officials.'

In October 1951, after Rajaji had left Nehru's cabinet to return to Madras, the prime minister sounded him out on the job of Indian high commissioner to the United Kingdom and, when he refused, asked Lord Mountbatten to try and persuade him. Mountbatten duly wrote to Rajaji, and in exchange got a blistering reply:

> My career is truly remarkable in its zigzag. . . . Cabinet Minister, Governor without power, Governor-General when the Constitution was to be wound up, Minister without Portfolio, Home Minister and . . . now the proposition is Acting High Commissioner in U.K.! Finally I must one day cheerfully accept a senior clerk's place somewhere and raise that job to its proper and honoured importance.

The job Rajaji did accept a few months later was that of chief minister of Madras. He stayed in that post until April 1954, when his party indicated that they wanted K. Kamaraj to replace him. Now Rajaji entered what neither his astrologer nor his own foresight had anticipated, namely, his retirement from politics. He settled down in a small house to spend his days, he said, reading and writing. But, in the end, philosophy and literature proved an inadequate substitute for public affairs. He was moved to comment from time to time on the nuclear arms race between Russia and America, with regard to which he took a line not dissimilar to that of Nehru. Then, when the Second Five Year Plan committed the Government of India to a socialist model of economics, he began commenting on domestic affairs too. Here, however, he came to be increasingly at odds with Nehru.

Consider now an article published by Rajaji in May 1958 under the title 'Wanted: Independent Thinking'. This examined the 'present discontent about the Congress' from the perspective of one who 'has spent the best part of his life-time serving the organization and who owes many honours and kindnesses to it.' He worried that 'as a result of tacit submission on the part of the people of emancipated India, a few good persons at the top, enjoying prestige and power, are acting like guardians of docile children rather than as leaders in a parliamentary democracy.' He went on: 'The long reign of popular favourites, without any significant opposition . . . is probably the main cause for the collapse of independent thinking' in India. But a healthy democracy required 'an Opposition that thinks differently and does not just want more of the same, a group of vigorously thinking citizens which aims at the general welfare, and not one that in order to get more votes from the so-called have-nots, offers more to them than the party in power has given, an Opposition that appeals to reason . . .' Such an opposition, even if it did not succeed in ousting the ruling party, might yet control and humanize it.

A year later, now touching eighty, Rajaji chose a public meeting in Bangalore to launch an all-out attack on the 'megalomaniac' economic and foreign policies of the prime minister. This was followed by the formation in Madras of a new political party, the Swatantra Party. This party focused its criticisms on the 'personality cult' around the prime minister, and on the economic policies of the ruling Congress. In a series of articles published in his journal *Swarajya*, Rajaji took apart these socialist pretensions. The prime minister's 'personal allergy' towards private enterprise, he commented, was both unwarranted and unfair. For 'it is as patriotic to start and manage a good private business concern, be it in industry or in transport or in distribution, as to be attached to a public managed industry either as an official or propagandist patron-saint.' But Nehru was moved instead by an admiration for Soviet Russia that was 'taking different and various forms at national cost'.

Rajaji also sharply attacked the 'megalomania that vitiates the present development policies'. What India needed, he said, 'is not just big projects, but useful and fruitful projects . . . Big dams are good, but more essential are thousands of small projects which could be and would be executed by the enthusiasm of the local people because they directly and immediately improve their lives.' Speaking more generally, 'the role of the Government should be that of a catalyst in stimulating economic development while individual initiative and enterprise are given fullest play.'

In September 1952, when Rajaji and Nehru were still friends, the American journalist and pioneeering Gandhi biographer Louis Fischer wrote to him of his belief that 'some straight talk to the power that is [Nehru], would do a lot of good, for I doubt whether time cures certain diseases. . . . You are the one man who . . . could appeal to his mind. . . '. At that time, of course, Rajaji was in the Congress; but now, seven years later, Nehru did not take well to criticisms from a colleague-turned-adversary. Sometimes he affected a cavalier attitude—when asked at a press conference about his differences with Rajaji he answered: 'He likes the Old Testament. I like the New Testament.' This was spoken in June 1959, but as the months went by the mood turned very sour indeed. In December 1961 Nehru told a group of newsmen that Rajaji 'stands on a mountain peak by himself. Nobody understands him, nor does he understand anybody. We need not consider him in this connection. All his policies in regard to India, if I may say so, are bad—bad economics, bad sense, and bad temper.' Eighteen months later Nehru claimed that the party Rajaji had started, Swatantra, was 'a mixture of the rottenest ideas imaginable'.

Sensitive observers mourned and worried about the gulf between the two. In May 1959, Rajaji's biographer Monica Felton told him that 'if I were the mother of you and the Prime Minister, I would bang your two heads together and tell you to stop arguing and to settle down and run things together.' Walter Crocker thought their differences real but by no means irreconcilable. Both loved freedom, both were deeply moral beings, and both were passionately committed to social and religious tolerance. Yet they fell out. 'Here was great drama', said Crocker: 'Two figures of Shakespearean scale in contest. And the drama was tragedy, for the contest was needless. Both men were required by India in the two crucial decades following Independence; and both men shared the blame, though perhaps not in equal measure, that there had been fission, not fusion, between them.'

The assessment by Nehru's sister, Vijayalakshmi Pandit, was not dissimilar. She wrote to Rajaji in June 1964: 'It seemed such a bad thing that two men like yourself and Bhai who had contributed so much individually and jointly to our beloved India should be apart at a time of national crisis. But the moment passed and now it is too late.'

This was written weeks after Nehru's death. That event had occasioned a brief obituary published by Rajaji in *Swarajya*:

> Eleven years younger than me, eleven times more important to the nation, eleven hundred times more beloved of the nation, Sri Nehru has suddenly departed from our midst and I remain alive to hear the sad news from Delhi—and bear the shock. . . .
>
> The old guard-room is completely empty now . . . I have been fighting Sri Nehru all these ten years over what I consider faults in public policies. But I knew all along that he alone could get them corrected. No one else would dare do it, and he is gone, leaving me weaker than before in my fight. But fighting apart, a beloved friend is gone, the most civilized person among us all. Not many among us are civilized yet.
>
> God save our people.

These words might serve as an epitaph to the relationship between these two remarkable men. Or one might choose instead the story of Edwina Mountbatten's visit to Madras in early 1953. Told about the visit, Rajaji drew up a punishing programme, whereby Lady Mountbatten would have to visit corporation slums, meet social workers, open a high school, have tea with army wives, see the temples at Mahabalipuram, and dine at the Raj Bhavan. When this schedule was sent back to Delhi it provoked this panic-stricken telegram from the prime minister: 'Programme sent by Mary Clubwalla for Edwina's visit to Madras is rather heavy. She has not been very fit. There is no mention in programme of her visit to you. This is main purpose of her going to Madras.'

This, read intelligently, might even be the most generous compliment ever paid by Nehru to a fellow Indian. If Edwina is to have stimulating conversation in India—Nehru is saying to Rajaji—and if it is to be with someone other than myself, then it must be only with you.

IV. Rajaji and the Bomb

Mahatma Gandhi once remarked that the atom bomb was 'the greatest sin known to science'. After India exploded a nuclear device in May 1998 and the nation swirled around itself in hysteria, it took a contemporary Gandhian to remember what the Master had said. Thus, the first dissenting article in the national press was written by the veteran architect Laurie Baker, who recalled three tests that an invention of science had to pass in a country such as ours: Is it non-violent? Is it eco-friendly? Is it poverty-reducing? The answers, in the case at hand, were No, No, and No.

India is now a certifiable nuclear power. This would have displeased Gandhi, and also displeased Rajagopalachari, the Gandhian who, in his lifetime, mounted the most sustained campaign against nuclear weapons. In 1945, after the bombs were dropped on Hiroshima and Nagasaki, he quipped: 'All this while we knew only of the chemist's bombs. Now we know of bombs made by physicists.' A decade later his tone was deadly serious. Rajmohan Gandhi quotes from a letter written by Rajaji to *The New York Times* at the end of 1954, in which he urged each party in the Cold War not to 'wait for the other', but to unilaterally 'throw all the atomic bombs in the deep Antarctic and begin a new world free from fear.'

In 1959, in a piece directed against nuclear tests, Rajaji wrote in disgust of

> politicians and technicians who do not believe in co-existence and mutual trust, but are convinced, and have been doing their best to educate the

people to believe, that the best defence of national existence is to make it clear that they have terrible weapons of retaliation. And this is naturally associated with a policy of armament manufacture to achieve that retaliatory strength and purpose.

He was speaking, of course, of America and Russia then, but he could as well have been speaking of India and Pakistan now.

Rajaji thought the making of atom bombs was the product of hubris, with man believing he 'had the rights and privileges of the sun or even of the Lord God himself.' It was, he remarked, 'an unfortunate day when science lifted the curtain of fundamental matter and trespassed into the greenroom of creation.' Rajaji made a distinction between a 'free science' which honestly documented the radiation effects of nuclear tests, and a 'hired science' which tried to doctor its results. These tests, he said, were 'a wholly illegitimate attack on the health of the present and future generations of the uninvolved millions, who have not yet written off their rights in favour of the nuclear pugilists.'

Rajaji's campaign against nuclear arms culminated in a journey he made to the United Kingdom and the United States in 1962, at the head of a three-member delegation travelling under the auspices of the Gandhi Peace Foundation. (The other members were R.R. Diwakar and B. Shiva Rao.) Rajaji was eighty-three, and this, believe it or not, was his first trip to the West. In America he met, among others, Henry Kissinger; Robert Oppenheimer (the man who had led the Los Alamos team that made the atom bomb, but had later thrown his hat into the peace camp); and the representatives to the United Nations of the Soviet Union and the United States. Rajaji also spoke at several universities and at the prestigious Council of Foreign Relations in New York. All through, he pursued his case against the Bomb with (to quote his biographer, Rajmohan Gandhi) 'the energy of a 40-year-old.'

The highlight of the trip was a meeting with John F. Kennedy, who had set aside twenty-five minutes but was so charmed by Rajaji that in the end they chatted for over an hour. Later, Kennedy told an aide that 'seldom have I heard a case presented with such precision, clarity and elegance of language.' He added that the interview had 'a civilizing quality about it.' A diplomat who was present, B.K. Nehru, recalled how 'the secretaries who came in with slips of paper reminding the President of his appointments were shooed away.' Kennedy, it appears, was 'fascinated' by Rajaji.

But Rajaji wasn't entirely sure that the president was convinced. A week later, the journalist Vincent Shean met him in New York and sought to gift him a stamp of Mahatma Gandhi issued just then by the U.S. Postal Department. 'You keep it', said Rajaji to Shean, 'and use it in a letter to Kennedy asking for the renunciation of the atomic bomb.'

After the delegation's return to India, B. Shiva Rao wrote to Jawaharlal Nehru of the impact its leader had made. When Rajaji spoke at the Council of Foreign Relations, the leader of the American delegation to the U.N. Disarmament Conference in Geneva told Shiva Rao: 'Why don't you send this man to represent India at Geneva?' Altogether, Rajaji made 'a deep impression on all the persons he saw in the U.S.A. and England.' He would, Shiva Rao told the prime minister, 'make an admirable representative for India . . . in Geneva.' He was 'extremely able and dignified in his presentation of the case for nuclear disarmanent.' Were he indeed to be sent as the government's representative to the talks, it would aid India in playing 'a constructive part in bringing about phased disarmament. . .'.

The suggestion was well meant and well merited. But by this time Nehru and Rajaji were in rival political parties. True, they agreed on the Bomb, but the older man's attacks on his economic and social policies the prime minister found hard to forgive. 'Rajaji is undoubtedly a person of high ability', replied Nehru to Shiva Rao, 'and we all have respect and affection for him. But I doubt very much if he will at all suit or fit in with the Disarmament Conference at Geneva which consists of senior officials. Also, unfortunately, he disagrees with almost everything in the domestic or international sphere for which some of us stand.' Partisan considerations would not allow India to send its best man to Geneva.

Strikingly, Rajaji was against atomic power as well as atomic weapons. When, in 1954, the *Times of India* insisted that nuclear energy was vital to a 'power-starved' India, Rajaji drew their attention to the 'terrible character of the risks necessarily attached' to this industry. Its process of production 'totally disregards the rights of those that do not in any way benefit from the enterprises.' Moreover, 'the general public is almost entirely ignorant of all that the new power source involves. It is not like coal or oil but comparable to a hypothetical case of using the thunderbolt to cook our breakfast.' This was characteristically acute, as well as prescient, for it took another two or three decades before science and society made a proper acquaintance with the risks and costs of nuclear power.

The anti-nuclear movement in India has witnessed the not always comfortable coexistence of Gandhians and Communists. However, after 1998, it has been more or less captured by the Left who, on the one hand, do not question the dangers of nuclear energy and, on the other, seem to think that nuclear weapons are somehow safe if placed in the hands of Red regimes. Rajaji's work has a more general relevance to questions of scientific ethics and nationalist military rivalry, but it also has a more specific relevance to the ethics of the anti-nuclear movement. He once expressed his wish to 'rescue the peace movement from the clutches of the Communist Party.' This is a task that remains unfinished.

The Environmentalist
of the Poor: Anil Agarwal

The Berkeley Nobel Laureate George Akerlof once remarked of his fellow economists that if you showed them something that worked in practice, they would not be satisfied unless it was also seen to work in theory. This insight explains much about the dismal science, including why, as late as 1980, the MIT economist Lester Thurow could so magisterially write: 'If you look at the countries that are interested in environmentalism, or at the individuals who support environmentalism within each country, one is struck by the extent to which environmentalism is an interest of the upper middle class. Poor countries and poor individuals simply aren't interested.'

It does not appear that Thurow looked very closely around the globe. For, seven years before he wrote his lines, the Chipko Andolan had decisively announced the poor's entry into the domain of environmentalism. Nor was Chipko unique: the decade of the 1970s saw a whole slew of popular movements in defence of local rights to forest, fish and water resources, as well as protests against large dams. These movements took place in India, Brazil, Malaysia, Ecuador and Kenya, and among peasants, pastoralists, and fisherfolk: that is, among communities even economists could identify as being poor.

Lester Thurow could write as he did because of the theory that environmentalism is a full-stomach phenomenon. In the West, the rise of the green movement in the 1960s was widely interpreted as a manifestation of what was called 'post-materialism'. The consumer societies of the North Atlantic world, wrote the political scientist Ronald Inglehart, had collectively shifted 'from giving top priority to physical sustenance and safety toward heavier emphasis on belonging, self-expression, and the quality of life.' It was thought that a cultivated interest in the protection of nature was possible only when the necessities of life could be taken for granted. As for the poor, their waking hours were spent foraging for food, water, housing, energy: how could they be concerned with something as elevated as the *environment*?

Movements such as Chipko challenged the post-materialist hypothesis, in practice. But its decisive theoretical refutation was the work of the campaigning journalist Anil Agarwal, who died in Dehradun on the 2nd of January 2002, aged fifty-four. Agarwal was a man of ferocious intelligence and commitment, these traits displayed early. At the Indian Institute of Technology, Kanpur, where he studied mechanical engineering, he was elected president of the students' gymkhana. After he graduated, he travelled in Europe but came back to join the *Hindustan Times* as a science reporter, this when his classmates were taking the already well-trodden route to the United States. His flair for communicating complex ideas in clear language was recognized by the *New Scientist*, for which he also began to write.

The story that changed Agarwal's life originated in a visit to the Alakananda valley sometime in early 1975. The Chipko Andolan was then less than two years old. But Agarwal was impressed by what it had already done and more impressed still by its leader, Chandi Prasad Bhatt.

Agarwal returned from Garhwal with an essay that, with a key word misspelt, was printed in the *New Scientist* under the title 'Ghandi's Ghost Protects the Himalayan Trees'. It might have been the first account of the Chipko movement in the international press. It was certainly a definitive moment in the career of its author. It was through Chipko that Agarwal came to understand that the poor had, if anything, a greater stake in the responsible management of the environment. That insight became the driving force of his work over the next twenty-five years.

In the mid 1970s Agarwal moved to London to join the International Institute for Environment and Development. There he came under the caring tutelage of Barbara Ward, the author with René Dubos of *Only One Earth*, the 'official' text of the first United Nations Symposium on the Environment. Then, encouraged by that remarkable civil servant Lovraj Kumar, he decided to return to India to found the Centre for Science and Environment (CSE) in New Delhi.

Not long after founding CSE, Agarwal went for a meeting in Malayaysia, a trip that was as definitive as his earlier trek to Garhwal. For his hosts in Penang had just published a report on the 'State of Malaysia's Environment'. It was a slim document, but suggestive. No sooner had he read it than Agarwal started planning a more ambitious Indian version. The material was at hand, if one cared to look for it. For the natural resource conflicts of the 1970s had been attentively and sympathetically documented by our journalists, writing in English as well as in the Indian languages. The academic community was by and large blind to the degradation of the environment, but here too there were exceptions, most notably the partnership of the ecologist Madhav Gadgil and the anthropologist Kailash Malhotra. These two had just completed an extended study on behalf of the newly instituted Department of Environment, which documented the shrinking access to nature in the villages and hamlets of India. There was also the work on fisheries by John Kurien and on common property by N.S. Jodha: two economists with a most atypical orientation towards fieldwork.

Drawing on these scattered studies, and aided by his colleagues Ravi Chopra and Kalpana Sharma, Agarwal and the CSE published *The State of India's Environment 1982: A Citizens' Report*. This was a landmark, in an intellectual sense—as the first serious overview of the use and abuse of nature in India. But its merits were as much about form as content. The report was attractively produced and imaginatively laid out: plenty of pictures interwoven with the text, boxes artfully designed to highlight salutary or egregious examples, numbers and tables sparingly but effectively used.

This work, often referred to as the First Citizens' Report was, in a word, a triumph. Two years later the CSE put out a Second Citizens' Report, edited by Agarwal and his colleague Sunita Narain, an effervescent young activist who had come to environmentalism through the Delhi-based students' group, Kalpavriksh. This report was presented as elegantly as its predecessor, but it was more thorough, and enriched by two essays on the politics of the environment, written by Agarwal and Dunu Roy.

The Citizens' Reports were a simultaneous wake-up call to an insular academy, a half-blind state, and a somnolent public. They were read, discussed, and acted upon, and came to enjoy an influence far in excess of what its editors anticipated: this influence not being out of proportion with their intrinsic value. Among the signs of how good the reports were was the fact that their Kannada and Hindi translators were Shivarama Karanth, the great Kannada novelist and polymath; and the respected environmentalist and Chipko historian Anupam Mishra.

In between the publication of the two Citizens' Reports, Anil Agarwal lectured in Calcutta. I lived then in that city. I was in the last throes of a Ph.D. dissertation on forests and social protest in the Himalaya. During the course of my research I had met Agarwal, interviewed him on his encounters with Chipko, and raided the files on the movement that he generously placed at my disposal. Like him, I had met and been captivated by Chandi Prasad Bhatt. My conversion to their brand of environmentalism, however, was interrupted at every stage by my milieu, by the dominance in Calcutta of a worldview that regarded ecology as a bourgeois deviation from the class struggle.

It was to such a sceptical audience that Anil Agarwal was asked to speak. The talk was held in the Mahabodhi Society, in a long low hall which, like all such places in Calcutta, had a marked scarcity of light. But this dark room was gloriously illuminated by the lecturer. Agarwal was a little man, five feet four inches at most, his figure made less prepossessing by a heavily banded pair of spectacles. Yet the glasses could not hide the sparkle, nor the slightness of his figure overshadow the manifest energy and enthusiasm. Bobbing up and down the podium, he delivered a missionary sermon to a bunch of pagans, piling up example upon example of the destruction of nature and its impact on the poor. The crowd, at first unbelieving, slowly came round, persuaded by the integrity of the man as much by the solid core of his message.

Agarwal was that rare bird, a superb public speaker who was also a skilled writer. (Indians who are good at the one form of communication are generally hopeless at the other.) He had a way of immediately attracting the reader's attention, most often through clever juxtaposition. Thus his flamboyant but also deeply insightful remark of how natural resources management in India was a case of 'nineteenth-century laws for twenty-first century realities'. Thus also his mischievous yet not entirely facetious desire to define GNP afresh as 'Gross Nature Product'. I recall, too, a piece on how the Maharashtra government had been forbidden by the Forest Conservation Act to construct water taps for pilgrims en route to the shrine of Bhimashankar. Agarwal suggested that the application to the Centre be reworded to claim that the taps were intended for migrating elephants. (The recommendation was acutely topical, for the environment minister at the time was the animal fundamentalist Maneka Gandhi.)

Under Agarwal's leadership, the CSE played a critical role in at least four environmental campaigns. To begin with, the Chipko experience informed his participation in the countrywide struggle for a democratic forest management. This struggle won a partial success when, in 1988, the Indian parliament accepted that ecological stability and people's needs, rather than commercial exploitation, were to be the cornerstones of the new, 'official', forest policy. Inspired by the same ideals of local participation and control were the CSE's seminars and reports on traditional water harvesting. These, emphasizing the creative partnership between indigenous knowledge and collective action, were compiled in a valuable volume with the characteristically catchy title, *Dying Wisdom.*

Admiration for the work of Anil Agarwal and the CSE was never confined to India. Nonetheless, their presence on the global stage was enhanced by the publication, in 1989, of *Global Warming in an Unequal World*, a pamphlet co-authored by Agarwal and Sunita Narain. This made a distinction between the 'survival emissions' of the poor, as for instance the methane released by paddy cultivation, and the 'luxury emissions' of the rich, such as the gases released into the atmosphere by the automobile–industrial complex. The conventional wisdom out of Washington sought to suggest that the poor were as responsible for global warming: thus, countries such as India and China needed to be as quick and ready in their remedial measures as, say, the United States and Germany. This wisdom had been restated in a report of the World Resources Institute (WRI), a report which Agarwal and Narain brutally took apart. They showed, first, that the WRI report erased the past, the historical responsibility for the build-up of greenhouse gases by the industrialized countries; and second, that in its prescriptions for the future the WRI made the unfair and illogical assumption that the carbon 'sink' provided by the oceans and atmosphere should be divided in proportion to the magnitude of greenhouse gases currently emitted by each country. A more just and tenable assumption, argued the Indians, would be to allocate each individual human being an equal share of the carbon sink.

The WRI report, in sum, sought to blame the victims and reward the polluters. This, said Agarwal and Narain, was an unhappy but by no means unique illustration of the 'environmental colonialism' that ruled international negotiations on climate change and the protection of biodiversity. As the CSE complained in a 'Statement on Global Democracy' issued specially for the Earth Summit of June 1992:

There is no effort to create new levels of power that would allow all citizens of the world to participate in global environmental management. Today, the reality is that Northern governments and institutions can, using their economic and political power, intervene in, say, Bangladesh's development. But no Bangladeshi can intervene in the development processes of Northern economies even if global warming caused largely by Northern emissions may submerge half [their] country.

Even so, at least one Indian was able to positively intervene in global debates. Sometimes his influence passed unnoticed. Thus, the World-watch Institute has reproduced, more-or-less wholesale, the frame-work of the CSE Citizens' Reports in its own *State of the World Reports*, issued annually since 1987. These follow the Indian example in dividing the work into thematic sections, using boxes as a key illus-trative device, and seeking to address multiple audiences—policy as well as popular. The imitation is so obvious that in a just world Agar-wal ought to have demanded compensation for his hard-won intel-lectual property.

On a personal front Anil Agarwal possessed an almost heroic deter-mination. He conducted a long battle against chronic asthma, and then in 1994 was diagnosed as suffering from a very rare form of can-cer which affected the eyes and brain. From his sick bed, while in re-mission he planned and carried out his last campaign. This related to the shamefully high levels of air pollution in Delhi. The CSE report on the problem was called—with an evocative economy so typical of the man—*Slow Murder*. This report almost singlehandedly forced the government to introduce remedial measures, these aimed both at vehicles and factories. Agarwal's insistence on Compressed Natural Gas (CNG) as Delhi's sole alternative to existing fuels became some-what controversial. The jury is still out on whether CNG or low-sul-phur diesel is the more suitable choice, yet there is no gainsaying the fact that, without Agarwal and the CSE, the citizens of Delhi would still be subject to the *ancien regime* of pollution unchecked and undiagnosed.

For more than twenty years Anil Agarwal was India's most arti-culate and influential writer on the environment. Viewing his career in the round, one is struck by several features. First, an ability to syn-thesize the results of specialized scientific studies. Second, a knack of communicating this synthesis in accessible prose. Third, the insist-ence that it was not enough for the environmentalist to hector and chastise: solutions had to be offered, even if the state was as yet un-willing to act upon them.

One is impressed, too, by the range of Agarwal's work. Forests, water, biodiversity, climate change at the global level, air pollution in a single city: he studied and wrote about them all. What unites these dispersed and prolific writings is Agarwal's approach—he looks at environmental problems from the perspective of the poor. His oeuvre provides an intellectual and moral challenge to the belief that the poor are too poor to be green. He demonstrates that, in the biomass economies of the rural Third World, the poor have a vital interest in the careful management of forests, soil, pasture, and water. (The rich can more easily shift to alternative fuels and building materials.) In his later work, he shows likewise that, the more prosperous the country or community, the more likely it is to insulate itself from the harmful effects of pollution while passing on this burden to the disadvantaged.

If I had to recommend only one essay by Agarwal, it would be his World Conservation Lecture of 1985, first published in *The Environmentalist*, 1986, and reprinted in an anthology I edited, *Social Ecology* (Oxford University Press, 1994). This essay presents a detailed picture of environmental destruction in India, against the backdrop of the rather different Western experience. The examples are drawn from across the country and deal with a variety of natural resources. The conclusions are crisply and unambiguously stated. The 'first lesson' is that 'the main source of environmental destruction in the world is the demand for natural resources generated by the consumption of the rich (whether they are rich nations or rich individuals and groups within nations) . . .' The 'second lesson' is that 'it is the poor who are affected the most by environmental destruction'; thus, the 'eradication of poverty in a country like India is simply not possible without the rational management of our environment and that, conversely, environmental destruction will only intensify poverty.'

Agarwal anticipates in this essay a theme later picked up by feminist writers. As he put it:

The destruction of the environment clearly poses the biggest threat to marginal cultures and occupations like [those] of tribals, nomads, fisherfolk and artisans, which have always been heavily dependent on their

immediate environment for their survival. But the maximum impact of
the destruction of biomass sources is on women. Women in all rural cultures are affected, especially women from poor landless, marginal and
small farming families. Seen from the point of view of these women, it
can be argued that all development is ignorant of women's needs, and
often anti-women, literally designed to increase their work burden.

The process of resource degradation, says Agarwal, has made it more
difficult and dangerous for women to go about the business of collecting fuel, fodder and water. He makes an inspired distinction between 'male' trees—species promoted by forest departments seeking
to increase their cash income—and 'female' trees, those species that
lighten the woman's load yet tend not to be favoured by public agencies. On the whole, Agarwal's understanding of the gender dimensions of the environment debate was indubitably ahead of its time. It
has always seemed to me that his precocity has not been adequately
recognized, perhaps because in this regard he happened to belong to
the wrong gender himself.

It was, I think, Voltaire who said that while one might seek to flat-
ter the living, the dead deserve nothing less than the truth. No assessment of Anil Agarwal as writer and activist can overlook his flaws.
These were personal as well as intellectual. Thus, while the first two
pioneering Citizens' Reports were being produced, Agarwal and the
CSE were catalysts to a genuinely collaborative exercise. Over the
years, however, Agarwal came to distance himself from many individuals and trends in the environmental community with whom he
had once worked and who had contributed to his reports. Perhaps this
alienation was related to his creeping cancer. Still, one could not altogether overcome the suspicion that the CSE would participate in a
campaign only if it could orchestrate and direct it. One example was
the organization's withdrawal, over the 1990s, from the continuing
struggle for forest democracy. Again, it is something of a pity that the
activities of the Narmada Bachao Andolan were never adequately
covered in the pages of the CSE fortnightly *Down to Earth*. Future

historians of this most important social movement will find more meat in the reports of daily newspapers than in this specialist environmentalist journal.

Agarwal had a deeply prejudiced attitude towards the bureaucracy, which he distrusted and seemed at times to despise. This is a trait shared by some kinds of Gandhians and some kinds of Marxists, and indeed Agarwal was a sort of socialist Gandhian himself. What made his prejudice unpalatable is that he had no difficulty courting ruling politicians. At various times he closely identified himself with the prime minister, Rajiv Gandhi, the environment minister Kamal Nath, and Madhya Pradesh's chief minister Digvijay Singh—with such men he kept in abeyance his sceptical attitude towards power and authority.

In an interview to *Seminar*, Agarwal described the bureaucracy as 'pig-headed, obstinate and stupid'. 'I don't expect the bureaucracy to do it', he added, speaking of natural resource management, adding: 'The only way the bureaucracy will work together is if there is a drive from the top.' These strictures appear to me to be excessive as well as false: forestry reform in West Bengal was initiated by capable and far-sighted officials without directives from the 'top'. There are good bureaucrats as well as bad ones. Agarwal hoped to dispense with the class altogether, a wish that seems naïve in light of the needs of a complex modern society. (Perhaps, in a long distant past, a benevolent raja could actually 'return the forests to the people'.) Our politicians need to be sensitized and—in my view more crucially—our bureaucrats humanized. This, of course, will take much persuasion and agitation. Still, a sustainable system of environmental management cannot come about by turning one's back on officials of the state, whether they be paid or elected.

There are environmental activists who were wounded by Agarwal's capricious behaviour, and there are environmental scholars who were obliged to state their disagreement with aspects of his work. Yet even when we stopped speaking with him, we read him. This is a measure of his continuing importance, but I hope I have adequately stressed the other measures too. It was a privilege to have known him, and a honour to have been a fellow traveller on a rocky road—the Indian road to sustainability.

Permanent Rebellion: The Story of B.P. Koirala

'Every man's life', remarked Dr Johnson, 'should be best written by himself.' Strangely, Johnson did not carry out his own injunction, and it was Boswell who set out for posterity the main contours of Johnson's life.

One must not unduly regret Johnson's failure. For one thing, it allowed Boswell to write what is still among the most widely read of all biographies. For another, the autobiography is the most perilous of literary forms. As the French scholar André Maurois pointed out, it is marked by a 'deliberate forgetfulness', a willed failure to remember failure, a desire to omit events that were unpleasant or that might undermine one's reputation. The autobiography, says Maurois, is a genre marked by lack of sincerity. It forgets and it rationalises. It gives order and retrospective coherence to decisions made *ad hoc* and more or less on the spot.

The memoirs that rationalise the most, Maurois further notes, are those written by military men and politicians. The general's victories in his re-telling owe nothing to accident and impulse, or luck: they are the product of planning and tactical skill alone. The prime minister's policies owe nothing to expediency or compromise; they are made exclusively on the basis of ideology and principle. I have no interest in military history myself, but the political memoirs I have read tend to confirm Maurois's judgement. For the most part, these are exercises in vanity and self-justification, and the less authentic (as well as readable) for that.

The autobiography of the Nepali politician and sometime prime minister B.P. Koirala is a stunning exception to this rule. It is a remarkable document of personal and social history, a vivid account of exile and rebellion which provides acute insights into the history and politics of the twentieth century. Koirala's memoirs were not written but spoken, dictated into a microphone held by his friend and associate—the Kathmandu lawyer Ganesh Raj Sharma. When he began the exercise, in December 1981, the politician was already in the advanced stages of throat cancer. The transcripts remained with Sharma for years; only when Nepal renewed its acquaintance with democracy, in the 1990s, was it deemed safe to place them before the public. A Nepali edition appeared in 1998, published by Jagdamba Prakashan in Lalitpur. Three years later appeared an English version, translated by Kanak Mani Dixit and published by Himal Books under the title *Atmabrittanta: Late Life Recollections.*

Born in 1914, BP was the son of Krishna Prasad Koirala, a poet, businessman and reformer who fought and made up—and then fought again—with the Rana rulers of Nepal. Krishna Prasad helped establish the town of Biratnagar in the Terai, where he made his money running a series of customs posts. He opened a school and a hospital, and promoted the uplift of women. He believed that girls must ride bicycles and horses, and learn to use daggers and guns—if only to keep away lecherous louts. He once remarked that 'women and men are like two wheels of a chariot' and 'you needed both wheels to run the chariot.' With ideas such as these it is not surprising that he fell foul of the Ranas and sought exile in British India. His son's memoirs narrate the ups and downs of the Koirala fortunes; the businesses bought by the father and sold or run into the ground; the homes fitfully occupied by the family in the towns of Bihar and the United Provinces.

BP grew up in the India of the 1920s, a place and time offering a plenitude of political choices. There was Gandhi and there was Lenin. There was also Ataturk, an appealing model for rationalists seeking to rid their society of tradition and custom.

Koirala chose Gandhi. After hearing the Mahatma speak, he told his father he would join an ashram school. The patriarch encouraged him, for he believed that the Indian national movement 'was also our movement because the autocracy of the Ranas was supported by British imperialists'. The boy, meanwhile, was soaking in the progressive writing of the Indo-Gangetic plain. He read the nationalist Hindi poets Maithili Sharan Gupt and Jai Shankar Prasad, and above all, the great Hindi novelist Premchand. Indeed, it was in Premchand's journal *Hans* that BP made his literary debut.

Along with his brother, Matrika Prasad Koirala, BP was arrested during the 1930 movement, suspected of being part of a terrorist ring. He was, however, released for lack of evidence. The father had meanwhile made up with the Ranas and gone back to Nepal. The son stayed on in India and turned leftwards. He read Marx, listened to Radio Moscow, and hung about with communists. The Assamese writer Dev Kanta Baruah (still an honest radical then, not the craven *chamcha* of Indira Gandhi that he later became) alerted BP to the exploitation of farm workers by landlords. Koirala was impressed by Marxist theory, but less so by communist politics. He could not accept the CPI's view that the national movement 'was nothing, that it was being masterminded by the British themselves, and that Gandhi was an unknowing agent of the British.'

It was at about this time that the Nepali radical made the acquaintance of that other oscillator between Gandhi and Marx, Jayaprakash Narayan. 'I was greatly impressed by him', writes Koirala: 'he did not use sophisticated language and exhibited a simple personality.' BP also befriended the socialists Acharya Narendra Dev and Ram Manohar Lohia. He was studying at Banaras Hindu University (BHU), a hotbed of Congress socialists. Like them, and like Jawaharlal Nehru,

he thought of going to Spain to fight on the Republican side in the
civil war.

After graduating from BHU, Koirala tried his hand at the law and
worked as a labour organiser in north Bihar. He was arrested for in-
citing workers but soon released. He was 'out' only for a little while,
for he now got caught up in the Quit India movement. He was lodged
in Bankipur jail, where one of his fellow prisoners was Dr Rajendra
Prasad. They engaged in friendly but vigorous debate; Rajen *babu* on
the side of spiritualism, the Nepali on behalf of scientific socialism.

Koirala was released in 1945 and began plotting a successful return
to his native land. The Second World War was over, and Indian independence seemed imminent. The formation of an Interim Government led by Nehru in September 1946 encouraged Nepali exiles to
think seriously of fighting for democracy too. Their country had for
a century been under the thumb of the Ranas. This lineage of aristo-
crats owned the land, controlled the army, monopolized the top
administrative jobs, and manipulated the hereditary monarch. According to the historian Aniruddh Gupta, 'the survival of Rana rule
mainly depended on its capacity to suppress the growth of political
awakening in the country.' The most effective way of retaining control was to deny the privileges of higher education to commoners.

To get himself a college degree, every ambitious young Nepali had
to travel to India. With education came political radicalism. By the
1940s there were plenty of young men like the Koirala brothers who
believed, to quote an emigré journal, that 'the salvation of the Nepa-
lese lies in struggle', that 'to hope for reforms from the Ranas is like
hoping for milk from a dry cow.' On 25 January 1947 these men established the Nepali National Congress with the help of funds from a
handful of disgruntled Ranas. In March of that year BP's younger
brother, Girija Prasad, helped instigate a strike of jute mill workers in
Biratnagar. BP crossed over to help. He was arrested and taken with
his fellow agitators to Kathmandu, a long, slow walk across the hills.
It took three weeks to get to the capital, the prisoners' march attracting much attention and helping to radicalize peasants whose villages lay en route.

The Koiralas were kept in a Kathmandu bungalow. Letters to the Rana prime minister by Gandhi, Rajendra Prasad and others helped bring about their early release. BP went back to India and began looking for arms to storm Kathmandu. He tells a lovely story, possibly embroidered, of how he journeyed to Calcutta in the last week of January 1948 to buy arms. He made contact with an arms dealer, and at 6 p.m. on the 30th was met on a Calcutta street corner by a stranger who passed him a parcel and vanished. The parcel was to be passed on, in turn, to a dissident Rana named Basanta Shumshere, who was to throw its contents at his assembled kinsmen in Nepal. As Koirala waited—the grenades wrapped in a hand towel—'from the radio of a cigarette and *paan* vendor nearby I heard the news—Gandhi has died.' The Rana arrived: the bundle was handed over. BP came back to his boarding house and wept with remorse through the night. In time he was consoled by the words of Ho Chi Minh: 'Whatever may be my disagreements with Gandhi, we are all his products. Wherever there is a struggle, he has given his support and moral leadership. Even as someone who believes in violence, I can say that we are all his progeny.'

The story has a tame ending: the Rana entrusted with the job was too scared to set off the grenades. So, later in 1948, BP entered Kathmandu himself, disguised as a pandit. He made contact with other democrats but was found out and put in jail once more. The conditions were awful. His feet were fettered and

a blacksmith was brought from outside to do the job. He had to hammer vertically in order to fix the fetters, but in order not to hurt my foot in case the hammer slipped, he was striking at a slant. Once, the hammer did slip and struck the stone on which the fetters rested. At that, the officer who was standing next to me scolded the blacksmith, 'Careful! You might break the slab!' The blacksmith replied, 'I was aiming at the foot but it slipped and hit the stone.'

'If his bone is broken it will mend, but will you give me money for this broken piece of stone?'

Such harsh words serve to illustrate the attitude of my jailers.

The blacksmith visited the prisoner twice a day, to remove and then rejoin his fetters before and after meals. The British jails he had been in, writes Koirala, were a model of decency and cleanliness by comparison. To draw attention to his condition BP went on a fast which stretched to nearly four weeks. He was then freed and trekked once more into India. It was now June 1949. After a hasty medical check-up the exile began planning his return. In April 1950 the coming together of two factions created a brand new party named the Nepali Congress. Then, in November, King Tribhuvan fled to India. The struggle accelerated. A band of Nepali Congressman stormed a treasury in Birganj. A tractor dressed up as a tank—its sides were dressed with metal sheets—forced its way into the governor's garrison in the key town of Biratnagar.

Meanwhile, the Ranas in Kathmandu were growing nervous. King Tribhuvan's flight, remarks Aniruddh Gupta in *Politics in Nepal*, 'not only dealt an irreparable blow to Rana prestige, it made the people anxious about the safety of their Monarch whom they regarded as a divine being.' From his exile the king published an appeal for reconciliation. The Indian government convened a conference in Delhi, after which Tribhuvan returned with honour to his capital and put in place a coalition of Ranas and the Nepali Congress. The union was uncertain from the start, plagued by mutual suspicion. BP was home minister, but had to resign after his policemen fired on a students' demonstration. The government fell, to be replaced by another with Matrika Prasad Koirala as its head.

A revealing aspect of these memoirs is the bitter rivalry between the Koirala brothers. One was cautious, the other hot-headed. One was a moderate monarchist, the other a republican. Their disagreements were political as well as personal: BP even alleges that his brother once tried to bump him off. Jayaprakash Narayan tried, without success, to effect a reconciliation. Eventually, the Nepali Congress split into two parties, one for each brother.

In 1955 King Tribhuvan was succeeded by his son Mahendra, a man of greater ambition and resolve. Politicians were all dismissed to the margins, powers were centralised in the hands of the monarch.

After half a decade of rule by puppet prime ministers, the king was forced to call a general election in 1959, Nepal's first. The Nepali Congress swept the polls, winning 74 out of 109 seats. BP took office as prime minister. He stayed in the job for eighteen months, visiting India and China on state visits, and consorting with Nikita Khruschev at the United Nations. King Mahendra was resentful of Koirala's popularity within and (especially) outside Nepal. Late in 1960 the king organized a coup, sending his royal guards to arrest the prime minister and put him in jail. Mahendra was being pushed by the landed aristocracy to act before the Congress put in place radical land reforms. And, like monarchs everywhere, he had a congenital suspicion of democracy.

While his brother was in jail, Matrika Prasad went off as King Mahendra's ambassador to the United States. His family was fearful that BP would be bumped off—and thus meet the fate of the independent-minded prime minister of the Congo, Patrice Lumumba. Nehru sent a message of reassurance through Koirala's sister. Nehru's 'level of personal interest', remarks BP, was 'a source of great and reliable moral support for us prisoners who were so suddenly isolated.'

In 1965, with BP in jail, the Oxford University Press published a book called *Heroes and Builders of Nepal*. The author, a civil servant and diplomat, Rishikesh Shaha, began his narrative with Janaka and Buddha and ended with Tribhuvan and Mahendra, paying his dues en route to the great medieval warrior-kings Pratap Malla and Prithvinarayan Shah. His last chapter, titled 'The Dawn of Democracy in Nepal', is a paean to the monarchy. The ending of Rana autocracy is attributed solely to Tribhuvan: 'never before had there been a king who staked his life and throne to secure the liberty of his subjects.' Mahendra is praised for his 'successful foreign policy' and his 'work on national construction'; 'his leadership and personality', it is said, 'have aroused a deep awareness of national purpose'.

Given its author's position and the timing of its publication, the book makes no mention of the Nepali Congress or of the real hero and builder of modern Nepal, B.P. Koirala. It would be interesting to learn if BP read Shaha's book. Alas, his memoirs don't say. In any case, the narrative of the *Atmabrittanta* flags perceptibly after Koirala's arrest. The eight years in Sundarijal jail are glossed over. The text ends with Koirala's release and exile to India.

The book could have done with an editorial epilogue on Koirala's later life which, as always, was chock full with incident and controversy. Exiled once more to India, Koirala prepared his comrades in the Nepali Congress for a fresh round of armed struggle. Thirty-five of his young followers perished in a single encounter, wiped out by the Nepali army while taking shelter in a cave. In 1976 Koirala returned to his country, sensing perhaps that he had not long to live. He was immediately arrested and made a remarkable speech at his trial where he defended armed rebellion. In these last years in Nepal, he also supervised a transition in his party's leadership before dying of cancer in July 1982.

B.P. Koirala came of age while in exile in India. He first went to prison fighting for the freedom of a country not his own. He struck close friendships with Indian politicians. Jayaprakash Narayan and Jawaharlal Nehru were to him like his own big brothers. But after his return to Nepal, India itself appeared as Big Brother. As home minister and prime minister, writes Koirala, he had to fight against three forces: the royal palace, the land-holding élite, and India. Nehru might have been kind and polite, but his government deeply resented Koirala's independent foreign policy. The Indian ambassador in Kathmandu 'believed that he was even greater than the King.' One envoy, C.P.N. Singh, so readily threw his weight around that Koirala was constrained to tell a press conference in Banaras that 'the Indian ambassador wishes that our country be like his district board, and he regards himself as chairman of that district board.' Once, in New York, V.K. Krishna Menon asked Koirala—a sovereign prime minister—to accompany him to the airport to receive Nehru, a gesture that would tell all the world that Nepal wished to be seen as a client state of India. Naturally Koirala declined, but the wound festered: twenty years later he mentioned the incident in his memoirs as an example of how 'they [the Indians] just did not understand clean diplomacy.'

B.P. Koirala's *Atmabrittanta* was formally released in New Delhi in April 2001. Its themes are compelling anyway, but they have been made more poignant by the regicide in the Kathmandu palace. The book enjoys a more than ordinary resonance, speaking as it does of the remarkable hold of the monarchy in the popular imagination, of the fragility of Nepal's democracy, of its endemic hostility towards India, and of desperate inequality in the countryside. (The rise of Maoists in Nepal is a consequence of the failures of previous regimes to more effectively carry out the land reforms that Koirala had called for.) And the prime minister of Nepal, at the time of these recent tragic killings, was none other than the leader of the Biratnagar strikers of 1947, BP's younger brother Girija.

Koirala's memoirs should be read for their insights into Nepali politics. His book should be read for what it tells us about India and Indians. It should be read as a moving testament of one who was caught, on the right side, in the great (and unfinished) battle of the modern world—between autocracy and democracy. And it should be read for its literary qualities. For BP was one of his country's finest writers as well as its most prominent political rebel. His works include six novels, two collections of short stories, and hundreds of essays. As the critic C.K. Lal points out, BP was a literary innovator, perhaps the first Nepali writer to sensitively portray women and look towards local dialect rather than Sanskrit for inspiration. 'It is baffling', writes Lal, 'that no writer in Nepal to date has been able to reach the depth of mind of characters in a story the way BP did.'

As for the *Atmabrittanta*, even in this English version it sparkles. The book is rich with scenes and people closely and penetratingly observed. I read, with a flash of self-recognition, these remarks on Kathmandu's intellectuals: 'They love to highlight unimportant matters . . . They are big on discussion, but do not give a *paisa* of support.' And again: 'Whoever came [to India] from Kathmandu in those days used to arrive with a great air of mystery, as if they alone were carrying the heavy burden of revolution.'

The narrative glows with images both precise and illuminating. Here is Koirala on one of the many places he was obliged to call home:

The jailer led me to my place of incarceration. There was no light other than one smoky lantern with a weak flame. I was led into a cell, but I could not see anything. There was a bedstead made of wood so unseasoned that it looked like it would drip water; half the room had bluish algae on the walls. This much I could see. The ceiling was very low, and because it had been newly plastered the cement was still wet. The walls were cold and damp. They put my rug on the ground.

Exile, jail, exile again; life underground and life as the prime minister of his people: only Nelson Mandela among modern statesmen could so completely have known the highs and lows of politics. But even Mandela was not attacked by his fellow freedom fighters. This book has a fascinating account of a demonstration orchestrated against Koirala by his brother Matrika Prasad. He was due to speak at the town of Palpa, but certain dissidents were determined to keep him out:

> 'Murderer! Go back!' was the slogan they used, but I insisted on entering the town. It was quite a climb to get up there, and the road was difficult. Along the road, they had tied bones and skeletons on bamboo poles, and had put up bamboo barriers across the path. They threw stones at us, tried to hit me from the trail-side, and also tried to splatter me with black paint . . . The copper and bronze *gaagri* put out for my arrival had all been damaged, as were the welcome arches.

His associates were suitably intimidated, but Koirala insisted on going ahead with the public meeting, working through the night to organise it. The meeting, in the end, was successful. In the crowd to hear Koirala speak was the wandering American ornithologist S. Dillon Ripley.

BP provides a chilling description of the lifestyle of those celebrated fighters for the world's poor, the Chinese Communists. In Beijing Mao Zedong and Chou En-Lai stayed in lakeside palaces in the former emperor's grounds, their dwellings marked by great marble staircases and wall-to-wall carpeting. 'The grandeur amidst which the Chinese leaders were living', remarks Koirala, 'could not have been matched by any ruler of a capitalist state.' The visitor was allowed a joyride in Mao's personal train, with its well-appointed bedroom and its porcelain bathtub. Koirala, like China's Chairman, spent his time watching the countryside from the living room, this a large hall with glass walls and a glass roof, with 'a library, a table for playing cards, a chessboard, and waiters serving tea. Also, a sofa and revolving chairs.'

Reading B.P. Koirala's memoirs, I was struck by the parallels between his life and Nehru's. Both were democratic socialists who learnt much from Gandhi and a little from Marx. Both had fathers who were strong-minded and authoritative, self-made men who had a great deal of money and a political orientation besides. Both were, as sons, traitors to their class. Their political choices exposed them to poverty and oppression. Nonetheless, both enjoyed the ceremony of power: the bowing and scraping at state visits, the meetings at the United Nations. Both were truly charismatic figures who towered over their colleagues. BP's description of the 1959 elections in this book recalls the role played by Nehru in the Indian elections of 1952. Victory for the party candidate was assured only after Koirala or Nehru had descended from the heavens to speak: each constituency had, so to say, to be sanctified by a speech by the Great Leader. Their names got their party into power, but once in office, both were hemmed in by more cautious men at their side. The programmes of economic and social justice that they were in principle committed to never seriously took effect—Nehru might well have written, as Koirala does here, that 'real and effective support I did not get from my own party'. And in both cases, politics became a kind of family business: Nehru's daughter and grandson, and Koirala's elder and younger brother, also held office as prime minister of their country.

To this already extensive list one must add another similarity: both Koirala and Nehru had developed literary sensibilities, their political obligations coming in the way of their secondary careers as writers. But there are some notable divergences as well. Koirala appears to have had a more satisfactory married life. His experience of jail was certainly more painful. And his experience of power was more fleeting. Nehru, writes this book's translator wistfully, 'survived and led India for 17 years after its independence. Fate would not extend a similar privilege to B.P. Koirala, and even as his co-equals settled down to enjoy the fruits of post-colonial India, BP's fight for his people was just beginning. Ahead lay years more of imprisonment and in exile.'

One is tempted to say: politics' loss has been literature's gain. Nehru wrote a fine work of autobiography, published in 1936, when he had years in jail ahead of him. Nehru's book is persuasive because it is the testament of a rebel. He never went on to write of his years in office, perhaps because he was too busy, or perhaps because he knew that any such account would necessarily be evasive and euphemistic. Now, had B.P. Koirala been prime minister from, say, 1952 to 1967, Nepal might today have been a more contented society. But we would then have been denied these extraordinary memoirs, this nearly unique combination of political candour and literary elegance.*

*I am grateful to C.K. Lal for his help and advice in the writing of this essay.

Vajpayee's Nehru

I n the spring of 1977, thirty years of Congress rule ended and a
new government took power in New Delhi. Politicians who had
expected to live out their days in the opposition were unexpect-
edly thrust into ministerial office. In preparation, sycophantic bureaucrats began to take away or hide any visible signs in the secretariat
of the party and the family that had for so long governed India. One
member of the new Janata Government was quick to notice this not-
so-subtle spring cleaning. He was the external affairs minister, Atal
Behari Vajpayee. When he first entered his office, Vajpayee looked
around the walls and immediately identified a blank spot. 'This is
where Panditji's portrait used to be,' he told his secretary. 'I remember
it from my earlier visits to the room. Where has it gone? I want it
back.'

'Panditji' was of course Jawaharlal Nehru, a politician the new
foreign minister had reason to dislike. The organization in which Vajpayee was reared, the Rashtriya Swayamsevak Sangh (RSS), detested
Nehru. They suspected his culture, distrusted his politics, and opposed his economics. For the RSS, Nehru was an Anglicized Indian
out of touch with the realities of the motherland, a pseudo-secularist
soft on the minorities, a weak-kneed administrator who 'gave up' half
of Kashmir. To cap it all, in matters of economics he took his cues
from that godless dystopia, the Soviet Union.

All this Vajpayee had imbibed with his mother's milk, so to speak. But more recently, the two years before he became foreign minister had been spent in a jail where he had been placed by Nehru's daughter, Indira Gandhi. He had, in sum, compelling ideological and personal reasons to reject Nehru and his legacy. And yet he asked for Nehru's photograph to be reinstated in his office. This was a gesture that would not have come easily to some of his fellow *pracharaks*—to L.K. Advani, for instance. Vajpayee is a softer man and he must have been embarrassed by this brutal casting into the dustbin of one who was India's longest serving foreign minister—Nehru held that office for seventeen years, for as long as he was prime minister—as well as its most effective and charismatic. Despite all that he had learnt in his *shakha*, once he became foreign minister Vajpayee would have wished to claim this part of his predecessor's legacy, thus to once more make India an articulate and influential voice in world affairs.

The story of Vajpayee's entry into South Block in April 1977 was told to me by a now retired member of the Indian Foreign Service. To this anecdotal evidence of our current prime minister's admiration of the first person to hold the office, let me now offer the authoritative proof of print. Published in the proceedings of the Indian parliament for the year 1964 is a speech delivered by Atal Behari Vajpayee after the death of Nehru. It is an extraordinary tribute, whose full import and flavour is properly conveyed only in its original Hindi. Still, as I hope to show, it is moving enough in translation.

In the third week of May 1964, Vajpayee and Nehru had clashed in parliament. The prime minister had released Sheikh Abdullah from detention, and even sent him to Pakistan to negotiate a settlement with Field Marshal Ayub Khan. The Jana Sangh naturally opposed any such talks with the enemy. They had always rejected the 'two-nation theory', but, said Vajpayee to Nehru, the Sheikh's release and recent utterances had given voice to the still more pernicious 'three-nation theory', whereby Kashmir would have some kind of autonomous or (God forbid), even independent status.

While Sheikh Abdullah was in Pakistan, Nehru died. The Sheikh received the news while addressing a press conference in the capital of Pakistan-occupied Kashmir, Muzaffarabad. The Lion of Kashmir, reported one newspaper, 'broke into tears and sobbed . . . He could not speak for a few minutes. In a muffled voice, he said, "he is dead. I can't meet him".' Abdullah returned to Delhi, and from Palam headed straight to Teen Murti House. Here, 'Sheikh Abdullah cried like a child and the wreath nearly fell from his hands when he saw the body of Mr Nehru.'

We do not know of Atal Behari Vajpayee's first reactions to Nehru's death. However, speaking in parliament some days later, he said that with the prime minister's passing

> a dream has remained half-fulfilled, a song has become silent, and a flame has vanished into the Unknown. The dream was of a world free of fear and hunger; the song a great epic resonant with the spirit of the *Gita* and as fragrant as a rose, the flame a candle which burnt all night long, show-ing us the way.

The loss, said Vajpayee, was not that of a family or community or party. Mother India was in mourning because 'her beloved Prince has gone to sleep'. Humanity was sad because its servant and 'worshipper has left it for ever'. The 'benefactor of the downtrodden has gone'. The 'chief actor of the world stage has departed after performing his last act.'

Vajpayee went on to compare Jawaharlal Nehru to the most hal-lowed of all Indian heroes. In 'Panditji's life', he said, 'we get a glimpse of the noble sentiments to be found in the saga of Valmiki.' For, like Ram, Nehru was 'the orchestrator of the impossible and inconceiv-able'. He too 'was not afraid of compromise but would never compro-mise under duress'. In remembering the deceased prime minister, Vajpayee celebrated the human being whom 'no one can replace'. That 'strength of personality', he remarked, 'that vibrance and inde-pendence of mind, that quality of being able to befriend the opponent and enemy, that gentlemanliness, that greatness—this will not per-haps be found in the future.'

But Vajpayee also saluted the statesman. With the foundations of the republic built by Nehru now in question, he said, it was time to rededicate ourselves to his, and its, ideals.

With unity, discipline and self-confidence we must make this republic of ours flourish. The leader has gone, but the followers remain. The sun has set, yet by the shadow of stars we must find our way. These are testing times, but we must dedicate ourselves to his great aim, so that India can become strong, capable and prosperous. . . .

Above all, were India to 'establish lasting peace in the world; we shall succeed in paying proper homage to him.'

I am fairly sure that Vajpayee will never read this essay, but I hope some of his admirers and followers will. They will probably be embarrassed by it. I myself think that the speech whose translated excerpts I have reproduced here was a rather fine one. It was beautifully worded. It displayed the ability to 'befriend the opponent and enemy'—for which Vajpayee singled out Nehru. It was warm and heartfelt and humane: in a word, *gentlemanly*. Judging by this speech, and by other evidence that has come to us over the years, it seems clear that in some obvious ways—such as the courtesy towards his peers and adversaries—the young Jana Sanghi consciously modelled himself on his older Congress counterpart. The personal influence is manifest, but of any political influence there is, alas, not a trace.

Nirad Babu's Nehru

On the 8th of September 1951, *The Autobiography of an Unknown Indian* was published in London. When the book finally arrived in India, several weeks later, the author sent a copy to his literary mentor, Mohitlal Majumdar. Majumdar soon wrote back with words of appreciation, and then asked: 'What does Jawaharlal Nehru think of it?'

The Autobiography of an Unknown Indian was received with considerable acclaim in the United Kingdom but almost universally condemned in India. *Swadeshi*-minded reviewers saw it as a prejudiced look at Indian nationalism, as another drain inspector's report in the manner of Katherine Mayo's book *Mother India*. Only in *The Statesman* did it get any praise: but then *The Statesman* was still an English-owned paper, and its reviewer was that discerning and literate expatriate Englishman, Verrier Elwin.

Now, Jawaharlal Nehru was an Indian nationalist in politics and an English gentleman in his cultural make-up. What did he think of Nirad Chaudhuri's book? Alas, there is no sign that he ever read it. However, no sooner was the book published than Chaudhuri's bosses at All India Radio started waving the rule-book at him. By law, he was told, all government servants had to take official clearance before publishing a newspaper article, let alone a book. Owing to this transgression, Chaudhuri did not get the extension for which he had been recommended. Then, after he had retired from All India Radio, an informal ban was placed on his talking on or writing scripts for the organization, in those days a valuable source of supplementary income for writers.

Then, and later, it was suggested that these acts of vengeance were wreaked by people anxious to please the prime minister. It was claimed that Nehru was jealous of the attention the book got in England, where it was praised almost as widely as his own autobiography, published fifteen years earlier. Where Nehru was a world statesman, the author of this new book was, in his own words, an 'unknown Indian'. But these suggestions, or innuendoes, were rejected by Nirad Chaudhuri himself. In his later memoir, *Thy Hand, Great Anarch!*, Chaudhuri wrote that besides officials in the ministries, the Indian high commissioner in the UK, V.K. Krishna Menon, had 'strongly criticized' the *Autobiography* in public. And Menon was known to be a close friend of the prime minister. But Chaudhuri insisted that neither his views, nor anyone else's, would have caused Nehru to take revenge. As he put it, 'Jawaharlal Nehru was not the man to be roused to action over a book.'

Chaudhuri was giving the great man the benefit of the doubt. But a friend who has had the privilege of seeing Nehru's papers tells me that while the prime minister may never have read *The Autobiography of an Unknown Indian*, he did see and was perturbed by the reports of what it contained. Its dedication to the British Raj seems particularly to have caught his attention. There is, it appears, a file noting by Nehru querying whether a man so favourably disposed to our former rulers could be trusted with the bulletins of All India Radio.

At any rate, while Nehru's comments are contained in files closed to the public, the unknown Indian's views on Nehru are a matter of printed record. *Thy Hand, Great Anarch!* is peppered with comments on his person and his politics. Nirad Babu admired Nehru for his unflinching and (in the Indian context) unfashionable hostility to Japanese militarism, and for being 'so sure of himself' that he could deal with all kinds of accusations 'in the most dignified manner'. He wrote with great acuity about Nehru's loneliness, about how 'throughout his life [he] never got rid of the sense of being alone, being only by himself.'

This was something to empathize with, but there was also much to criticize. Nehru, said Chaudhuri, was 'completely out of touch with the Indian life, even of his time, except with the life of the self-segregating Anglicized set of upper India who lived in the so-called Civil Lines.' While he was 'repelled' by the 'crude Hinduism of northern India', Nehru had 'no understanding whatever of even the highest forms of contemporary Hinduism as preached in Bengal and Maharashtra.' This man of the people, wrote Chaudhuri, was actually a snob, with an undisguised condescension 'towards anyone who had the Hindi or Bengali accent in his English', towards whom 'he would always behave like an Englishman to a "native"'. Nehru was also said to be prone to giving 'elegant verbal embodiments to [his] obsessions' (a charge which, of course, can be laid at the door of Chaudhuri himself). To these comments one must add the claim, expressed in *The Autobiography of an Unknown Indian*, that 'collectively, we shall never achieve anything like the greatness and individuality of the Hindu civilization': a claim that seems almost a direct challenge to Nehru's hopes for modern India.

Let me turn to a now forgotten essay on Nehru by Nirad Chaudhuri, published in *The Illustrated Weekly of India* in the second week of May 1953. The writer was by this time a moderately well-known Indian, but his subject still towered over him, and everybody else. Nehru's leadership, remarked Chaudhuri, 'is the most important moral force behind the unity of India'. He was 'the leader not of a party, but of the people of India taken collectively, the legitimate successor to Gandhiji'. However, if 'Nehru goes out of politics or is overthrown, his leadership is likely to be split up into its components, and not pass over intact to another man. In other words, there cannot, properly speaking, be a successor to Nehru, but only successors to the different elements of his composite leadership.'

As Chaudhuri saw it, the Nehru of the 1950s helped harmonize the masses with the classes.

> Nehru is keeping together the governmental machine and the people, and without this nexus India would probably have been deprived of stable government in these crucial times. He has not only ensured co-operation between the two, but most probably has also prevented actual conflicts, cultural, economic, and political. Not even Mahatmaji's leadership, had it continued, would have been quite equal to them.

'If, within the country, Nehru is the indispensable link between the governing middle-classes and the sovereign people', continued Chaudhuri, 'he is no less the bond between India and the world.' He served as

> India's representative to the great Western democracies, and, I must add, their representative to India. The Western nations certainly look upon him as such and expect him to guarantee India's support for them, which is why they are so upset when Nehru takes an anti-Western or neutral line. They feel they are being let down by one of themselves.

Subsequent issues of the *Illustrated Weekly* carried many letters by readers, some appreciative of Chaudhuri's essay, others less so. The more critical mails seemed to come from Bengal. S.M. Chakravarty of Calcutta complained that Chaudhuri had 'painted Mr Nehru without the warts'—these being his tolerance of corruption and provincialism and his encouragement of personal favourites. Moni B. Majumdar, also from Calcutta, insisted that 'the Nehru of the old days is dead'. Where once he identified and mingled with the poor, now he moved around 'surrounded and protected by the police and the military', reminding one 'of the days when a British Viceroy travelled in India.' And K.C. Chatterjee of Bankipore rejected the argument that Nehru could have no successor. There were two worthy candidates in Bengal itself: B.C. Roy, who 'has shown a spirit of sacrifice in leaving his lucrative practice to lead the troubled and mutilated state of West Bengal'; and the 'constructive' and eloquent leader of the parliamentary opposition, Shyama Prasad Mukherjee.

Chronologically in-between, between his *Weekly* essay and the second volume of his autobiography, comes a review Chaudhuri wrote of the first volume of Sarvepalli Gopal's life of Nehru. This review was published in the *Times Literary Supplement* of 14 November 1975—an interesting date, this, Nehru's birth anniversary, but falling in the middle of the Indian 'Emergency', with Nehru's daughter having assumed dictatorial powers. Nirad Babu was now based in Oxford, where reports would have reached him of the detention of opposition leaders and the more general climate of fear and suspicion across northern India. This must explain why Chaudhuri made his review into a generalized attack on the Nehru clan. The Nehrus, he said, were never really Indian—they did not know Sanskrit, and learnt of Hinduism and India from the books of Englishmen. Worse, they imitated Muslim manners and wore Muslim dress. The Nehrus, wrote Chaudhuri, 'so far as they were not English, were Islamized Hindus.' Some of the ire was directed specifically at the most famous of the Nehrus. Jawaharlal Nehru's 'worst surrender', wrote Chaudhuri, 'was to have accepted partition, the greatest betrayal of India in history.' Here a man celebrated for his detachment seems to have completely abandoned it, by making an individual the scapegoat for a decision that was the product of complex historical forces. By 1946 no one—not Jinnah, not Gandhi, not Nehru, not Patel, and not even Mountbatten—could have stopped partition.

Nirad Babu was known to be a meticulous record-keeper, filing away all that he wrote and all that people wrote about him. I wonder whether, when he came to write *Thy Hand, Great Anarch!*, he consulted the file marked 'Writings and Correspondence for 1953'. Certainly, his retrospective assessment of 1987, by which time Nehru's reputation had dropped precipitously, is far more qualified than the one he offered while Nehru was alive. To celebrate Nehru when he was in his pomp and to have mixed feelings about him when he was in the doghouse—this somehow goes against the grain of the image that Chaudhuri cultivated about himself. The anomaly can be explained in one of two ways. A cynic would say that this writer, who claimed to stand alone and apart, was actually quite prepared to lose himself in the herd. More likely, to my mind, is that while the ambivalence of *Thy Hand, Great Anarch!* reflected Chaudhuri's real feelings towards Nehru, the gushing admiration of his *Weekly* essay stemmed from a desire to spite and provoke the Bengali *bhadralok*, known to detest Nehru (and Gandhi) for depriving their province of the moral and political leadership of free India.

The Good Scientist:
Satish Dhawan

In India's halting march to modernity, Bengal and Bengalis were for a very long time in the forefront. Then, in the early decades of the last century, three unconnected events helped deprive the province of its vanguard status. First, in 1911, the Raj shifted its capital from Calcutta to Delhi. Later, in 1920, the supporters of Mohandas K. Gandhi shouted down C.R. Das's opposition to non-co-operation, this presaging a more general shift of nationalist passion west-wards. Finally, in 1933, Chandrasekhar Venkata Raman left his chair in Calcutta University to take up a job in Bangalore.

The consequences of the first two events are long known, and—in Bengal—perhaps too long complained about. But what of the third? Till the 1920s, the only decent scientists produced by India had been Bengalis. One generation gave us Prafulla Chandra Ray and Jagadish Chandra Bose; the next generation, Satyen Bose and Meghnad Saha. Before all these men there had been Mahendralal Sircar, founder of the Indian Association for the Cultivation of Science. True, Raman was a Tamil, but his great early experiments had all been done in Calcutta. In retrospect, his departure for Bangalore seemed to signal a more general decline of the scientific spirit in Bengal. J.C. Bose and Acharya Ray were dead. Saha had moved out, to Allahabad. Satyen Bose stayed, but his best work lay behind him.

Raman had left Calcutta to join the Indian Institute of Science (I.I.Sc). In a country where centres of learning rise and fall with its founders, this institute has managed to maintain its high standards for close to a century. In my fairly wide experience of Indian research institutes and universities, I would place the I.I.Sc. comfortably at the top. Possibly 80 per cent of its faculty are engaged in serious research; absorbed in their work and in their students, these men and women are found in their laboratories on weekends too. Recruitment to posts in different departments is hardly ever affected by considerations other than intellectual merit. Many of the scientists are genuinely world class. There are some faculty who take it easy, but these are made to feel low and shameful.

In the history of the I.I.Sc. there are perhaps three men who deserve special mention. The first was the philanthropist and patriot Jamsetji Tata, in whose mind the idea was born and through whose money the first buildings came up. (In grateful recognition, the common citizens of Bangalore still refer to the place as the 'Tata Institute'.) The second was C.V. Raman, whose presence in the institute first endowed it with the respect and reputation it has since enjoyed. The third was the scientist, visionary, and institution-builder Satish Dhawan, whose death in Bangalore in the first weeks of 2002 was widely and justly mourned.

Born in Lahore in 1920, Dhawan took degrees in engineering and English literature—a lovely combination!—before proceeding to the United States for higher studies. After being awarded a PhD in aeronautical engineering from the California Institute of Technology, he returned in 1951 to join the I.I.Sc. Here he did important work in fluid dynamics and led the building of India's first supersonic wind tunnel. In 1962 Dhawan was appointed director of the institute and a decade later persuaded to also serve as chairman of the Space Commission. This was an executive, hands-on job which he held and executed while serving simultaneously as the full-time director of the I.I.Sc. He retired from both positions in 1981, but not before being awarded the Padma Shri and the Padma Bhushan.

Such are the bare facts, but there is more to be said. It was during Dhawan's long tenure that the I.I.Sc. consolidated its reputation and made secure its standing as the finest centre of scientific research in all of Asia. He encouraged the creation of new interdisciplinary laboratories in areas such as molecular biophysics, microbiology, and atmospheric science. He was much concerned with promoting work of quality in established areas of science, but, at the same time, sensitive to the relevance of the institute's work to Indian conditions. It was Dhawan who recruited the young, and at the time relatively unknown, Madhav Gadgil: an act of faith rewarded in due course, as Gadgil founded a first-rate school of field-based ecological research. It was also Dhawan who supported the electrochemist A.K.N. Reddy in the creation of a centre for the development of technologies appropriate for rural areas. This centre, named ASTRA, has since done pioneering work in the promotion of low-cost housing and renewable energy.

Dhawan's interest in ecology and rural technology was characteristic of the man. So far as I can tell, he was interested in two kinds of science: the science that advanced the frontiers of human understanding, and the science that helped augment human welfare or mitigate human suffering. As a patriot, he would have appreciated the use of advanced technology in the defence of our national security. But he must have been disgusted at the way in which some of our scientists crowed at the nuclear tests, putting on military uniforms and posing for photographs in them.

So long as Dhawan guided the space programme, its orientation was clear: satellite technology must be used to garner information useful in agriculture and other sectors of the economy, and to promote distance learning in remote areas not easily served by other forms of communication. His humanitarian instincts were deep and finely honed. It is no accident that one of his closest friends in the scientific community was Vikram Sarabhai, who had the same—that is, non-militaristic—expectations of space research, and who was the only chairman of the Atomic Energy Commission who had no interest in bombs whatsoever.

Growing up in Bangalore in the 1960s and 1970s, I admired Satish Dhawan from a distance. My father and grandfather had both studied at the I.I.Sc. I did not study there only because I displayed, at a very early age, a colossal ineptitude with regard to science; a failure that, of course, made me venerate the place all the more. In those pre-globalized times the state and the better kind of public institution had a glow and prestige that is almost impossible to convey to the young Indian today. As director of the I.I.Sc. and as the head of India's space programme, Dhawan commanded a unique position among the conscious middle class of this science-minded city. Yet he wore his honours lightly. Unlike techno-icons of the present time, he did not use his status in one sphere to assume expertise in another. He knew his limits, whereas his epigones are always willing to explain to the rest of us how the economy might be better run or how to improve our personal conduct. In this respect, Dhawan might have endorsed the dictum of his near-contemporary, the anthropologist and fellow Bangalore resident M.N. Srinivas, that 'media attention is the enemy of scholarship'.

The only time I recall Dhawan appearing in the media was when he was interviewed along with other leading Indians on the golden jubilee of our independence. Two remarks he made then have stayed with me, not least because they contrasted so sharply with the plati-tudes offered by the other featured luminaries. Why do Indians so ad-mire Singapore, he asked, and why do they want to exchange life in a culturally diverse and robust democracy for a boring and homoge-neous little country that was autocratic to boot? And, addressing the Non-Resident Indian (NRI) in general, he said that whenever he heard NRIs criticize their native land, he asked them to come back and help improve the functioning of its institutions. I suppose that, in most cases, Dhawan's request would have been met with an embar-rassed silence.

Dhawan's obituaries were appropriately steeped in stories of his integrity and rectitude. When he built his own house, cement was in short supply and regulated by the government, but this director of the I.I.Sc. and this head of the Indian Space Research Organization (ISRO), stood in the queue with the next man, patiently waiting for his allotment. We heard of how, when the SLV satellite was launched and fell straight into the sea, Dhawan appeared alone before the press to take the blame. But when, the next year, the SLV soared successfully into the sky, Dhawan stayed home and instead asked the men who had actually designed the satellite to take the credit. Best of all was the story of a high official of ISRO visiting his home weeks before he died. When he heard his former boss had to go to hospital for a check-up, he said he would send a chauffered car. 'You are always tempting me', answered Dhawan, and refused the offer.

In his last years I got to know Satish Dhawan. Our acquaintance was very slight, and we met not more than half a dozen times: each occasion, however, adding to my knowledge and understanding. I was impressed by his concern for the displaced of the Narmada Valley; alone among our top scientists, he signed a petition circulated in 1988 asking for a fair and independent review of the dam project. I was moved by his concern for the villages that, willy-nilly, had come to share the same territory as the space station in Sriharikota; one of his last initiatives was to urge an anthropological study of what impact, positive and negative, this high-tech endeavour had had on traditional lifestyles. Most of all, I was struck by the complete absence of cynicism, by his hopes for our land, his vital interest in the young and his willingness to be challenged by their ideas.

A German thinker once suggested that while a patriot is someone who loves his country, a nationalist is someone who scorns other countries. It was a distinction that Satish Dhawan would have appreciated. He was a patriotic and, in his time, much celebrated Indian, but also a very good man.

Ideas of India: 1884, 1931, 1997

In the winter of 1883–4, the British poet Wilfrid Scawen Blunt came 'seeking the germs of self-governing power in India'. Landing in Madras, he travelled through Southern and Eastern India up to Calcutta, the financial and political capital of the Raj. He then went north to the Punjab and the North-West Frontier, before coming South again to visit the princely state of Hyderabad. In five months he had covered a huge chunk of the subcontinent, speaking to educated opinion Indian and British, but also visiting a number of villages. He took along a local interpreter to talk to the peasants, thus to be 'strong in the testimony of the people themselves.'

Blunt's methods were unusual, his conclusions daringly unorthodox. In a series of essays entitled 'Ideas about India' and published in the *Fortnightly Review*, he presented an unforgiving and deeply unflattering portrait of British rule. 'There is no love whatever lost between the Indians and ourselves,' he wrote, 'whether they be Mohammedan, or Hindu, or Parsi, or native Christian. We do nothing to gain their affection, and they waste none on us.' Let 'India once be united in a common sentiment of hatred for all that is English, and our rule will ipso facto cease. . . . The huge mammal, India's symbol, is a docile beast, and may be ridden by a child. He is sensible, temperate, and easily attached. But ill-treatment he will not bear for ever, and when he is angered in earnest, his vast bulk alone makes him dangerous, and puts it beyond the strength of the strongest to guide or control him.'

From Blunt's account there seemed much to hate and much to unite around. The peasantry (then as now the bulk of the Indian population) lived and died in desperate poverty—'Of luxuries other than the red pepper they seem wholly destitute.' The causes of their misery included the high land tax (estimated at 35 to 40 per cent of produce) and the destruction by British rule of the small industries that were an essential supplement to farming. Then there were the new forest laws, which were 'needlessly violent and most injurious to the people.' The Forest Act of 1878, that by one stroke of the executive pen reserved all woodland to the state, had 'much to answer for in the present state of discontent among the peasantry.' An even greater 'theme of complaint' was the salt tax. The price of salt was a thousand times its cost, its sale earning the government six million rupees as revenue. This tax, remarked Blunt, 'touches the people most dearly and is most injurious in proportion to the poverty of the sufferer by it.'

Blunt was directed by 'native economists' to the underlying roots of Indian poverty, the fact that 'whereas in every other country the finance minister looks solely to the interests of the country he serves, in India he looks principally to the interests, not of India, but of England'. 'Manchester must be appeased before India can hope to live,' he remarked bitterly. 'Debt in India unfortunately means dividends in Lombard Street'. Adding to the burden was the self-centred profligacy of the white ruling class. Blunt wondered 'whether anyone has calculated the number of miles of macadamised road in the various Anglo-Indian cantonments, not a yard of which has ever served any purpose beyond that of enabling the officers' wives to pay each other visits in their carriages. I wonder whether any one has calculated the number of absolutely useless clock towers and Gothic memorials erected by Sir Richard Temples to Sir Bartle Freres, and Sir Bartle Freres to Sir Richard Temples in the various Presidencies. I wonder whether any one has calculated how many hogsheads of champagne

the water-drinking ryot has paid for in the last half-century as an un-
accounted item of his yearly budget.'

Blunt was clear that 'the present system of finance and the exploitation of India to the profits of Englishmen would have to be abandoned.' Some of his Indian friends had 'complete administrative
independence' as their goal: this he endorsed, if in stages. The Civil
Service would be remodelled to make Indians gradually replace Englishmen in 'all but the highest posts.' Local parliamentary institutions
would be set up in all the provinces, at first with a 'large English ele-
ment.' But as 'the Indian mind educates itself with great rapidity,' in
another generation Indians might 'be entrusted with the sole care of
their own domestic legislation, and the sole control of their finances.'
He hoped thus to see 'each province of India entirely self-managed as
regards all civil matters, raising its own revenue in its own way, providing for its own needs of internal order, public works, and administration of all kinds, and controlled by the constant supervision of its
own provincial assembly.' He held out the example of the Austrian
empire, which within a generation, had transformed itself from a
bureaucratic despotism into a harmonious federation of once-feud-
ing races. 'If this has been possible through the gift of self-government, all things are possible; and India by the same means of honest
government, each province for itself, may become happy and thank-
ful, as the Austrian nations are.'

That monument to the Victorian Establishment, the *Dictionary of
National Biography*, complained gently that Wilfrid Scawen Blunt
'came to speak and write as if England were always in the wrong, and
her opponents invariably wise and reasonable men.' In the England
of his time, Blunt stood out for his sympathy with the colonised
(he also advocated independence for Egypt and Ireland). But note
also that he was ahead of the advance guard of Indian opinion. His
'Ideas about India' appeared a year before the Indian National Congress was formed, and years before Dadabhai Naoroji and Romesh
Chunder Dutt began to compute the costs to India of British rule.

Naoroji and Dutt must certainly have read Blunt, and so (I would
like to think) might have Gandhi. For the poet believed 'it to be an

axiom in politics that all social convulsions have been preceded by a period of growing misery for the agricultural poor, combined with the growing intelligence of the urban populations. . . . Where there is complete ignorance, misery may be accumulated almost without limit by a despotic power. Where the mass of the population is prosperous, no growth of knowledge need be feared. But it is at the point where education and starvation meet that the flame breaks forth.'

Blunt might have been writing of the non-cooperation movement of 1928–32, which was founded on the poverty of the peasantry and coordinated by the flock of educated young townsmen (and women) who responded to Gandhi's call. The Mahatma, indeed, mobilised his people around the land tax, the forest laws, and state monopoly over salt, the three core injustices identified by the poet almost half a century previously.

Non-cooperation was in mid-career when another British traveller-writer, Robert Byron, came to investigate the present and the future of India. Arriving in early August 1929, Byron toured widely through the towns and cities, talking to a cross-section of responsible and radical opinion. While we may admire his industry we must fault his timing, for he boarded a ship in Bombay two days before Gandhi reached Dandi, there to break the law prohibiting the making of salt by individuals.

Byron saw himself as a liberal and reconciler, but it is striking how reactionary his views are when compared to Blunt's. In the book that came out of his travels (*An Essay on India*, 1931), he claims that the East had always disregarded the craft of politics, concentrating 'first and foremost on the discovery of good by thought and ecstacy.' (Blunt, by contrast, remarked of the better-ruled princely states that they 'afford indications of the real capacity for self-government possessed by the indigenous races.') Byron thought that the Indian offered the purest specimen of *Homo Hierarchicus*—'The equalitarian idea of democracy is repugnant to all his most deeply ingrained instincts.' He did not see self-rule as a reasonable possibility, even in 100 years. In any case, the idea of India was a British one: 'it is the Englishman who has invented and kept the balance between the creeds, races, and castes, and maintains connexion between the province and the states.' The problem, such as there was, lay in the fact that the ruler tended to play the part of an 'unpalatable if salutary schoolmaster,' whereas he (and India) would be better served if he would act as 'a university tutor to his undergraduate pupils.'

Blunt, in 1884, ended his series of essays with a noble vision of a self-governing India, the provinces taking care of themselves but coming together in contented unity. Byron, in 1931, concluded his book with an extraordinary paean to British rule in India: 'It stands by itself in history, proud and incomparable, a work of art, a treasure to be put against a velvet cloth in the world's gallery of politics. . . . To see a great race given scope for the exercise of its greatest strength, to see it conduct the art of government on a scale and with a perfection accomplished by no previous race, is to achieve that sublime pleasure in the works of man which, ordinarily, is conferred only by the great artists. This I saw in India'.

In the event, democratic self-government came much sooner to India than Byron thought likely, though later perhaps than Blunt might have wished. As Sunil Khilnani explains in his *The Idea of India* it did not come as a gift of the departing British. But nor was it wrested by the masses; rather, 'it was given to them by the political choice of an intellectual elite'. Khilnani has not, it seems, read either Blunt or Byron, but their essays might usefully serve as a background to his own. His title recalls Blunt's, whose essential hopefulness he shares. And his brief is to argue the case for democracy in India, to dispose once and for all of the belief—exemplified by Byron, but by no means unique to him—that the hierarchy-obsessed Indians would not reconcile themselves to a system that accords each of its members the same political rights.

Indian history since 1947, writes Khilnani, has been the 'adventure of a political idea,' that is, democracy. He suggests that the pre-independence Congress had not meditated seriously on the political regime it would create when it came to power. 'The possibility that India could be united into a single political community was the wager

of India's modern, educated, urban elite'—an elite led by Jawaharlal Nehru. Pandit Nehru himself had no clear idea of what form
democracy would take, and improvised as he went along, sometimes
'against the inclinations of Indian society'. Central to his idea of India
was a 'tolerant, common, Indianness'. In his reading, the history of
pre-British India had moved 'by a logic of accommodation and acceptance,' the task now was to recreate that tolerance, if on an egali-
tarian and more economically secure plane. Nehru rejected the belief
that any city or region could be the centre of the Indian nation, or that
any language or religion could contain the essence of Indian culture.
The federal system he helped create gave space for the idea of a layered
Indianness, an accretion of identities so that being a Muslim or a
Kannadiga was perfectly consistent with being Indian. The Congress
under Pandit Nehru was itself a 'kind of translation machine,' maintaining a 'kind of tenuous mutual intelligibility' between state and
society, centre and province.

Jawaharlal Nehru was a hero of his age who has become an outcast
in ours. Khilnani's rehabilitation of his role and reputation is an act
of courage, and carried out with considerable skill. It is something of
a pity, therefore, that he goes along with the postmodern trend of
opposing Gandhi to Jawaharlal Nehru. He too easily accepts the view,
promoted by neo-traditionalists for their own sectarian purposes,
that Gandhi rejected science, industry, the state, and other artefacts
of modernity. He insufficiently acknowledges Gandhi's influence on
Nehru's idea of India, whose defence of plurality and inclusiveness
seems to have been directly inspired by the practice and example of
the Mahatma.

It might be said on Khilnani's behalf that he approaches the
Gandhi/Nehru polarity from the unfashionable or Nehruvian side.
All the same, his acceptance of the polarity is a serious weakness in
what is otherwise a fine book. The great Austrian polymath Joseph
Schumpeter once remarked that 'a political scientist is one who knows
no history, no sociology, no law, and no economics'. I too have always
believed that political science is a non-discipline, a pseudo-science. It

is a field to which Khilnani owes a formal allegiance, but his book
shows that he also knows the other and more worthy ones. *The Idea
of India* is a brilliantly concise and distilled history of the career of our
democracy, one of the very few books released in the year of com-
memoration that will actually be read the year after.

Khilnani is a polite writer, unfailingly courteous to icons as well as
adversaries, but also capable of a sudden decisiveness. He can be ironic or Socratic as the occasion demands, with the ability to sum up
an individual or institution in three or four words. Thus Ambedkar
was a 'thinker of lucid and focused anger,' Jagmohan (Lieutenant
Governor of Delhi during the Emergency) merely a 'vain sycophant'.
Sanjay Gandhi's Youth Congress was 'a delinquent boys' club', while
the Indian National Congress after his mother took charge of it 'swift-
ly degenerated into an unaudited company for winning elections'.
The Public Works Department has 'a unique styleless style of its
own', while another institution also too powerful for our good, the
Bharatiya Janata Party, wants to create a state that has 'both God and
nuclear warheads on its side'.

Nehru's idea of India, notes Khilnani, 'did not monopolise or
simplify the definition of Indianness'. Proof of its success is the fact
that 'India, an ungainly, unlikely inelegant concatenation of differences, after 50 years still exists as a single entity'. But what of fifty years
hence, or a hundred? For as Khilnani himself acknowledges, Nehru's
'theoretically untidy, improvising, pluralist approach' is now being
strongly challenged by the 'neatly rationalist and purifying exclusivism'
of the BJP. Will India remain united and free, or will it degenerate
into a battleground of antagonistic forces? As of 1997 Wilfrid Blunt
seems vindicated. But Robert Byron could be proved right yet.

The Coconuts of Bengal;
Brown Men, White Affinities

Back in the 1970s, a group of political scientists advanced the
theory that India was a 'multinational' state rather than a
simple 'nation-state'. It was said that like the Soviet Union
the Republic of India was an artifice of history, the product of accident rather than of willed circumstance, an unhappy and unstable
coalition of different nationalities forced to cohabit by a strong state.
There, the Leninists had brought together Ukrainians, Latvians,
Georgians and others under the control of a dominant nationality,
the Russians. Here, the British and the Congress had forced the Bengalis, Andhras, Tamils and others to accept political union with, and
political subjugation to, the Hindi-speaking nation.

I was reminded of this theory when, in July 1995, I visited Nirad
Chaudhuri at his Oxford home. For two hours we spoke—rather,
Chaudhuri spoke and I listened—about English literature, English
crockery, English monarchs, English wars and French wines. Just before I left the telephone rang. The lady attending to the great little
writer picked up the phone and told him it was his son calling, from
'desh'. *Desh*, not *ghar*, homeland, that is, not home. Other clues—for
instance, his preference (a sensible one!) for *maccherjhol* over fish and
chips—led me to conclude that Nirad *babu* had two distinct nationalities, Bengali and English.

A friend of mine once described Nirad Chaudhuri as the President for Life of the Coconut Club of Bengal. The members of this (in Calcutta, at any rate) well subscribed club were, like the coconut and Chaudhuri, brown on the surface and white within, Bengali by birth but English by habit and taste. In truth, the brown sometimes seeped into the skin, for the bhadralok intellectual would not wholly disavow his roots. Even when he studied at Oxford or declaimed Shakespeare, a part of his soul remained pledged to Bengal. This was true of Nirad *babu*, and this was also true of roughly a million others. In this respect at least the writer who thought he stood alone was wholly representative of his time and class.

As a young man, Chaudhuri knew the Mother Country only from afar, but sons and daughters of better-heeled families were sent there to study. Once upon a time, it was not enough to take a PhD in history or chemistry from Dhaka or Calcutta; one had to obtain a second doctorate from Oxford or Cambridge. Meanwhile, the less scholarly minded *bhadralok* went to Oxbridge to get a BA, or qualified for the bar from the Inner Temple or Lincoln's Inn. These journeymen effortlessly fused English ways with Bengali ones, practising and promoting their dual nationality. On their return, they would appear suited and booted in the office but stay *dhoti–punjabied* at home. They would waltz when in the club but tunefully sing the works of Nazrul Islam in their *bari*.

A significant minority of these Coconuts converted to Communism while still in England. Thus they abandoned one foreign allegiance for another, Mother England for Father Russia. These turncoats included such well-known figures as Susobhan Sarkar, Hiren Mukherjee, Nikhil Chakravarty, and Jyoti Basu. However, one part of their self remained unchanged. That is, the bhadralok communist adopted a new foreign master without abandoning his language, literature, and cuisine.

Just as one did not have to cross the *kaala paani* to be Bengali and English, one did not have to leave Calcutta to become Bengali and Russian. Some of the finest bhadralok film-makers, thinkers and writers of the post-Second World War era have displayed a pathetic loyalty to the Soviet Union. A Calcutta scholar of my acquaintance, an educationist of distinction now in his late sixties, once told me of his visit to the Party headquarters during the time of Stalin's last illness, in 1953. There he joined the ranks of his anxious comrades, all scanning the news communicated by telex and telegraph from the Kremlin, their Vatican. When the message came that Stalin had breathed his last, recalled this scholar, he felt more lonely than when his own father had died.

Three years later, Stalin's successor announced that the Father to generations of Bengalis was actually the greatest mass murderer in human history. The educationist, to his credit, left the Communist Party of India, and has retained a sturdily independent existence ever since. Numerous other bhadralok denounced Khruschev's 'revelations'—revelations known to the non-communist world for decades—as bourgeois lies. There was also a section that went in search of a substitute fatherland. The Soviet Union now stood exposed as a land of grisly Gulags, but there might yet be a Communist Utopia someplace else. A good proportion of the renegades settled on China, whose Chairman, it was suggested, was actually our Chairman too. Others, who could not ignore the casualty lists of the Great Leap Forward and the Great Proletarian Cultural Revolution, went looking for more exotic locations. And so there are activists and artists who have been Bengali and Russian, Bengali and Chinese, Bengali and Cuban, Bengali and Vietnamese, and Bengali and Albanian.

All told, the Bengali has shown a keener and more durable interest in other cultures than, for example, the Marathi or the Tamil. The foreign nationality might change, but not the native one. Thus, Satyajit Ray was at one point in his life both Bengali and British, but at another point, Bengali and French. (With the emergence of the EU, Ray, were he alive now, would perhaps be considered Bengali and European.) More recently, the collapse of the Berlin Wall and China's march down the capitalist road has caused some surprising shifts of allegiance. The United States of America, the Great Satan, the country so massively demonised in Bengali literature, art and cinema, has become an alternative homeland for numerous bhadralok thinkers. Emblematic here is the case of the Subaltern Studies project, the movement of new historical writing which was originally inspired, back in 1981–2, by the *Collected Works of Chairman Mao*. Within a decade, the project had been laid to rest in the universities of Chicago and Columbia. The very historians who were once Bengali and Chinese have now become Bengali and American.

From one point of view, this unique blending of nationalities could be called cosmopolitanism, illustrating a rare and untypical interest in ideas and movements originating outside India or, indeed, outside Asia. Moreover, the bhadralok dual national has embraced a foreign culture while holding steadfast to this own—he (and she) is a *rooted* cosmopolitan. From another point of view, however, this must be seen as a form of parochialism—as a characteristically Bengali lack of interest in other parts of this land. Thus, a well-regarded scholar who lives in Calcutta will not visit New Delhi, which he dismisses as 'that imperial city'. However, he is happy enough to spend half the year in New York.

Perhaps one man's internationalism is another man's chauvinism. And perhaps the last bhadralok thinker to be both Bengali and Indian was Rabindranath Tagore.

II

The first section of this essay was earlier published in that respectable bhadralok paper of Calcutta, *The Telegraph*. It was intended to provoke, and it did. The letters I received in response were a charming mix of approval and dismissal. I was accused of being a self-hating Bengali, or (if the writer in question knew that my surname actually conceals a Tamil identity) of being a professional 'Bong-basher'. 'Have you ever seen anyone from Tamilnadu or Maharashtra derogating their own people in public', asked one correspondent. 'Don't Tamils go in a herd to the US for IT jobs', asked another. These critics at least had the courage (and courtesy) to use their own names, unlike the two letter-writers who sought to hide themselves under those authentically Bengali titles, 'Gabbar Singh' and 'M.O. Gambo'.

The most damaging criticism came from a lady who pointed out that 'if you take a survey of the people who leave their homes on a regular basis either to travel around the country or to work elsewhere you will find Bengalis topping the list.' She then quoted from a letter written by her son, in temporary exile in Scotland: 'Late last night I was looking at the map and suddenly the tremendous romance of these places hit me once again: Peshawar, Aligarh, Allahabad, Meerut, Ambala. I will return I know for sure, and soon. I want to see Sasaram too.'

This was a salutary reminder, and indeed while writing my article I was not unmindful of the Bengali penchant for travel, as witness the bus companies and special railway compartments reserved exclusively for their journeys to temple towns and historic sites. I have an enduring memory of a cold bus ride up to Naini Tal with a Bengali tourist, dressed in shirt and *chappals*, his conversation periodically interspersed, as gusts of snow-laden air hit us, with a flick of the cigarette and an expressive '*ai, shala!*'. My *Telegraph* essay, however, did not really deal with these patrons of Kundu and other Travels; rather, it focused on the cultural aristocracy of Bengal, the writers and scholars and film-makers whose journeys, both mundane and imaginative, have generally been made overseas.

One correspondent, agreeing with me, succinctly suggested that for the Bengali dual national 'the rest of India is a geographical obsolescence. Dum Dum connects straight to JFK or Heathrow.' Juxtaposing this endorsement with the chastisements, I thought I should perhaps reformulate my thesis as follows: the ordinary folk of Bengal, the *sadharan lok*, are genuinely interested in other parts of India; the self-proclaimed intellectual, hardly ever.

This amended thesis finds confirmation from the remarks and comments of other correspondents. One asked how I could forget the renaming of Calcutta, that Marxist-inspired act of linguistic chauvinism. He then recalled how the dismantling of a statue outside the KGB headquarters in Moscow had brought forth an instant rebuke from the Chairman of the Left Front: 'We condemn this act of disrespect to Comrade Dzerzhinsky who is one of the greatest Marxists of all time.'

Other writers amplified the theme of bhadralok hypocrisy. I was told of the romantics who wished to merge Bangladesh and West Bengal into a 'Sonar Bangla', but who would not care to travel to the eastern side, while happy enough to exchange a comfortable life in Kolkata for a more comfortable life in London. Another correspondent passed on a delightful story of how the eminent historian Irfan Habib was once introduced at a public meeting by a bhadralok Communist: not by his books, nor even by the length of his party membership, but by how he was linked by descent to the most sophisticated of Indian Muslim families, the Tyabjis.

Finally, there were those letter-writers who argued that my thesis, even if valid, really applied to the past. The question I should have addressed more directly was this: how would Bengalis fare in the homogenizing and globalizing world of the twenty-first century? One writer to the newspaper felt that they were indeed already 'fast shedding or disguising their Bengali-ness in an attempt to internationalize themselves'. On the other hand, an economist friend believed that their history of rooted cosmopolitanism would stand them in good stead. The Bengalis, he perceptively remarked, were 'actually survivors and the ones who can do so in new and hostile environments are those who can adapt.' They had become coconuts—white inside, brown outside—to better cope with British rule. This ability to retain elements of your own culture while absorbing elements of another, suggested the economist, was a 'special case of the general theory of adaptability that we are increasingly going to see in a borderless world.'

Altogether the most curious letter came from a South Indian who claimed that the bhadralok 'were merely self-deprecating slaves of some foreign master or the other, whether British, Russian or Chinese. All of them deserve to be held in the most profound contempt

by all self-respecting people.' For this correspondent, 'a "rooted cosmopolitan" can exist only in the imagination.' Further correspondence revealed him to be an admirer of Bal Thackeray and Nathuram
Godse, and the upholder of a chauvinism so extreme that even
Gandhi was suspect for the sin of respecting the human rights of
minorities.

I would recommend, to this gentleman in particular but also to all
readers who might not have seen it, a book titled *The Mahatma and
the Poet* published by the National Book Trust. Edited by Sabyasachi
Bhattacharya, this contains the complete correspondence between
the two greatest modern Indians. Better than anything else I have
seen, this exchange reveals both the perils and promise of what I have
here termed 'rooted cosmopolitanism'. For, more urgently than ever
before, the world we now live in forces us to declare our cultural affi-
liation—or affiliations. We really have only three choices: to reject
everything 'foreign' (as the Hindu and Muslim chauvinists pres-
cribe); to unthinkingly absorb everything 'foreign' (as American
advertisers ask us to do); or to work out an honourable accommodation between cultures, thus to discard what is useless or reactionary
in 'ours' while absorbing what is genuinely useful or progressive in
'theirs'. In this vital and profoundly challenging exercise there can
be no better—and still relevant—guides than the Gujarati-patriot-
internationalist Gandhi, and the bhadralok-Indian-world citizen
Tagore.

Tigers in the Alps

The revolutionary who succeeds underground is not the one who hides like a mouse under the floor-boards, shunning the light of day and social involvement. The successful and resourceful underground worker takes a most active part in the everyday life of those around him, he shares their weaknesses and their passions, he is in the public eye, in the hurly-burly, with an occupation which everyone understands... The wisest way is also the simplest: to combine your secret and your overt activity easily and naturally.

—Alexander Solzhenitsyn, *Lenin in Zürich*

On the outskirts of the ancient Swiss town of Bern lies an open space traditionally used as an *allmend,* or collective pasture; acres and acres of grass set against a dramatic backdrop of rocky hills. The southern part of the field has been converted into an exhibition hall, used off and on to display and sell agricultural machines. The open ground is still large enough to be known as the *grossé allmend.* However, no cows graze there anymore. Empty during the week, on Sundays the field is home to groups of little boys playing football, or frisbee, or flying kites, or simply taking a walk with their fathers and their dogs.

Every year, in August, this Swiss field is colonized for a weekend by a crowd of Tamils. Some are resident in Bern, others come from

Zürich and Luzern, still others from the Netherlands and Germany and England. But they all came, originally, from the northern districts of Sri Lanka, and many still hope one day to return there. That the civil war in their island does not yet permit; hence this annual get-together in Bern, where four or five thousand Tamils gather to underline and affirm their spirit of community.

When I went to the Bern *allmend* this past August, the weather was wet, but the celebrations were unaffected. Across the large field the Tamils divided themselves by age and gender: teenage boys in one circle, teenage girls in another, here some families with little kids, there a cabal of sari-clad *paatis* (grandmothers), gossiping. The food, the music, the exuberant colours that the people wore and which also adorned the shops: to collectively describe these the English word 'festival' seems somewhat antiseptic. Indeed, so completely Tamil was the atmosphere that a Swiss friend who accompanied me to the *allmend* quietly left after half an hour.

I stayed the whole day, and came back the next. The ostensible focus of attention, all the while, was a series of sporting contests, between teams of Tamils representing different parts of Europe. The games played included cricket, volleyball, football, and a traditional sport called *killitata*, a hybrid that mixes running with wrestling. Football took pride of place, with six different cups at stake: separate championships for boys under 10, under 13, under 15, under 18, and over 35, as well as one for girls. The ground was slushy underfoot, ideal for a hard game of soccer. The teams sported vivid colours: blue and white, red and black, yellow and dark green. As they played their supporters crowded the touch-lines, shouting in Tamil, while a man with a microphone urged them to keep away from the grass. Some fans chose not to yell but to play their drums, rhythmically.

The ambience was Tamil but the referees were Swiss and the style of the game German. The boys played the focused, physical football of the Bundesliga, short passes and bold body checks, rather than the long, hopeful balls up front that mark the game in South Asia. Their heading was first-class. And their spirit ferociously competitive. It had to be, with teams bearing names such as Super-Eagles, Germany, and Tamil Eelam, Poland. In the under 18 final, I watched Young Royal Sports Club, Zürich, play the Tamil Football Club of Denmark. The coach of the Young Royals kept up a continual stream of advice and (it has to be said) abuse: 'apdi ille' (not like that), 'Ramesh ku kudu, paithiyo' (pass to Ramesh, you imbecile), and such like. The object of his ire, a boy with streaked hair, was at length substituted. He came out swearing—in Swiss German.

For each championship there were twelve to fourteen teams in the competition. On the Saturday there were often half a dozen matches being played simultaneously. In the centre of the *allmend* flew the red-and-yellow flag of the putative homeland, Tamil Eelam. Under the flag, on a table shielded from the rain by a red canopy, rested the prizes of the competition: a row of large silver cups, all looking alike, with 'TAMIL EELAM CUP' inscribed at their base, and a portrait of a man holding a flag on the side, his face pencilled inside a map of the island, the Tamil homeland's borders marked.

Towards the northern end of the *allmend* the cricket tournament was being held. This was altogether more genteel, the game played with a soft tennis ball, by men almost all the wrong side of thirty-five. There was one young boys club: Eela Stars C.C., Bern, formed by eighteen-year-old Mahesh in memory of his dead father. But they lost early, to men who had learnt to play cricket under English-trained coaches back in Sri Lanka. The cricket final was played between two German teams. After the match the winners and losers joined in an impromptu sing-song, featuring hits from movies made in Madras.

All through the weekend, the weather was gloomy and punctuated by showers. But late on Saturday evening the sun came out. I looked out over the field. To the north and east, there was a row of grass-covered hills with cypresses on their crest, and, above them, steeper slopes and rocky outposts. Across the *allmend*, a whole series of football and cricket matches were being played, accompanied by shrieks and shouts, loud but some quite musical, especially where the drums were in operation. On a distant slope a Swiss man was soberly taking his Alsatian for a walk.

As foreign as the shouts were the smells. The food was superb: those Tamil staples, rice and *sambaar* and *dosai*, for lunch, as well as snacks such as *shundal* (spiced chick pea) and *bida* (betel nut leaf with grated coconuts and other condiments wrapped inside). (There was however one hamburger stall, patronized by the Swiss football referees on duty.) Other shops were selling saris and *salwar kameezes*, bangles and other kinds of jewellery, videos and cassettes of film songs, and medallions of the leader of the Liberation Tigers of Tamil Eelam, Velupillai Prabhakaran, cradling a leopard cub.

There was one shop selling books. The titles on display included a compendious edition of the *Kural*, the thousand-page text on life and good conduct by the Tamil sage, Thiruvalluvar. Tamil-French and Tamil-Deutsch dictionaries were also on offer, as were some computer manuals. But, right in front, on the desk that first caught the casual shopper's eye, were the recommended political texts. These were the Tamil translation of Lapierre and Collins's *Freedom at Midnight*, a biography of Ché Guevara, and the newly printed memoir of Adele Balasingham, the Australian wife of the Tiger theoretician Anton Balasingham. There were also two books about Balasingham's boss, Prabhakaran. The cover of one book showed the Tiger supremo in a forest clearing, wearing fatigues, surrounded by a bunch of adoring boy cadres. The second book's cover had a large portrait of Prabhakaran in the foreground, with that other successful freedom fighter, Sheikh Mujib of Bangladesh, looking on indulgently from atop.

I don't read Tamil, and had to judge the contents of the books by the photographs on their jackets. I turned for help to the bookshop attendant, a sweet, smiling twenty-year-old from Holland, named by his father after the great Indian cricketer of the 1970s, Sunil Gavaskar. I pointed to a book whose cover featured a man in khaki drill, wearing a khaki cap and dark glasses. 'Who is this?', I asked Gavaskar Mahendran. 'Nehru?', he replied, uncertainly. After I had left I realized who it actually was: Subhas Chandra Bose, the Bengali leader who had allied with the Axis powers during the Second World War, and formed an 'Indian National Army' composed chiefly of prisoners of war.

A father who named his son after Gavaskar would be the kind of man who admired Jawaharlal Nehru. But, of course, the moderate Nehru would scarcely appeal to the Tigers. (For one thing, he never held a gun.) Bose, on the other hand, would: his story, made suitably heroic, sat well with stories of Guevara and Mujib and, of course, Prabhakaran. The bookshop was a manifest display of the real intentions of this sports festival, but there were other signs, too. One was the dress code of the organizers: black trousers, white shirt, and a black jacket with 'WTCC' on the back (standing for World Tamil Co-ordination Committee), and the logo of the Liberation Tigers of Tamil Eelam in front. There were perhaps some two dozen such men, all dressed alike, spread out across the *allmend*, co-ordinating the various games and acting as ports of authority and call.

The black-and-white outfit somehow seemed appropriate, given the uncomplicated ideology of the Tamil Tigers and the unforgiving nature of their political practice. A slight variation on this dress code was permitted to Parthiban, the man assigned by the WTCC to escort and direct visitors such as myself. Parthiban was short, dapper, and—for a Sri Lankan Tamil—unusually fair and conspicuously clean-shaven. He also had a better-than-average facility with the international language of spin, English. He wore dark-grey trousers on both days, with a light cream bush-shirt on the Saturday and a light green shirt on the Sunday—shirts that were almost, but not quite, white. He had his lines well prepared: he himself was a 'development consultant' working in Geneva, specializing on issues of 'sustainable development'. The aim of this festival he glossed as 'telling our youth about their culture and traditions'. As we passed the various games, he would repeat: 'culture and tradition', 'culture and tradition'. Only once did the guard drop, when, in answer to a question as to why girls were playing football, he answered that the uplift of women in all respects, including the physical, was part of the 'agenda of the revolution'.

On instructions from above, Parthiban stuck closely to me. Clearly it would not do to let an 'Indian journalist from Bangalore' go about on his own. Fortunately, though, early on Sunday he was taken away by his girlfriend to meet her parents, his prospective in-laws, and I never saw him again.

Parthiban's exit allowed me to make the acquaintance of Astrid, a large-boned and genial Swiss lady who had married a Tamil and adopted both his culture and his football team. Now twenty-nine, Astrid had met her husband Jeyakumar ten years earlier while playing volleyball: he, a refugee, had been assigned by the Swiss authorities to a village near her own. She was doing a PhD in geography at the University of Zürich; her topic, the impact of Sinhala colonization on the civil war. In her free time, Astrid helped her husband run his soccer team. She spoke Tamil adequately, had learnt the complex script, and had visited the island six times—though not yet, she said sadly, the northern city of Jaffna, the heartbed of Tamil pride and rebelliousness. She seemed quite starry-eyed about the Liberation Tigers of Tamil Eelam. 'Every Tamil here supports the Tigers', she told me: 'They have to, if they want to support the struggle back home. Only the Tigers run the schools, and take care of the orphans'. I reminded her that the Tigers were still a banned organization in many countries. 'Not here in Switzerland', she replied, with uncharacteristic sharpness.

The Tamil boys on the field all called Astrid 'akka', elder sister. Seeing this big, blonde lady with her arms around little black boys in football dress, my companion that day, the film-maker Sabine Geisiger, exclaimed: 'She is the Mother Teresa of the Tamils!' Astrid's acceptance was aided by precedent: like Adele, the wife of Anton Balasingham, here was a white lady devoted to their language and their cause.

Astrid Jayakumar is a Swiss woman who wants to become a Tamil. Then there was Tommy, the Tamil boy who would much rather be Swiss. He was a slim and athletic seventeen-year-old, with a glowing skin. Sporting large ear-rings, Tommy was actually named 'Karthik Sambasivan'. He looked askance at his native culture: the Tamils, he said, were disorganized, unpunctual, hierarchical and—in their attitude to women and children—authoritarian. His sister was not allowed to go out alone or date Swiss boys. He would go out with Swiss

girls, but was still too scared to tell his parents. He had come to the
festival hoping to run in the short sprints, but, to his disgust, the
events had been cancelled. There was a consolation: his athletic skills
had already put him on the fast track to a Swiss passport.

The motto of this annual festival on the Bern *allmend* might very
well be: 'No more Tommys'. Its chief public purpose was to allow
the exiles, spread in small numbers across Europe, to congregate as
Tamils, to play their games, eat their food, listen to their music, meet
old friends and make new ones, and make or break matrimonial alli-
ances. But behind this social bonding was an aim rather more sinis-
ter—for to consolidate the Tamils as a community was also to remind
them of the unfinished struggle back home, thus to forcefully direct
their attention to the needs and claims of the Liberation Tigers of
Tamil Eelam. Each team had to pay an entrance fee; each shop had
to pay a cash deposit; and other collections for the Tigers were undoubtedly being solicited on the side. The skill with which the whole
show was organized left one in no doubt as to who was in command.

II

There are 45,000 Tamils in Switzerland, a number larger than it
might at first appear. For there are less than three and a half million
Tamils back in Sri Lanka. And there are only about six million Swiss
people. Thus, one in every eighty Sri Lankan Tamils lives in Switzerland. Some live in isolated villages, but most in the cities of the north.
In parts of Zürich and Bern one in every twenty residents is Tamil.

How did so many Tamils get so far? They came, in the first instance, fleeing the civil war in Sri Lanka. This is a conflict as bloody
and brutal, and as apparently incapable of resolution, as the troubles
in Palestine and in the Kashmir valley. In the twenty years that the war
has been on, an estimated 70,000 people have lost their lives. Perhaps
five times that number have fled, seeking refuge in India, Australia,
Canada, and the countries of Western Europe.

The Tamils of Sri Lanka are concentrated in the north and east of
the island. These, the so-called 'Jaffna Tamils', are to be distinguished

from the much smaller population of 'Estate Tamils', nineteenth century migrants from South India who came to work in the tea gardens of the Central Highlands. The Estate Tamils seek only rights of citizenship within a united Sri Lanka. But the Jaffna Tamils seek political autonomy, and, increasingly, independence.

As in the Middle East and Kashmir, the roots of the Sri Lankan conflict lie in British colonial policy. The British patronized the Tamils, seeing them as more reliable allies and more efficient workers in the administration. The Tamils took quicker to English, and thus came to monopolize the occupations of petty bureaucrat, schoolteacher, and clerk. When the British left, in 1948, the Sinhala-speaking majority moved to redress the balance. In 1956, Sinhala was made the sole official language of the island. Two years later, there was an anti-Tamil riot in the capital city, Colombo. The Tamils began to feel insecure, and to lose the edge they had in the professions. They protested, at first through the parties that represented them in the Sri Lankan Parliament. This they followed by Gandhian-style civil disobedience outside government offices. The Sinhala were unyielding. It didn't help that the two groups were divided by religion as much as by language (the Sinhala are chiefly Buddhist, the Tamils largely Hindu.)

In 1972, a new constitution confirmed the pre-eminence of the Sinhala language, and of the Buddhist religion as well. Slowly, the Tamils began to seek more radical solutions. In 1977, the Tamil United Liberation Front (TULF) swept the polls in the north and east, its election plank being the creation of a separate, sovereign, state, 'Eelam'. In response, the more extreme Sinhala began to speak of revenge. The incidence of violence grew. In the north the Sri Lankan army began to behave like an army of occupation. On the last day of May 1981 the army and the police burnt down the great Public Library in the premier Tamil city, Jaffna, which contained thousands of books as well as rare palm-leaf manuscripts. The next day, the soldiers went on a rampage through the streets of Jaffna, destroying statues of celebrated Tamil poets and saints as well as a bust of the Indian prophet of non-violence, Mahatma Gandhi.

The scholar A.J.V. Chandrakanthan was one of the Tamils who witnessed this 'unforgettable act of barbarity'. Chandrakanthan is now in exile—he is currently a Professor of Theology at Concordia University in Montreal. As he recalled, 'on 1 June 1981, at about 8.00 a. m., I was standing close to the main gate of the library premises, as were a few hundred Tamils of all ages and professions in shock and disbelief, looking helplessly at the smoke and smouldering fire whose tongues took more than a night to swallow those treasures of inestimable value. The Sinhala reserve police who doused and torched the library could be seen relaxing a few hundred yards away at the pavilion of the Jaffna stadium overlooking the burnt library'.

The burning of their cherished library was to deeply scar the Tamil psyche. No longer could they trust the other side; nor could they square this barbarity with the faith the Sinhala professed to follow. Their feelings were eloquently expressed in a poem written shortly after the event by a Jaffna teacher. The translation is by R. Cheran:

The Killing of the Buddha
by M.A. Nuhman

Yesterday,
in my dream
Buddha was shot dead.
State forces in civies
killed him.
His blood splattered body
lay on the steps of
Jaffna library.
Ministers came in the darkness
'why did you kill him?
this name is not on our list?'
They asked
angrily.
'No, Sir,
No crimes committed.
We could not kill
even a fly

without first killing him
That's why...'
The forces replied.
'O.K., O.K.
Get rid of the body
Quickly'.
Said the Ministers at once, and
vanished instantly.
The body was dragged in.
They covered the body
with 96,000 books
and made a funeral pyre.
They lit the pyre
with *Sihaloka Sutra.*
Not only the body,
The *Dhammapada* too was burnt.

The Sinhala soldiers who vandalized Jaffna effectively drove the Tamils to violence. Increasingly, the TULF had to make way for more militant groupings. The younger Tamils insisted that Gandhian methods were of no use: they might have worked in India, but that was because they were used by the majority against the minority. Here, where the Tamils were a minority, there was no recourse other than armed struggle. The mid 1970s saw the formation of several new groups: the Eelam Revolutionary Organisation (EROS), the Peoples Liberation Organisation of Tamil Eelam (PLOTE), Tamil Eelam Liberation Organisation (TELO), and the Eelam Peoples Revolutionary Liberation Front (EPRLF). These were Marxist or quasi-Marxist in inspiration, as was the group that came to dominate the struggle, the Liberation Tigers of Tamil Eelam (LTTE). In the summer of 1983, mines laid by the LTTE killed about a dozen Army soldiers. The bodies of these soldiers were taken back to Colombo, where a large crowd waited to receive them. Over the next week, the capital was convulsed by violence against the Tamils. Directed by senior Sinhala politicians, and aided by election lists, mobs identified Tamil homes and businesses and systematically torched them. More than 3,000 Tamils perished in the rioting.

In his authoritative study of the insurgency, M.R. Narayan Swamy writes that the Colombo pogrom 'opened a floodgate of young Tamils to various Tamil militant groups'. Like the torching of the Jaffna library, it was the work of a 'Sinhalese mobocracy [which] did more than anything else to give a facade of respectability to the militants'. After 1983 there was an intensification of the war in the north. Slowly, the LTTE acquired an edge, in both weaponry and fearlessness, over other groups. In well-directed actions it eliminated hundreds of cadres of its main rivals, TELO and EPRLF. It mounted daring raids on banks and police stations. And it also attacked civilians in the south, this seen as necessary retaliation for atrocities by the army in the north. Thus in May 1985 the Tigers killed 146 civilians in Anuradhapura. The choice of location was deliberate: for Anuradhapura was once the seat of an ancient Sinhala kingdom, while one of the town's most visited sites marks the legendary victory (back in the second century BC) of the Sinhala King Dutugemenu over his Tamil rival Elara, a victory seen by the classical text, the *Mahavamsa*, as 'the consummation of Sri Lanka's manifest destiny as the bulwark of Buddhism'.

While prime minister of India between 1980 and 1984, Mrs Indira Gandhi had allowed Tamil militants to run training camps on Indian soil. Her more-than-willing aide was the chief minister of Tamil Nadu, M.G. Ramachandran, who thought that the weight of the sixty million Tamils of India should be thrown behind the Eelam cause.

However, when Rajiv Gandhi succeeded his mother as prime minister, there came about a one-hundred-and-eighty degree shift in Indian policy. Rajiv and his advisers had ambitions to make India the United States of South Asia. One step in this direction was to mediate in the internal conflicts of neighbouring countries. Support to the Tamil Tigers was withdrawn. An invitation was extended by (perhaps extracted from) the Government of Sri Lanka, and in 1987 an 'Indian Peace Keeping Force' (IPKF) was sent to restore civic order in the north of the island. At this time the LTTE had a fighting force of about 3,000, and were in effective control of Jaffna.

Under the terms of the accord the Tigers were supposed to disarm. They made a show of surrendering their arms, but in actual fact gave up only old and dud weapons. There was never much trust between the Tigers and the Indian army, and whatever there was disappeared once allegations became rife of soldiers' violations of the human rights of civilians. The Indians began to be seen as the new army of occupation. The Tigers resumed their struggle, on terrain they knew so much better than their adversaries. The LTTE's skill and courage in battle are testified to by the general in command of the IPKF: while he condemned their 'senseless, mulish, destructive insistence on continuation of military means', he confessed to 'a high regard for the [LTTE's] discipline, determination, motivation and technical expertise'.

As the bodies of soldiers began returning to the mainland, the Indian government withdrew the IPKF. But, in May 1991, Rajiv Gandhi paid for his folly with his life, when he was assassinated by a Tiger human bomb. This was only one of several successful assassinations carried out by the Tigers. Other people killed in this fashion include the Sinhalese politicians R. Premadasa, Gamini Dissanayake and Lalith Athulathmudali, and the moderate Tamil leaders A. Amirthalingam and Neelan Tiruchelvam.

The departure of the IPKF signalled a resumption of the war between the LTTE and the Sri Lankan army. In the bid to control key positions, both sides partook of an unspeakable savagery. Sri Lankan forces bombed and shelled civilian areas. The Tigers retaliated with land mines and human bombs. Jaffna fell out of army control, and then came back to them. For fifteen years the north and east of the island lived under the shadow and sound of a more-or-less continual crossfire. As a consequence, wrote one recent traveller, 'towns and villages, in most instances, are ghost towns and ghost villages. One can see the ruins of buildings through the shrubs grown over the townships and villages. Now many of them are actually like archaeological sites'.

Some of the most spectacular Tiger actions have been conducted in the heart of Sinhala power, Colombo. In October 1995 they set ablaze the city's major fuel depots. Three months later they bombed the Central Bank. Most dramatic was their attack on Colombo airport in the summer of 2001, when a dozen Tigers entered the premises by boat, via a lagoon, and destroyed half the civilian fleet of Sri Lankan Airlines, as well as several military planes and helicopters. This operation was carried out on the 24th of July, the eighteenth anniversary of the anti-Tamil riots of 1983.

The main axis of conflict in Sri Lanka is between Sinhala and Tamil. But there are other conflicts too. One pits the Hindu Tamils against the Muslims, another the LTTE against those who dare dissent from them. The Muslims are chiefly traders and artisans. Traditionally, they were well integrated with the Hindus in the north and east. But the LTTE did not regard them as reliable, and resented their unwillingness to pay taxes. The conflict simmered, till in 1990 an estimated 90,000 Muslims were expelled from Mannar and Jaffna, their houses looted and ransacked by LTTE cadres. Most ended up in refugee camps in the south of the island.

The Indian journalist Nirupama Subramanian, who has followed the Sri Lankan conflict for years, writes that 'from assassinating rival Tamil leaders . . . and stifling all forms of dissent, to recruiting children and extorting money and assuming the role of cultural guardians and moral police of the Tamils, the LTTE has made a fine art of preying on its own people'. Sri Lankan army brutalities have been well documented by Tamil activists. Notably, it is also Tamils who have recorded, in print, the excesses of the LTTE. Particularly active in this regard are the University Teachers for Human Rights–Jaffna. Their reports speak of public executions by the Tigers, with woman cadres used, for instance, to shoot women suspected of being informers. In the early 1990s, the LTTE held 4,000 prisoners, most of whom were Tamil, many sympathizers or members of rival groups. Torture was rampant. As one former prisoner recalled:

> There were four boys, armed with batons. I am pretty certain they were less than 15 years old. They . . . started to beat me . . . [and] continued to beat me till I was unconscious.

Ten by ten, we were taken to another place. They chained our legs
with a chain made out of six heavy metal balls... Keeping the prisoner
chained to a tilted concrete slab they will roll a wooden roller with an iron
bar inserted in it from top to bottom all over the body. The roller weighs
about 300 lbs. When they do that, bones will crack and the skin of the
body peel off.

On the Sri Lankan side generals and presidents have come and gone.
But on the Tiger side the leadership, civilian as well as military, has
remained in the hands of Velupillai Prabhakaran. Born in Jaffna in
1954, the son of a minor government official, in school Prabhakaran
became acquainted with stories of Subhas Bose and Bhagat Singh,
Indian freedom fighters who had eschewed Gandhian methods in
favour of the gun. Other heroes were the comic strip character, Phan-
tom, and Kattaboman, a Tamil warrior-chieftain who died fighting
the British.

Like other young Tamils, Prabhakaran was stung by the decision,
in 1973, of the Sri Lankan government to favour Sinhala students in
college admissions. Since Tamils dominated the science, medical and
engineering faculties, they were now required to get higher marks
than their counterparts. Prabhakaran joined in street protests against
the move, and soon became involved in more radical actions. What
really brought him into prominence was the 1975 killing—with his
bare hands, it was said—of a mayor of Jaffna regarded as being too
ready to talk peace with the Sinhala. The next year Prabhakaran
founded the LTTE. For its logo he chose the head of a roaring tiger,
ringed by guns and bullets. The tiger was the insignia of the once
extensive Chola Kingdom of South India. While Prabhakaran was
inspired by memories of ancient Tamil glory, the idea of the logo actually came to him from a matchbox label. Curiously, the symbol of
Sinhala pride is the lion, which is displayed on the Sri Lankan flag.
The parties to the conflict thus each have their own King of the Forest.
It is another matter that neither the lion nor the tiger are to be found
in the island's jungles.

A reclusive figure, who has hardly ever been interviewed by the press, Prabhakaran has a command over his cadres probably unequalled by any other guerrilla or terrorist leader in modern history. He is a brilliant military strategist, and also a technological innovator. The Tigers were probably the first, and have certainly been the most effective, suicide bombers. At a mere word from him, boys and girls of eighteen will strap themselves with explosives or swallow a cyanide tablet. Not even Osama bin Laden or Ché Guevara have exercised such a total hold over their following. As the former Tamil militant Purnaka L. de Silva has written, 'in the LTTE, Prabhakaran demands absolute loyalty, which gives him something akin to total control over the actions and (physical) bodies of his paramilitaries, with the ultimate sacrifice to his will, being martyrdom and the oblivion of the hereafter.'

A considerable tribute to the Tiger leader comes from the pen of J.N. Dixit, Indian high commissioner to Sri Lanka between 1985 and 1989 (the IPKF years), and a man known as the 'viceroy' for the awe and authority he commanded. Prabhakaran, writes Dixit,

> is disciplined, austere and passionately committed to the cause of Sri Lankan Tamils' liberation. Whatever he may be criticised for, it cannot be denied that the man has an inner fire and dedication and he is endowed with natural military abilities, both strategic and tactical. He has proved also that he is a keen observer of the nature of competitive and critical politics. He has proved his abilities in judging political events and his adroitness in responding to them.

Prabhakaran is completely fearless, but also deeply vengeful and somewhat paranoid. Over the years, he has eliminated all others who may claim to speak with any authority for a section of the Tamils. In July 1989, while the LTTE was having formal talks with the president of Sri Lanka, Ranasinghe Premadasa, a Tiger murdered the long-time leader of the TULF, A. Amirthalingam. A few months later a Colombo journalist met with Prabhakaran's deputy, Mahendirarajah *alias* Mahatya. 'If you stand for the multi-party system', he asked Mahatya, 'why did your men kill Amirthalingam and other TULF leaders?' This was the reply he got: 'They were not killed because they held views different from that of the LTTE but because they were acting as the agents of India, in short, [as] traitors, collaborators. In that background, the LTTE kills those who betray the cause. . . . In a national struggle, the battle is everywhere, the traitor anywhere.'

Mahatya himself had a reputation for fearlessness second only to his leader's. It was he who had directed the Tiger's successful operations against the IPKF. But then, in 1995, he fell foul of the boss. Perhaps he harboured thoughts of the top job, or perhaps Prabhakaran was nervous of his growing popularity. Anyhow, one day agents from the LTTE's intelligence wing arrested Mahatya. He was accused of being an agent of the Indian government, and of conspiring to assassinate Prabhakaran. Video-taped 'confessions' were obtained from Mahatya's colleagues. It is said that Prabhakaran then had his former deputy put in a dog kennel. There he lay for some days, before being taken out and executed.

'In the battle, the traitor is anywhere . . .' However, one Tiger who has steadfastly enjoyed his leader's confidence is Anton Balasingham. Thick-set and dark-skinned, with a goatee, Balasingham was a Tamil journalist in Colombo who worked as a translator with the British High Commission. Then he went to London to study, and became fascinated by Marxism. It was his translations into Tamil of texts on guerrilla warfare by Mao and Ché that first brought him to Prabhakaran's attention. They met in 1979, in the Indian city of Madras, and seem to have hit it off instantly. For the next twenty years Balasingham has served as the spokesman for the Tigers, based variously in India, London, Colombo and (for a brief while) with his master in the *Vanni*, the arid scrub jungles of northern Sri Lanka. It is he who briefs the world's press on Tiger actions and demands, and it is he who represents Prabhakaran whenever the leader chooses to talk directly to the enemy.

It was in London that Balasingham met his future wife, Adele, a girl from the La Trobe valley of Victoria then studying sociology at South

Bank University. (This union, and its consequences, seem to vindi-
cate Margaret Thatcher's vendetta against sociology, a subject she
thought fomented instability and revolution.) When she wed Balasingham in London in 1978, Adele 'married the collective consciousness and history of a people'. Adele has followed Anton everywhere,
even to the *Vanni*. Prabhakaran likes her too, calling her 'Auntie'.

The best-selling title at the Tiger bookshop in Bern was Adele
Balasingham's latest offering, *The Will to Freedom: An Inside View of
Tamil Resistance*. I quickly discovered that this is a work which gives
the word 'partisan' a new meaning. I looked in the index, and found
the intriguing entry: 'assassination attempt'. I followed the four page-
references listed there to the text. These, I regret to say, did not tell
me anything about the Tiger-directed killings of Premadasa or Rajiv
Gandhi or Amirthalingam, but dealt rather with 'plots' aimed at the
Balasinghams, 'hatched' by the intelligence agencies of India and Sri
Lanka.

Still, despite its inaccuracies, this book by Adele Balasingham is as
close to a printed rendering of His Master's Voice as we are likely to
get. (Prabhakaran is not the kind of man who will write, or even
dictate, his own *Mein Kampf*.) The Tiger supremo, writes his Australian disciple, is a man of 'meticulous grooming', who dislikes the 'long
beards and scruffy dress' of Western revolutionaries. He has a 'high
moral character', and displays 'exemplary behaviour in personal life'.
He is 'a warm and courageous human being' who, meeting the Balasinghams in a stuffy hotel room in Madras, insisted on shifting them
to better accommodation. 'One of his favourite interests is science
and he encourages the cadres to learn new technologies and scientific
knowledge'. Among his other interests are 'Tamil liberation literature
and arts', English war films, and, more surprisingly, cooking. For,
'most of all, Mr Pirabakaran is a connoisseur of good food . . . He
views cooking as an art . . . For me, a vegetarian, he thought hard before deciding on a tasty dish he could prepare for me . . .'

Early in her book Adele Balasingham describes the first meeting
between 'these two now historical figures', her husband and her

leader. What struck her then were Prabhakaran's 'huge black eyes'. 'Indeed one gets the feeling that he is peering right through to your soul and it is this depth in his eyes, which mirrors his mind and thinking too. . . . [T]here is no way untruth or deceit can creep into a conversation when these probing eyes are watching every word.' Twenty years on and three hundred pages into the narrative, Adele tells us that she asked her husband what it was he most admired in Prabhakaran. Anton said it was his 'supreme self-confidence in times of adversity', and his belief in 'Dharma, the law of righteousness'.

In April 2002 the Balasinghams were in Sri Lanka, and so was I. Except that I was holidaying in Colombo, while they were in the depths of the *Vanni*, orchestrating Prabhakaran's first live, televised press conference. After 9/11 the Tigers had decided to try and make themselves respectable. The Norwegian government had brokered a cease-fire, and talks were being planned later in the year in Thailand.

However, the world would believe the Tigers were serious only if the word came from the leader. Thus it was that Prabhakaran faced the press, with Balasingham at his side, translating and occasionally embellishing his words. Indian journalists who passed through Colombo told me of the intense security and paranoia, of how they had their cameras opened and their shoes confiscated lest they be inspired by the 'journalists' who had not long ago killed the Afghan resistance leader, Ahmed Shah Masood.

Much meaning was being read into what Prabhakaran said or did not say that day, and into how he looked. Gone was that trademark of Tamil masculinity, the moustache. In India or in Sri Lanka, in peace or in war, it is almost impossible to find a Tamil male without a moustache. (The largest one is worn by the notorious forest brigand, Veerappan.) But Prabhakaran had now taken it off. Another indication of his wish to appear respectable, or shall we say bourgeois, was that he had come dressed not in battle fatigues but in a businessman's safari suit.

My Sri Lankan friends were certain that these changes in appearance were at the behest of his adviser. They joked that since Prabhakaran claimed he did not want political office himself, Balasingham might one day be appointed the first president of Tamil Eelam. What stood in the way was his health. Balasingham was in the advanced stages of diabetes, and required several insulin shots a day. No one knew how long he would live. 'Next in line in succession', said a Tamil friend, 'is his wife. Then we will have as our leader [the Australian] Adele Balasingham, and you will have [the Italian] Sonia Gandhi.'

III

From the early 1980s, as the civil war in Sri Lanka became more bloody, Tamils in the north began looking for ways of escape. Typically, each family wanted one of its younger male members to seek refuge abroad. This was a classic peasant strategy: the spreading of risk. Those who stayed back pooled their resources and bought a one-way ticket for their young man. In the early 1990s, the Oxford anthropologist Christopher McDowell interviewed Tamil refugees in the German-speaking parts of Switzerland. Among the testimonies he collected was this representative one from a refugee named Jeya-kumara Sinnathamby:

> I left Colombo in May 1984 on an Aeroflot flight to Abu Dhabi and then on to Moscow. From Moscow I went straight to East Berlin. I travelled alone because my friends had decided not to come at the last minute. My father paid 15,000 [Sri Lankan] rupees for the journey and I carried US$300 in cash.
>
> I arrived in East Berlin at 9 o'clock in the morning, and I purchased a 24 hour visa for US$3 at the airport. Then I took a train to West Berlin: I had no problems because of the visa. At about mid-day I arrived in West Berlin where I was approached by a Pakistani man. I told him I wanted to travel to Switzerland and he said he would show me the way. The Pakistani bought me a train ticket to Neuss and gave me the photograph of another Pakistani who would meet me there.
>
> Later in the afternoon I took the train to Neuss. For the whole journey I hid myself under a bench in the carriage. I had left my passport with the Pakistani man in Berlin. He said I could have it later. I met the other

man in Neuss and he let me stay at his house for a few days. There had been other boys there a few days before. I didn't like the house. Others said that Tamil boys had gone to work in hotels as roomboys. Two days later the Pakistani put me on a train to Switzerland. He said it went all the way to Zürich, but I should get off at Bern.

Again I hid myself under a bench. There were four people in the carriage. I did not notice the border . . . then there were four more people in the carriage . . . they may have been guards. I arrived late in Bern and spent the night in the station. The next day I went to the Aliens Police and asked for asylum. They asked me where my passport was . . . I told them it had been stolen.

An alternative route was to flee to India from the Jaffna Peninsula, across the Gulf of Mannar. From Delhi one could take a flight to Belgrade, which like Moscow did not, in those Cold War days, require an Asian to have a visa. Sometimes *schleppers*, or agents, were paid money to ensure safe passage across the Iron Curtain to Italy or Germany and, finally, to Switzerland. As McDowell found, most refugees did not, to begin with, have firm political affiliations. It was just that the civil war had made life intolerable for the ordinary civilian, and the asylum seeker had been chosen by his family as being the most likely to make some kind of life overseas.

The Tamils came to Switzerland alone or in small groups. They were interrogated by the police, before being assigned to hostels with refugees from other countries. They received a living allowance of four francs a day. After a few months they were assigned to cantons willing to receive them, and also allowed to work. Slowly, the Tamils from the remoter valleys somehow found a way to the city, where jobs paid less poorly, where they were less clearly marked out by their colour, and where they might find some more of their fellows. Now, two decades after the first lot arrived, the bulk of the Tamils in Switzerland are to be found in the German-speaking cities of Zürich, Basle, Luzern, and Bern.

The Tamils who made it to Switzerland in the early 1980s were mostly men. Later, they were joined by young girls coming to make an arranged marriage. The Swiss Tamils are, overwhelmingly, from the Vellala or Kariayar castes, that is, from farming or fishing backgrounds. Very few could speak a language other than their mother tongue. Those Tamils who spoke English generally found their way to the United Kingdom or Canada.

As it turned out, most of the Tamils in Switzerland ended up not, as Jeyakumara Sinnathamby had feared, as roomboys in hotels, but as something very adjacent: cooks and cleaners in restaurants. The *pizza-olo* of the Italian restaurant I patronized in Zürich was a Sri Lankan Tamil, as were several of the waiters. Indeed, almost all the Tamil men I met in Switzerland worked in the catering business. That was where, when they first came, they got work most easily; and that was where, for want of other options, they stayed. The authorities encouraged this, for native-born Swiss did not take readily to these dreary and comparatively low-paying occupations. The other trade where there were openings was construction, but the Tamils were deemed too slight to drive cranes or help build offices in the cold. To these jobs were directed refugees from Eastern Europe instead.

How do the Swiss view the Tamils? Emblematic here are the shifing views of the popular tabloid, *Blick*. In the early 1980s, *Blick* vigorously denounced the incoming refugees as different and strange, and wanted them deported. But by the mid 1990s *Blick* and its readers had started seeing the Tamils almost as a 'model minority', as hardworking and docile, and doing essential jobs that no one else would, at any rate not for those wages. The ordinary Swiss liked to contrast the Tamils with Yugoslavs and Balkan peoples more generally. These other immigrants had also come in the 1980s, but were regarded as a perfect nuisance: as loud, aggressive, involved in drugs and excessively covetous of Swiss women.

Back in 1843, Jacob Burckhardt complained of his native Basel that it was in danger of silting up 'without stimulating life-giving elements from outside. There are learned people here but they have turned to stone against everything foreign'. Writing a century and a half later, another fine historian, Jonathan Steinberg, commented that 'if Swiss democracy has some ugly features, it shows them to its foreigners'. But the ordinary Swiss, I found, has really no interest in Tamil culture whatsoever. He didn't know of, and wouldn't care about, the richness of their classical literature or the subtle beauties of their classical music.

Still, of overt racism towards the Tamils there are few signs. In retrospect, the Tamils were certainly lucky that the Kosavars and the Yugoslavs came at the same time as they did. I asked a Zürich anthropologist what the future held. Would there develop an influential far-right party on the French or Austrian models? The anthropologist pointed out that there was already a party whose one-point programme was: 'Out with the Foreigners'. But, he added, their support base was trifling, and unlikely to grow. Was this because their tradition of humanitarian work made the Swiss more tolerant of difference, or because Switzerland had never been a colonizing power? The anthropologist felt that more important by far was the fact that this was the most prosperous country in Europe. The Swiss, he said, were simply too rich to be racist.

IV

In Zürich I stayed in the 'Industriequartier', a district located a mile downriver from the main railway station. Its four-storeyed stone apartments were built in the nineteenth century, but the workers who once lived in them had long since departed. What remained was a large (and now empty) church named for Josef, and the original street names: Heinrichstrasse, Fabrikstrasse, and Quellenstrasse. This was now perhaps the most racially mixed of Zürich's districts, with a fair representation of Italians, Turks, Yugoslavs, Bangladeshis and, not least, Tamils.

On my first night in the city I had dinner at the Santa Lucia restaurant, with its Tamil-speaking *pizza-olo*. I sat at a table outside and observed the street. A Tamil man with an umbrella, aged about fifty, parked himself on a cylindrical pillar meant to mark off the road from the pedestrian area. He bobbed his umbrella up and down, and chatted up the passing Tamils: three boys carrying videos (of Bollywood movies, perhaps), a couple out on a date. Two men in their twenties came and joined him, sitting likewise on those parking pillars. A car stopped for ten minutes, on the road, the driver leaning out to speak to his fellows. This was so Tamil (or South Asian) and so un-Swiss: the use of public space to 'take the air', to stand on the road or a street corner in anticipation of other members of the community—whether rich or poor, young or old, men, women, or children.

Another evening I was walking along Josef Park, in front of the old working-class residences. I came across a group of Tamil teenage boys, walking and playing with a football. They must have spoken Swiss German at school, but among themselves they conversed in Tamil: surely, I thought, a unique form of bilingualism. They seemed to know the locality intimately, and appeared very comfortable on the street, gossiping in their own tongue as they kicked the ball off the parapets and dustbins. Their attention was momentarily diverted when four (white) Swiss girls came and sat on a bench in the plaza. The Tamils cast shy and sly glances in their direction, but made no move to talk or flirt. They could have been a group of loitering boys in any South Asian town, out on the road between six and eight in the evening, after school but before dinner, home-work, and bed. As in South Asia, this group was strictly male. For the girls had returned home directly from school. They had to help with the cooking and housework, and in any case it was not deemed safe or proper for them to wander about in the streets.

Exiles everywhere tend to stick together, at least in the first generation. But in this case, the natural desire to hang out with one's (likewise vulnerable) fellows is strengthened by conscious and directed social organization. In the heart of this immigrant ghetto of Zürich is an office which runs no less than seventy-three Tamil schools in Switzerland. These schools hold classes twice a week: on Wednesday afternoons, when the regular Swiss schools close early, and on Saturdays. The children come in after they turn five, and sometimes stay until the age of twenty. The kids start with Tamil songs and stories, before moving on to the alphabet and the construction of sentences. They use well designed and lavishly illustrated textbooks, printed in Bielefeld in Germany, but with their content supervised by a committee of Tamil professors from Jaffna, Colombo, Thanjavur, and Madras.

The association that runs the schools calls itself the 'World Tamil Education Service'. Its office, on the corner of Josefstrasse and Langstrasse, is equipped with computers and a xerox machine, and even an airy and well-lit conference room. One afternoon I met the two main office-bearers: Mahindran, a well-built man about five feet nine inches tall, and Sudhaharan, who was much shorter, balding, and with glasses. Both wore moustaches, both said they were thirty-three, and both had come in the late 1980s from Jaffna, abandoning their college degrees halfway. And both had worked as cooks in Zürich: Sudhaharan, who helped out part-time at the education service, still did so.

In the early 1990s, some Tamil schools were started in Switzerland on an individual and uncoordinated basis. In 1995 Mahindran took the initiative to hold a Tamil language exam, in which 315 students took part. The next year he held a meeting of Tamil teachers from across the country, which decided to formalize the curriculum and seek proper textbooks. By 1998, there were 35 Tamil schools in Switzerland, and about 1400 students. Now there were 73 schools, with 4000 students enrolled in them. The teachers worked mostly for free, but a few were paid from a grant given by the aid agency, Caritas.

I asked Mahindran and Sudhaharan whether their schools taught history and politics. No, they said, we want only to focus on language and culture. When pressed, they admitted that the boys and girls did get a political education at home, from their parents, who naturally had ideas of their own about the civil war. I then asked about the recently enacted cease-fire on the island. Both of them, mild mannered and gentle as they appeared to be, were firm and decisive in their political views. They were for the Tigers, completely. When I asked about

Tamils who might have reasons for not supporting the Tigers, Sudha-háran answered: 'In the early 1980s, there were other armed groups, but these were agents of the Sri Lankan or Indian governments. Fifteen years of struggle have shown that only the Tigers are trusted by the Tamil people. Of course, thieves and crooked businessmen don't like the LTTE. But all others do.' Then he added, as an after-thought: 'Of course, they [the Tigers] are strict.'

I asked whether the Sri Lankan situation could be compared to Palestine. At one level the parallel held: both the Tamils and the Palestinians faced dispossession and a colonizing army. But Sudha-haran, small and slight as he was, insisted that the Tamils were far superior. 'Look at the Palestinians', he said, 'they are fighting among themselves—one for Hamas, another for Arafat. And some of them are still throwing stones at the Israelis! They must build a united *military* force.' The contrast could not be clearer: on one side the disunited Palestinians, on the other the Tigers, sole spokesmen for their people and ferocious fighters to boot.

At one point, nervous about the turn in our conversation, M. and S. clarified: 'These are our personal views. We don't teach them in our schools—no politics there, only language and culture'. Whether they seeped into the schools or not, their own views were pretty direct. Almost my last question related to the aim of the peace talks now being overseen by the Norwegians. I asked whether they would be satisfied with autonomy within a united Sri Lanka, or whether they would still insist on independence. The answer, from Mahindran, was immediate and resonant with feeling. 'We have lost *everything*— homes, lands, forests and families. What for? In 1985, we might have accepted autonomy. But now, after all this struggle and sacrifice, what can we accept? Only Eelam.'

V

An abiding memory of my time in Zürich is of church bells pealing. I lived across the street from a Protestant church, but elsewhere, too, conversations were interrupted by the sound of bells rung faithfully every quarter of an hour. Who was listening, or answering the call? Here, as elsewhere in Western Europe, few people under fifty were practising Christians. The indication of this was not merely falling attendance in church. It lay also, for instance, in the divorce rate, which was more than sixty per cent.

In this city of the great theologian Zwingli, the community that seemed to most seriously follow their faith were the Tamils. One day I called on a temple priest in the suburb of Adliswil. Dedicated to Shiva's second son, Subramaniam, the temple was sited on the banks of a gentle and green river, which was nice, and the priest was short and with a pronounced paunch, which was reassuring. When I had visited Sri Lanka earlier in the year, an experienced political journalist told me that malnutrition was rife in the north: 'The only well fed people there', he said, 'are LTTE cadres, traders, and Hindu priests.'

Priests in Indian temples are also always over-fed. But the story of Sharma *vadhyar* of Adliswil was anything but typical. Although from a family of priests, he had rejected the trade and worked in a firm in Colombo for fourteen years. He was at the same time an activist with a group affiliated to the Fourth International. When the going got hot in Sri Lanka, fellow Trotskyists in Germany helped him seek asylum there. He found his way to Zürich, where the Tamils urged him to resume the family calling. He taught himself the scriptures, and started naming the odd baby. He graduated to marriages and deaths, and eventually was able to persuade the Swiss authorities to allot him space for a temple.

Fat, affable, wearing a *dhoti* but with his upper body bare, Sharma was a bit of an operator, but a charming one, and also highly successful. He wore large gold-and-diamond ear-rings, obviously a post-Trotskyist accretion. We spoke in his office, drinking orange juice in plastic cups, amidst a pile of Tamil books. Among them was a new edition of the Ramayana as retold by the legendary poet Kamban, which Sharma said had been gifted to him by the chief minister of Pondicherry.

'Communism is Service. What we are doing here is also Service.'
Saying this, Sharma took us to his temple. Here, dozens of young men
were cutting vegetables and cleaning idols, in preparation for a prayer
to be held later in the day, for which four hundred people were expected. We couldn't stay, so Sharma asked that we come instead for
the opening of a ten-day festival, to begin the next Friday.

When I got there the following week, the place had been transformed. The entrance now had a twenty-foot-high tower made of
cardboard affixed to it, mimicking the traditional *gopuram* of the
South Indian temple. The cardboard was coloured and painted over
with deities. On either side flew a flag: the red-and-white Swiss flag
to the right, the yellow-and-blue Adliswil cantonal flag to the left. It
was nine o'clock when I reached, but the ceremonies had begun.
Inside, musicians specially flown in from Sri Lanka were playing their
clarinets. Sharma was anointing the idols behind an orange curtain.
The devotees patiently waited: women and kids sitting on the floor,
the men standing to a side, separately.

After half an hour the curtain was lifted, to reveal both Lord Subramaniam and his attendant. Sharma wore a richly embroidered gold
dhoti, and a red-and-gold sash on his head. Half-a-dozen assistants
began chanting. A young pig-tailed priest with a fine tenor voice did
a solo number, reading from a book in which Sanskrit had been rendered in the Tamil script. Altogether, the priestly functions seemed
rather *ad hoc*, learnt from books and improvised rather than traditionally learnt. Yet there was no mistaking the devotion. One of the
poems read out was a long invocation to the rivers of the Indian heart-
land, the waters that had given birth both to the language of Sanskrit and to classical Hindu civilization. 'Ganga, Yamuna, Saraswati,
Narmada!', chanted the tenor, 'Godavari, Mahanadi, Tungabhadra!'
The action was moving southwards, to rivers added on (I suspect) by
a medieval Tamil saint. We finally reached as close to Eelam as 'Tam-
baraparani', a river that runs in the southern parts of the Indian state
of Tamil Nadu.

Worshippers were streaming in all the time, making their way
from the outlying cantons. Little boys in handsome *kurta-pyjamas*,

girls in shimmering *salwar kameezes*—the preferred colours red and
silver or bright green—women bedecked in jewellery, as if for their
own weddings. They came in twos and threes, unobtrusively and
spread out in time, then suddenly revealing themselves to be a consolidated and surprisingly large force. By eleven o'clock, there were at
least eight hundred people present. It was at this hour, as Sharma had
previously told us, that a Swiss Christian priest of the vicinity was
expected to come and hoist the temple flag.

The churchman didn't come ('caught in a traffic jam', was one
rumour we heard) so, at 11.15, Sharma came out of the temple, accompanied by young men carrying the deity under an umbrella
embroidered in scarlet. The priest hoisted the temple flag, in between
those of Adliswil and the Swiss Federation, broke a coconut, and
formally announced the inauguration of the festival.

Why did the Swiss padre back out of the event? Perhaps he was too
busy, or perhaps too lazy. Perhaps a colleague had told him that it
would be theologically unsound. It was as well that he stayed away.
Had he come, the crowds and their religiosity would have made him
very depressed as well as terrribly envious.

I did, however, meet a Swiss priest who sees Tamil worshippers
on a more or less daily basis. His name is Father Patrick, and he is
the Rector of the Abbey of Einsiedeln, a Catholic shrine in the hills
outside Zürich that dates back at least to the tenth century, and whose
most famous feature is a Black Madonna. The Madonna receives
Catholic pilgrims from all over the world, but she also receives a
steady stream of Hindu Tamils settled in Switzerland, who have come
to revere her as a Mother Goddess.

I drove to Einsiedeln from Zürich, with friends. On the way the
weather changed. The sky darkened, and by the time we arrived there
was a mist over the mountains. We waited in the long driveway, where
Father Patrick came out to meet us, his black habit silhouetted against
the monastery. He was a tiny man, with eyes glinting behind silver-
rimmed spectacles. Now about thirty-five, he had joined Einsiedeln
after high school, before going off to Rome to do a doctorate, in
atheism. ('You must know the other side', as he put it.) After his PhD

he had returned to the monastery, to take charge of the theological school and otherwise help in the administration.

We went inside to view the Madonna. She was Black, Father Patrick explained, not by design but because the absence of light and the wax dripping from candles had darkened her. She was dressed in a cheery frock, red roses printed against a pink background. Father Patrick said the Madonna was dressed afresh six or eight times a year, the operation performed behind a curtain by a priest. Just like Sharma and his Subramaniam, I thought: the air of mystique, the distance between the deity and the worshipper, with the priest as the essential intermediary. The dressing up of Mary, her black visage, and the riot of colours in the baroque church itself—this, I reflected, must explain why the Tamils come here. On this single afternoon twenty or thirty Tamils arrived, alone, as couples, or as families. Sometimes they came in larger numbers, in busloads visiting on Sundays from Zürich or Bern.

I hopped out of the enclosure to speak to the Tamils. Most, as I had suspected, were Hindu. I went back to Father Patrick, and asked him why he thought the Tamils came to worship in Einsiedeln. 'Of course, our Madonna is black', he said, but then added innovatively that 'besides, Mary was herself a refugee [a reference to her fleeing her native Nazareth for Bethlehem], and had known so much sorrow herself [as in the loss of her only child]'. 'I don't know much about Hinduism', he went on, 'but doesn't it quite easily absorb gods from other faiths?' When I pressed him as to whether the Tamils came to the Madonna seeking a specific blessing—a male child, or a cure for an illness—the priest answered, somewhat evasively, that Christianity did not believe in intercession with God.

Forty years ago the Einsiedeln monastery had as many as two hundred monks. The number was now down to eighty-two, their average age in excess of sixty. Father Patrick had told us that they employed Tamils in their kitchen. He was unconvinced by our suggestion that perhaps taking in Tamil novitiates would be a better idea. As we prepared to leave, there was a rush of Swiss people coming into the church. An older monk standing by said, 'It must be raining', a cynical comment validated when we went outside, and were drenched in reaching the car.

VI

In the Adliswil temple the Tiger presence was muted. There was no Eelam flag anywhere. I did see some teenage boys wearing black and white, but their fathers were dressed in gayer colours. Still, the Tigers must on the whole approve of a devotionalism that brings the Tamils together, that endorses their unity as well as their separateness from the Swiss mainstream.

Also in Adliswil, and just fifteen minutes walk from the temple, lives a man who is both a devout Hindu and a committed Tiger. His name is Mathialakan, and he is the prime mover behind the annual sports festival of the Tamil diaspora. The chief chef in a Swiss restaurant, Mathi has the sleek and trim body of an athlete. His eyes are soft, almost dreamy, his hair thick, his manner quiet but utterly self-assured. We spoke in his house, amidst a clutter of papers and files from the recently concluded Bern meeting. Mathi's English was as dodgy as my Tamil. So, for the most part, he spoke in Swiss German, his words translated by Yumi, a Swiss student of Japanese extraction who had come with me. Also in the room were his wife and their sixteen-month-old son. On the wall hung photographs of his parents, a red LTTE poster with a growling yellow tiger on it, and a Tamil calendar dominated by a portrait of Prabhakaran.

Mathi had studied in Mahajana College near Jaffna, a place which was, as he put it, 'famous in Sri Lanka for its football team'. They had won the district championship eight years in a row. He himself played at that pivotal position, centre-forward. In 1987 he was doing his A levels in Jaffna, and hoped to become an accountant. But, like so many others, his studies were interrrupted by the IPKF. The oppressions of the IPKF, remembered Mathi, 'had united all the previously quarrelling Tamil groups against them'. A fellow student, Thileepan,

went on a fast-unto-death in protest against the alliance of the Sri
Lankan army and the IPKF. 'Even Mahatma Gandhi drank water during his fasts', said Mathi, meaningfully, 'but not Thileepan'. After
Thileepan died, the students exploded in support of the Tigers. With
hundreds of others, Mathi was also put in jail. His mother would
come to see him every day, till, taking pity, an Indian Tamil soldier
called Narayanaswami allowed him to escape. He made his way to
Colombo and, in 1990, to Switzerland.

As an exile in Zürich, Mathi was struck by the divide between parents and children. The problem was that parents simply gave or-
ders—eat this, dress like that, etc.—without explaining what the
culture was. So, thought Mathi, we need to more systematically teach
our children about the homeland:

> Five hundred years ago, we Tamils had our own country, our own govern-
> ment, our own state. Colonization by the Europeans and oppression by
> the Sinhalese destroyed it. Now we are struggling for the reclamation of
> our land. Even while we are here, we must prepare to go back to Eelam.
> Eventually that will be our home, not Switzerland. Here we can never
> escape being foreign.

In 1996, Mathi started an association called Tamilar Illam, or the
Tamil House. He focused on sport, a medium that would best bring
parents and kids together. He enforced a 'Tamil only' rule on the
football field. In 1998 he held his first tournament, for under-15s,
with seven participating teams from five cantons. Slowly, the scope
expanded to include other age groups—under 10, under 13, and
under 18. There was no need, in his mind, for a 18 to 35 category,
since those who fell within it were, like him, already Tamil in spirit
and sentiment. There was, however, an over 35 group for the parents,
who would take their kids to the club and end up playing themselves.

The first transnational sports festival was held in 1999. It was a
master-stroke: bonding the old with the young, pleasing those parents whose boys played, spurring the ambition to participate in the
parents of those who didn't. 'How does this link to the struggle for

Eelam?' I asked. 'Our war is not only for the separation of territory',
said Mathi. 'It is for the maintenance of language, culture and religion—all together (*alles zusammen*). The festival brings parents and
children together, renews cultural ties, and promotes a unity of outlook among éxiles in different countries'. 'I had my own dreams destroyed', he added: 'My own life is effectively finished. But these boys
can still, with our help, realize their dreams.' I suppose he meant that
he had now to live out his days as a chef in Adliswil, when he hoped
to have been an accountant in Sri Lanka. This was said with such
finality that it unnerved Yumi, with her own life ahead of her. 'It is
astonishing, the casual way in which he said "my life is destroyed", she
told me later: 'That was almost like kicking me off the sofa.'

I asked Mathi who he had supported in the recently concluded soccer World Cup. 'Brazil, naturally', he said. It appeared that he was a
fan of the game of cricket, too. 'I support the Indian cricket team', he
told me: 'even when they play Sri Lanka, and despite the doings of the
Indian Peace Keeping Force'. The memory of Thileepan's martyrdom could not completely efface the attachment to India, the mother
lode of his language and religion. He hoped next year to take his son
to the sacred shrine of Tirupathi in South India, to make the traditional offering of his first-born's lovely crop of black hair.

On that planned visit Mathi would be accompanied by a bunch of
boy footballers from Zürich. 'Here we can only teach them so much
about our culture', he said: 'they have to go to Jaffna to experience
it.' Another (and larger) ambition was the creation of a full-fledged
Tamil football team, entered under its own colours in the Swiss
National League. Did not, I ask, this dream clash with the other
dream of return? In his eyes this was not a contradiction. 'All I hope',
he said, 'is that our boys should be proud of our culture and history.
They can be Swiss by nationality, but they must still be Tamil in
spirit.' A Tamil team in the Swiss league would also be consisent with
what was still a possible, if worst-case, scenario: 'If the war gets worse,
and there are no Tamils left in Sri Lanka, they will at least be here, with
their culture intact.'

Mathi, like other of his fellows, refused to admit of any reason for a Tamil not to support the Tigers. 'Without the Tamil Tigers there would be no Tamils', he remarked, implying that they would all have been killed by the Sri Lankan army. After I had finished interrogating him, Mathi said, 'Can I now ask you a question? Why is *The Hindu* [the Madras newspaper he was told I wrote for] so against the Tigers?' I answered, weakly: 'I don't know—I only write on cricket, for the magazine section, not on politics.' 'Surely', he went on archly, 'you read the rest of the paper? *Why* is *The Hindu* so hostile to the Tigers?'

I now decided that I must be at least half-way honest. 'Perhaps because they have more sympathy with the Tamil moderates, such as the leaders of the TULF'. 'Then', continued Mathi, 'let me ask you another question. What do *you* think of the Tigers?' 'I share their dream of a just solution for the Tamils', I began. 'I admire their courage. But why did they have to kill Tamils who might have differed from them? The assassination of Sinhala prime ministers and ministers—even that can be understood in the context of army atrocities. But why kill Amirthalingam and Tiruchelvam?'

Mathi turned to his wife, sitting discreetly behind him, and asked her to refresh his memory. She recalled for him who the two men were, and then he proceeded: 'Amirthalingam—he was elected on a platform of Tamil Eelam in 1977. But he forgot about it—started looking out for his own interests instead. Tiruchelvam—he might have been of Tamil blood, but he lived in Colombo and couldn't speak Tamil. And he was working with the Sinhala and the Americans and against the Tamils'. This was crude propaganda, but he seemed to believe it completely. I thought I had to protest, for Tiruchelvam was a scholar of much integrity. I had been to his house in Colombo, and had many friends who admired and even worshipped him. A brilliant legal scholar who had trained and also taught at Harvard, he was drafting a devolution package for the north when he was murdered by the Tigers. Ironically, in his last public lecture, Tiruchelvam had spoken out against what he called the 'absurd contradiction of imposing a mono-ethnic state on a multi-ethnic polity.' 'No, no', I said now to Mathi, 'he was working for autonomy. Maybe not independence, but surely that was not enough reason to kill him?' I tried to explain what 'autonomy' meant, but Mathi either didn't understand, or chose not to.

Not in twenty years—since I lived with Marxists in Calcutta—could I remember having had political discussions of such intensity. Still, Mathi was not, in the formal sense, a 'party man'. His admiration for the Tigers was born out of his experiences as a student under the IPKF, and it deepened in exile, as alternatives to their path were crushed or faded away. Even more intense was a talk I had with the leading Tiger ideologue of Switzerland, Anton Ponnarajah. He called himself a 'human rights activist', a now almost ubiquitous pose adopted by sympathizers of revolutionary groups across the globe.

I met Anton in the restaurant of the Luzern railway station, as he waited to catch a train to Geneva. The one hour he had allowed me was extended to two, and then to three. Anton was stocky, with puffy cheeks and the obligatory moustache of the Tamil male. His hair was well oiled and combed backwards. Like Mathi and Mahindran, he was full of charm. He laughed and smiled easily, and refused to allow me to pay for the drinks. Of all the Tamils I met he was the most articulate and well read. He had studied in a top Jesuit school in Jaffna where, I guess, he had learnt how to state and defend a case.

Anton left Sri Lanka in 1985. At the time he was in the middle of a degree course in Mechanical Engineering. But, he insisted, 'by profession I am an actor.' He had trained at a once vibrant theatre school run by A.C. Tarsesius in Jaffna. (The school was a casualty of the civil war, and Tarsesius himself was in exile in London.) After coming to Switzerland, he founded a mixed theatre group, acting with Arabs and Africans in plays with inter-cultural themes. Now he had shifted over to human rights work, but still managed to supervise a theatre school for the Tamil diaspora. He had designed a one-year course, with five hundred hours of contact time, funded by the exiles, and with a dozen full-time students. This past year, his students had put on two plays for their Commencement, one dealing with the Sri Lankan conflict, the other with the position of foreigners in Switzerland.

Twice a year, in April and August, Anton went to Geneva to meet with delegates to the U.N. Commission on Human Rights. I asked him whether, in addition to the violations of the Sri Lankan army, he also mentioned violations by the Tigers. 'No', he said, 'because the Tigers are reacting to their actions'. 'What if reaction becomes over-reaction', I asked. 'We are not promoting human rights abuse by the Tigers', answered Anton, 'but you have to understand it as a response to army excesses. You can call it "over-reaction", but others will view it differently'. Then he adduced a string of army crimes, the bombing of churches and schools among them.

Anton liked to tell Swiss friends who criticized their country: 'For me your political system is Heaven. I came from Hell.' In this land's past lay perhaps a lesson for his own. 'Look at Swiss history', he told me, 'these cantons hated each other, they massacred each other. But finally they have learnt to live with and respect one another.' For all his partisanship, Anton seemed hopeful of a political solution. As we spoke, the warring parties were preparing to talk in Thailand. 'Are the Sri Lankan politicians more sincere than in the past?', I asked. 'No', said Anton, 'but their military is now certain that they can't win the war.' He didn't think the independence vs. autonomy issue would pose a problem. 'If the two parties are willing, a solution can be found: federal, confederal, two countries, or whatever.'

This political realism towards the future was, however, markedly absent in Anton's understanding of the past. I asked whether he felt the Tigers should apologize for having killed Tamils such as Amirthalingam. 'He gave a clean sheet to the IPKF', Anton answered, immediately. He then compared the TULF leader to Vichy collaborators who were later hanged. 'Whoever is a betrayer will be punished by the masses'.

But what about Tiruchelvam? Why murder a fine and internationally respected scholar? 'Because he was working against the interests of the Tamils', came the very quick reply. 'Tiruchelvam said he was against the LTTE, but it is the Tigers who represent the whole community, the whole of the Tamil people. He talked against human rights violations of the Tigers, but never about the army.' He reminded me again of what the French and the British had done to their 'betrayers' after the Second World War: 'If you are willing to be used by the enemy's propaganda machinery, you should be prepared for the consequences.' Anton added, spitefully: 'Tiruchelvam did not know Tamil, did not even know where Jaffna was.' (At least one of these statements I knew to be a lie. When I visited Tiruchelvam's house, in Colombo, his still intact study was lined with rows upon rows of Tamil books.) Later in the conversation, Anton told me of a speech at which Prabhakaran had apparently said: 'If I betray the Tamil people, I too will be killed.' This was a chilling justification of political murder, here being quoted with pride.

I insisted on seeking some admission of Tiger frailty. In parts of Mannar and in the eastern region around Batticaloa, the LTTE had mounted savage attacks on Tamil-speaking Muslims who had resisted being taxed. Independent reports suggested that whole villages had been ethnically cleansed. 'What about the Tigers' treatment of the Muslims', I asked. Pat came the answer, patiently prepared over years, and articulated many times before:

> There was *never* any conflict in the past. It has been created by the Government. As Lenin says, the oppressors always try to create clashes between sections of the oppressed. But as Tamils we know what it means to be subjugated by a majority. Give us the chance to decide our own future. Wait for the political solution. Then the Tiger leadership will never allow oppression of another minority.

The only time Anton stumbled, very slightly, was when I raised the question of Rajiv Gandhi's assassination. He first blamed it on the IPKF (original action causing a justifiable over-reaction). In any case, if the Sri Lankan prime minister was now willing to talk to the Tigers after all the killings of Sinhala politicians, why couldn't the Indians do likewise? But this was different, I answered. One couldn't so easily justify the murder of a leading foreign politician in his own land. This single act had wiped out all sympathy for the Tigers among the sixty million Tamils of India. Besides, Prabhakaran himself was an accused in the Rajiv Gandhi murder case, and the Indian government had demanded his extradition. Rajiv's widow, Sonia, was leader of the opposition in the Indian parliament, and a likely prime minister-in-waiting. Wouldn't this be a problem for the peace talks? Wouldn't those talks require, for their success, the benign approval of the regional Big Brother?

Anton sought refuge in his leader's choice of words. 'In his press conference [of April 2002], Mr Prabhakaran referred to the killing of Rajiv as a "tragic event" ', he said. 'Not, mind you, as a successful suicide operation'. Then, like a good Leninist, he insisted that these questions were at bottom political, not personal or emotional. 'Sonia Gandhi or even Mr Prabhakaran will not live for ever. A way will be found to resolve this.'

As Anton prepared to pick up his things to catch the train to Geneva, I asked him three questions in quick succession:

Q: 'Are you a Christian?'
A: 'A Catholic by birth, but I don't follow any religious observances or go to church, although my wife does.'

Q: 'Are you a Marxist?' (this provoked by the several references to Lenin).
A: 'No, because what Marx and Lenin did or said were appropriate to their context. We have to design solutions relevant to our context.'

Q: 'Are you a Tiger?'
A: 'I am a Tamil, and all Tamils are Tigers'.

Q: 'Really?' (this said quizzically).
A: 'Let me explain. I see myself first and last as a Tamil. I will always be a Tamil, even if I live fifty years in Switzerland. In my homeland the Tamil people are being oppressed, and only the Tigers are fighting this oppression. So I am a Tiger.'

Anton Ponnarajah had abandoned his baptismal faith for another. Still in the Church, and a priest no less, was Father Peppi, who had been sent by his bishop to minister to the 4,000 Tamil Catholics in Switzerland. A round-faced and ever-smiling man, Father Peppi had studied in a seminary in Jaffna during the bloody days of the 1980s. The students, he recalled, had read their texts by candlelight, sometimes with the sound of shelling in the background. The priest seemed to view the IPKF much like any Tiger did. He was himself picked up one morning by Indian soldiers—at 6.30 a.m., while he was praying, and released only late at night.

After his ordination, Father Peppi was asked to look after a refugee camp in Vavuniya. There were 30,000 inmates: Hindus, Muslims, and Christians. Each family lived in a tiny room, ten feet by ten feet, and with no education or health facilities. He remembered a cholera epidemic in which thirty babies died in a month. 'Always panic, that time', as he put it. One of his fellow priests had estimated that there were 30,000 war widows in the North. But, Father Peppi added at once, 'other side also there are many widows in the South.'

The Father was proud of the efforts of his Church towards reconciliation. His own patriarch, the Bishop of Mannar, had collected money for the Sinhala poor. The Bishop of Colombo had collected blood for Tamil victims of the war. The Catholics were a minority on both sides, but in the vanguard of the moves for peace.

Father Peppi's present job was to hold Tamil language services for the exiles. The first and third Sundays of the month he took Mass in Zürich, the second Sunday in Luzern or Bern, the fourth Sunday in Geneva or Lausanne. The Swiss Church had given him a flat—which is where we spoke—but their flock was completely segregated from his own. They met only once a year, on the second Sunday in November, observed as a 'foreigners day' in Zürich, when the Tamil Catholics, along with the Albanians, Serbians, and others, were granted ten minutes of a multilingual service that ran for a whole morning. Once this was over the Tamils retreated to their ghetto.

In Switzerland Father Peppi stayed away from the Tigers. He did not attend their functions, and they left him alone, assured that he had no political axe to grind. When I asked why they had such a following, he said it was because they were the only organization now fighting for the Tamils. 'They are the only redemption for their sufffering. My bishop recognized this, hence he urged the government to talk to them.' But, I asked, were there problems back home with the Tigers? 'Yes, for in their own areas they are like a government. They control everything. They want obedience to their rules. Their pass system proved difficult for us. Our people would sometimes complain about the taxes they levied.' Are they taxing refugees, too? I asked. Father Peppi said he didn't know.

How much money do the Tigers in fact get from the exiles? One published account said they collected 50 Swiss francs per month per family. This, accumulated over the community, would amount to five million francs annually. A university professor in Zürich knew someone who paid, he said, as much as 200 francs a month. A Swiss journalist said that a great deal of money was also collected on events like Heroes Day, observed annually on 27th November, when thousands of Tamils would meet to hear patriotic speeches and to commemorate their dead. A male nurse in Basel told me simply that the 'Tigers ask many, many money. They ask a lot if you have or if you don't have.' He claimed to know a family who had made a one-time payment of 10, 000 francs. Two or three years later, the Tigers came back to ask for more.

The nurse was a Muslim, originally from Mannar. Between 1989 and 1991 he was a medical student in Jaffna. It was hard for him to go home on vacations, travelling to and fro between areas controlled by the Tigers and the army. Then, suddenly, there was no home anymore. His father's thriving fish business was destroyed by the Tigers, as part of a wider attack on Muslims. The family fled to Colombo and the boy, on his parents' advice, escaped to Europe. Helped by an agent, he finally reached Switzerland, via Italy, Yugoslavia and Austria.

I spoke to this Tamil Muslim—let us call him Arif—in a Movenpick café outside the railway station. Here, in Basel, he could more easily become a nurse than a doctor. The authorities encouraged educated

Tamils to move into this profession, since the Swiss could not decently look after their own elderly. Arif did a four-year course in nursing school, helped by loans from friends, Hindus as well as Muslims. 'Among us there is no problem', he said. 'The Tigers are the problem. They profit from a conflict. They incite Hindu–Muslim clashes in the Eastern Province, so that they can gain control.' He now stayed clear of the Tigers, but said he knew other exiles who paid money regularly. This was to prevent harm coming to their families back home. 'They pay as otherwise they are worried the Tigers will take away everything—land, jewellery, houses. No one talks about these things because they are afraid. I am also afraid.'

I asked Arif whether he welcomed the ceasefire. 'No, not really. I never believe these things. This is to allow Tigers to plan for the next stage of the war. Now they can move freely, bring in weapons and money into the North.' 'If they really wanted peace', he told me pointedly, 'why were they still collecting money? After the ceasefire, Swiss Tamils visited Jaffna and Mannar but came back to tell us: "Don't go home. The Tigers will take your money."' Arif said he didn't believe that the Tigers were for the Tamils, since they had made so many of them suffer. Then he added: 'The other side [the Sri Lankan army] is also not good.'

The café where we met was crowded. Arif looked worried whenever I spoke loudly, as I have a tendency to do. He himself spoke in a low voice, but with deliberation and absolute clarity. Arif was reflective and philosophical, wise beyond his years, the wisdom born out of his own, and his people's, experience. I should say the same for his almost exact contemporary, Mathi of Adliswil. Yet, how different were their perceptions of the Tigers. One hesitates to ascribe this difference simply to their respective religions. Leonard Woolf, who worked as a civil servant among the Jaffna Tamils in the first decade of the twentieth century, wrote of 'their strange mixture of tortuousness and directness, of cunning and stupidity, of cruelty and kindness'. Thus the people, and thus also their leaders. The Tamil Tigers are both liberators and oppressors, heroic fighters for freedom as well as authoritarians brutally intolerant of dissent. How one judges them depends on which side you happen to see first, or see longest.

VII

Twenty years of war in Sri Lanka has produced many deaths and no winners. When a cease-fire was agreed upon in February 2002, both sides had their reasons to temporarily put away arms. After 9/11, the pressures on the Tigers to remake themselves as political moderates increased. It was also said that Prabhakaran was keen that his three children, already in their teens, not have to replicate his own experience of life in the jungle. As for the Sri Lankan government, the war had hugely dented its finances. Debt-servicing—chiefly to pay for arms bought abroad—exceeded government revenues. Rates of desertion in the army were alarmingly high. And it was clear to the top Sinhala commanders that while this was a war they could not lose, they didn't appear to be winning it either.

At the time of the ceasefire, there were 35,000 government troops stationed in the Peninsula. The fighting strength of the LTTE was 15,000, many of these in the 14 to 18 age bracket. The Tigers controlled two districts in full and chunks of five others. Here they ran their own police stations under the Eelam flag.

On the 23rd of February 2003 the ceasefire entered its second year. In this time there have been several rounds of talks, held in Thailand, Norway, and Germany. The main Tiger interlocutor is, as ever, the London-based Anton Balasingham. He has been assisted by top Tiger cadres, including the head of the political wing, S.P. Thamilselvan, and the eastern military commander, Karuna—both of whom had to get Sri Lankan passports in order to travel overseas. The government's pointman was the scholarly, silver-haired G.L. Peiris, who before he joined the cabinet was a professor of constitutional law at Colombo Univesity.

At the second round of talks, in Thailand in early November 2002, the parties established three committees: to deal with rehabilitation of the north and the east, with de-escalation, and with political questions. In these committees were representatives of the government, the Tigers, and, most notably, the vulnerable minority, the Muslims.

At the next round of talks, in Oslo in December, both parties agreed, as their joint statement put it, 'to explore a political solution founded on internal self-determination based on a federal structure within a united Sri Lanka'. Balasingham hailed this as 'an unprecedented historic decision'. The Norwegian special envoy to the talks more cautiously called it a 'major step', and suggested that 'a long and bumpy road still lay ahead'.

'Internal self-determination' seems, on the face of it, to be an abandonment of the ideal of Eelam. This is a major concession by the Tigers. Another hopeful sign is their willingness to talk to the Muslims. The LTTE and the Sri Lankan Muslim Congress reached agreement that Muslims in the East would not be harassed and could freely engage in fishing, agriculture, and trade. Later, as a gesture of goodwill, the LTTE transferred three commanders perceived to be biased against Muslims and indulging in extortion.

However, gesture and rhetoric has to contend against some harsh ground realities. In the third week of January 2003, the University Teachers for Human Rights–Jaffna issued a report listing instances of continuing child conscription by the LTTE and the abduction of political rivals. In the first week of February, the Sri Lankan navy apprehended a Tiger boat carrying arms and ammunition. Two Norwegians of the monitoring mission were called in; as soon as they boarded the boat, the Tigers set it on fire. The Norwegians jumped overboard and escaped unhurt. Ten days later there was a scuffle between Sri Lankan soldiers and LTTE women cadres who refused to take off their military-style belts when moving in government-controlled areas. Balasingham, in London, called the clash 'an intolerable provocation'. In Jaffna itself 8000 Tamils marched in protest, shouting slogans and burning effigies of Sri Lankan politicians. Then in early March the navy sunk another boat they suspected had weapons. The LTTE claimed it was a merchant ship, and said its sinking would have 'far-reaching implications for the peace process'.

The political scientist Jayadeva Uyangoda—a close observer of and occasional participant in the peace process—says that the year since arms were downed have seen 'negotiations without any reconciliation.' Confirmation comes from the proposed reopening of the great Jaffna Library, rebuilt and restocked with funds from UNESCO, the Ford Foundation, and the Sri Lankan government. Two Sri Lankan cabinet ministers were due to fly in for the event, which was scheduled for the second week of February. However, local protests instigated by the LTTE led to the function being called off. A pro-Tiger group locked the godown where the books were kept, to prevent them being shifted to the new premises. Evidently, the Tigers did not want a symbolically significant act of reconciliation to take place under the patronage of the Sri Lankan government.

Will the peace hold? Will a federal solution be workable and acceptable to all parties? The stumbling blocks are many, and various. The president, Chandrika Kumaratunga, who heads a different party from the prime minister, Ranil Wickramasinghe, has opposed the talks, saying the Tigers cannot be relied upon. (One can see Mrs Kumaratunga's point of view, since she narrowly escaped being killed by a suicide bomber.) Then there are the Sinhala chauvinists, who view any kind of devolution as dangerous. It was with these people in mind that Mr Wickramasinghe issued a statement refuting allegations that his government was 'kneeling before the LTTE'.

In between the talks, Anton Balasingham has visited the forest to consult with his leader. Ultimately, the fate of the negotiations might very well be decided by this one man, Velupillai Prabhakaran. On the 27th of November 2002—a week before talks were held in Oslo—Prabhakaran delivered his annual Martyrs Day address. It was here that he put forward the idea of 'internal self-determination [which] entitles a people to regional self-rule'. Yet this undeniably significant, even historic, concession, was rendered suspect by caveat and innuendo. Thus he contrasted the Tigers' 'sincere and dedicated commitment to the peace process' with the 'hardline and deceitful political approaches of previous Sri Lankan governments' as well as the continuing 'provocative attempts by certain elements of the armed forces and anti-peace racist forces'. There were several references to 'Sinhala chauvinist forces', and an assertion that 'it is the politics of the Sinhala nation that will eventually determine whether the Sinhalese could peacefully coexist with the Tamils . . . But if our people's right to self-determination is denied and our demand for regional self-rule is rejected we have no alternative other than to secede and form an independent state'.

On the 1st of November 2002, as talks were proceeding in Thailand, a Colombo court convicted Prabhakaran in the Central Bank bombing case. His sentence: 200 years in prison. The talks continued regardless. When the time comes, the Sri Lankan government might get the sentence annulled. Remembering the crimes committed by their own army and air force, they might forget the bombings carried out by the LTTE as well. More difficult to overlook is the assassination of Rajiv Gandhi. The Indian government has an extradition request out for Prabhakaran, who masterminded that particular murder, as he did so many others.

Sri Lanka's need for peace thus clashes with India's need for justice. The parties to the current talks have all finessed the question, but if a solution is reached they will have to face it. It seems that Prabhakaran has one of three options. He can continue to stay in hiding. Or he can turn himself in for trial in New Delhi. Or the Sri Lankans, both Tamil and Sinhala, can approach Rajiv Gandhi's widow to drop the matter in the interests of South Asian unity and solidarity. This last is the most attractive, although it might be as hard for Prabhakaran to ask for forgiveness as it would be for Sonia Gandhi to grant it.

'Oslo' is a word associated with a famous peace initiative that later ran aground. Will the Norwegians have better luck with these historic enemies? And if they do, what would a post-autonomy administration look like? There would be few lawyers or teachers or scholars or engineers, for the professional classes and the intelligentsia have been driven to exile. Besides, these are not the LTTE types, ready to exercise a right of return. Even if the peace holds, and a framework for power sharing is agreed upon, how would the Tigers rule? Could these men, and boys, who had known only war, know how to maintain civic order and assure essential services? Would they allow elections where other parties can participate?

But perhaps these questions will not need to be asked just yet. For previous ceasefires—in 1987, 1989–90, and 1994–5, the last extending over fourteen months—were all broken, their fate captured in some tartly ironic verses by the Tamil poet Balasoorian:

> Dust rises in the streets.
> Sounds of gun shots cease,
> Guns disappear in waist belts,
> Jeeps growl,
> Dust rises . . .
>
> All the same
> The world stands still
> Embracing the peace.
>
> In an instant
> Gun shots will explode
> The quiet will shatter
> Flies
> And street dogs sometimes,
> Will take up arms.

Indeed, as this book gets ready to go to press, in the third week, of April 2003 the Tigers have pulled out of the peace process, citing 'slow implementation of decisions taken at earlier talks.' The sceptical president, Chandrika Kumaratunga, has put the Sri Lankan army as full alert. The dialogue-seeking prime minister, Ranil Wickramasinghe, has sent an emissary to the Norwegians, asking them to get the Tigers back to the table.

VIII

Sometimes, walking the streets of Zürich in between appointments, I would compare the Tamil predicament to others I knew or had read about. The Tamils were certainly not like the Indian professionals in the United States, who came from élite backgrounds and mostly chose to turn their backs on the problems of their country. In some respects they were like the Jews of early-twentieth-century Brooklyn: labouring away in low-paying jobs, but determined to educate their kids, to make them doctors and lawyers when they had themselves been cooks or bricklayers. At other times I thought the Tamils were akin to the Tibetans in India: likewise fleeing persecution, likewise committed to maintaining their language and culture in exile, as preparation for an eventual return. But there was one essential difference: here there was no Dalai Lama. Nor could the Tibetans claim a continuing opposition within their homeland. Their leader preached non-violence from an Indian hill town, whereas the Tiger chief was based in the jungles of Sri Lanka, directing a violent and (it seemed) not unsuccessful battle for survival.

Where would that struggle finally lead? I put the question to Martin Sturzinger, a journalist who is probably the foremost Swiss authority on the Tamils. Now forty-five, Sturzinger has been following the Sri Lankan conflict since 1983. He had made more than twenty trips to the island. He had never met Prabhakaran, but knew Anton Balasingham very well. Back in 1989, when the Tigers prepared to talk to President Premadasa, he had presented Balasingham with a book in English on the Swiss Constitution. 'I don't know whether he read it', commented Sturzinger: 'But he didn't look too happy with the gift!'. On another occasion, he told the Tiger ideologue: 'You are socialists, so why don't you also take up the cause of the poor among the Sinhala and the Muslim?' Balasingham replied: 'We are first nationalists, only then socialists'. Sturzinger thought to himself: 'Nationalists, then Socialists, does that equal National-Socialist?'

Martin Sturzinger described himself as 'very sympathetic to the Tamil cause'. He had seen that they had no equal status within Sri Lanka. But to the question, 'Do all Tamils in fact support the Tigers?', he replied: 'There are now half-a-million Tamils in Colombo. Many of them are migrants from the Jaffna or Batticaloa areas. Would they be in Colombo if life was so good in territories controlled by the Tigers?' Here, in Switzerland, Sturzinger worked as an adviser on

Tamil affairs to the Refugee Council. 'Sometimes the Swiss people are so naive', he remarked. A Swiss NGO, wishing to show its interest in 'refugee culture', invited a group of Tamils to put on a dance show. They came, and staged a drama with girls in fatigues, singing while brandishing sticks. The audience didn't understand the language or the context, viewing it merely as a pleasing display of immigrant culture.

Sturzinger had spent the better part of a lifetime educating his countrymen about the plight of the foreigners in their midst. About his understanding or empathy there could be no question. Yet he said, 'I have reservations about their leadership'. In May 2002, Balasingham visited Switzerland to speak to the exiles about why the Tigers had decided to sue for peace. There was a large rally in Freiburg, organized by Anton Ponnarajah, and attended by more than 3000 Tamils. As in the Bern *allmend*, there were LTTE cadres placed strategically among the crowd, wearing black trousers and white shirts. 'It was almost fascist', said Sturzinger.

If we settle for less than Eelam, remarked Balasingham back in 1989, our own people will kill us. But now it increasingly seemed that autonomy on the Swiss model, rather than independence, was the most feasible option. Would the exiles accept this? Would their dreams of sovereignty and freedom be satisfied with a solution that had been on the table from before the Tigers were born? An answer was on offer in the place where Sturzinger and I met, the Thamillar Restaurant, off Aemtlerstrasse in central Zürich. Here, one wall had a large photograph of Prabhakaran, captioned: 'Tamil Eelam National Leader'. He was wearing a bush-shirt, and was smiling. It seemed to be a studio photograph. As I stepped up to have a closer look, a waiter commented: 'There are thousands of such photos in Sri Lanka'.

More revealing still was what met the eye as one first entered the restaurant. This was a board along whose top ran the legend, 'Eelam'. Below was a map of the homeland, coloured green. The borders were marked by a row of blinking lights. The territory claimed extended to at least 150 miles south of the eastern port, Trincomalee. On the western sea board, too, it extended well below the town of Puttalam, way beyond what any Sri Lankan would concede. The major settlements were well marked on the map: Killinochi, Mannar, Batticaloa, and Jallappanam (Jaffna). Just south of Trinco, a little red dot identified the proposed new 'Capital'. Why, I wondered, had they chosen this place and not the old historic cultural centre, Jaffna? Was this to keep peace with the Muslims, or because of its proximity to the key port of Trinco? Or did it merely reflect the ambition of a new state to build a new capital?

While the territory of Eelam was painted over in green, the rest of the island was coloured a dull brown. On the southern part of Sri Lanka was painted the logo of the LTTE, a fierce yellow tiger against a deep red background. The tiger's eyes were a pair of orange lights. And what was the symbolism of *this*? The LTTE logo sat atop, or rather squashed, where Colombo would be on the map. The snarling tiger, with its eyes flashing, seemed to act simultaneously as the watchdog and guarantor of the territory placed above it.

What I had read about the Tigers before I came to Switzerland did not endear them to me. What some Tigers told me in Zürich and Luzern dismayed and even chilled me. And yet, with the exception of the oily spin doctor Parthiban, I hardly met an exile who did not charm me. Despite their profound ambivalence towards India and Indians, I was always treated with respect and courtesy. My sometimes impolite questions were always answered with an equal directness.

An Indian brought up to admire Gandhi and Nehru cannot easily warm to the Liberation Tigers of Tamil Eelam. My experiences in Switzerland did not quell my reservations: on the contrary, as when faced with the inflexible ideology of the cadres or the odious dishonesties of Adele Balasingham's book, it only confirmed them. But perhaps I might still be allowed to separate the person from his faith, thus to remember with affection the cook-cum-sports organizer Mathialakan, the actor-cum-activist Anton Ponnarajah, the school-and-curriculum builder Mahindran. One memory, above all others, shall stay with me. On the second evening of the Bern festival I witnessed the final round of that famous Tamil game, 'musical chairs'. Its organizer was a little man named Manoharan, clad in black trousers, white shirt, and Tiger jacket. With me was a Swiss television crew who wished to film the event. Manoharan ran to call us from the food stall, placing us strategically in the middle of the ring. We stayed there for forty-five minutes, watching a field of twenty-five women dwindle to two. Also watching were hundreds of Tamils, standing four rows deep, with individual voices alerting wife, mother or daughter to a vacant chair when the music stopped. All the while Manoharan busily supervised the game, signalling to the music with a code of his own, chastising participants who tried to cheat by walking too slowly. He executed his responsibilities with an appealing mixture of charm and authority, and with an absolute and seemingly natural fairness. I cannot speak for his leader in the forest, or of how that man might come to run his Tamil state, but little Manoharan's conduct of his modest musical chairs did not seem inconsistent with the path of *dharma*, or righteousness.

The Greatest Criminal
in History: Joseph Stalin

There was a great Marxist called Lenin
Who did two or three million men in
That's a lot to do in
But where he did one in
That great Marxist Stalin did ten in.

—Robert Conquest

Dictators, whether of left or right, have a way of totally iso-
lating themselves from their subjects. The historian Robert
Conquest thus writes of Joseph Stalin that 'his social life
was an imperfectly maintained pretence, which eventually degenerated into forced jollity with coarse and terrified toadies'. On
28 February 1953, Stalin had his last supper in his *dacha* with four
of these toadies: Beria, Malenkov, Khruschev, and Bulganin. They
watched a film, and then had a five-course meal with plenty of liquor.
The meal ended at five in the morning, with Stalin 'pretty drunk and
in high spirits'—as he would be, having done much of the drinking,
and all the talking.

After dinner Stalin took a steam bath and crawled into bed. When
he had not emerged until ten at night, his bodyguards broke into his

room, to find him lying on the carpet, conscious but unable to move or speak. Doctors were now sent for, who plied him with injections and pills and fed him with a spoon. The Lord of Greater Russia had regressed to being a child. Indeed, according to one eyewitness, almost the only gesture he made in these last days was to point at a picture on the wall of children feeding a little lamb from a bottle, as if to say—that is what I have now become.

Stalin eventually died on the 5th of March, the cause, as officially diagnosed, a burst blood vessel in the brain. The Central Committee of the Communist Party of India sent a message to their Soviet counterparts:

> With sorrow too deep for tears, we pay our homage to the memory of Comrade Stalin. Mankind has lost its noblest representative, the movement for human liberation its greatest leader, the cause of Peace its indefatigable champion . . . Stricken with grief at the passing away of this titan of human thought and action, we, Communists of the present generation, shall ever recollect with pride that we have lived in the same epoch as Comrade Stalin, have been guided and led by him, have been taught by him how to serve the working class and the people to the last drop of our blood.

Only slightly less effusive was the tribute offered by the ex-communist M.N. Roy. Roy had once known Stalin, while they worked together in the Comintern not long after the Bolshevik Revolution. But then Roy returned to India, and by the late 1930s had left the Party altogether. Yet, as Gene Overstreet and Marshall Windmiller write in their history of Indian communism, Stalin never lost his hold on him. Roy always remained, as he put it, 'a personal admirer of my ex-friend'. When Stalin died, Roy penned an extraordinary apologia in his journal *Radical Humanist*. He admitted that his friend was widely hated both within and outside Russia, but argued nonetheless that

> No great man has ever been an angel. Greatness is always purchased at the cost of goodness. . . . Our plea is that some justice should be done to the most maligned man of our time. He deserves better justice; because, but for his caution and wisdom, and also his fanatical faith in the

inevitability of revolution, war might have already overtaken the civilized world. If the charitable obituary notices on his death do not acquit Stalin of the charge of preparing a war against the democratic world, they would be hypocritical and unrealistic . . . He was the greatest military genius of our time . . . Stalin was undoubtedly the tallest personality of our time, and as such is bound to leave his mark on history.

Roy seems here to be suggesting that Stalin somehow played a role in preventing the Cold War from becoming Hot. This thesis was also accepted by the Indian prime minister, Jawaharlal Nehru, in the course of an over-generous tribute to Stalin in the Rajya Sabha. While allowing that 'people may differ in their judgement' of the Russian leader, and while acknowledging that he could be 'ruthless in the pursuit of his objectives', Nehru argued that, on balance, 'it is right to say that Marshal Stalin's weight and influence had been cast in favour of peace'.

Consider now a less charitable obituary notice, this the handiwork of Philip Spratt who, as it turns out, had once been a member of the Communist Party of India, and later an adherent of Roy's brand of Radical Humanism. By 1953, however, he was a confirmed, perhaps even obsessive, anti-communist. (He was a leading light in the Indian wing of the Congress for Cultural Freedom.) He lived now in Bangalore, where he edited the liberal weekly *MysIndia*. The weekly carried an editorial, ostensibly anonymous but clearly written by Spratt, which began with a brilliant burst of sarcasm: 'The official announcement of the death of Stalin is conclusive proof that Soviet science has not yet conquered death, that Jewish doctors had no hand in it, and that he died in the natural course like almost everybody in the still unregenerate parts of the world groaning under the sway of capitalists, exploiters and warmongers.' The editorial went on to critically assess Stalin's career, before rounding on Nehru for praising him. 'Of all the pronouncements made on the death of Stalin', remarked Spratt,

> the most unnecessary, fulsome and fatuous was that perpetrated by our unique leader in his official capacity as the head of the Government of India . . . To say, as the Pandit has done, that Stalin has been a power

making for peace all these years, is a howler of a type that would be amusing in an examinee; but coming from the head of a government . . . [it is] a blunder of the first magnitude.

Was it in pursuance of the love of peace that Stalin entered into the notorious pact with Hitler when he denounced the war as that of imperialists? Was it his love of peace that enabled the Chinese to get a prodigious supply of arms and equipment from the Russians in the course of the present Korean diversion? Was it the love of peace that prompted Stalin to traduce the Indian proposal for Korea as a Democratic trap?

In praising Stalin, Nehru had not only ignored the cynicism of his manoeuvres in the international arena, but also his crimes against his own people. Spratt suspected that, in a 'moment of perversity', Nehru had

given the go-by to the basic ideas which he says he has learnt at the feet of Gandhiji. Chief among these is that the means and ends should correspond or cohere or harmonise. Stalin waded his way to the throne of the Czars through slaughter and the shedding of an ocean of blood. The latest purge of a handful of doctors is as much his doing as the liquidation of millions of Kulaks, of bands of dissidents, deviationists and traitors all through these dreadful years which are hailed as the years of glory. Are we to take it that Pandit Nehru subscribes to the view that the ends justify the means? On no other basis can we account for that extraordinary performance with which he has compromised himself and the country by an eulogy . . . which was so blatantly at variance with the facts and the truth.

M.N. Roy and Philip Spratt were once very close friends: through the 1940s they worked together in the Radical Humanist movement. I don't know whether they were still in touch at the time Stalin died. They wrote their pieces at the same time; for both appeared in the issues of their respective journals, bearing the date 15 March 1953. But their assessments could not have been more different. Roy appeared to believe that the ends justified the means. Spratt disagreed; nor did he share the optimism about Stalin's ends themselves. Besides, the life of Mahatma Gandhi demonstrated that greatness was not necessarily incompatible with goodness.

Here then are three contemporary responses to Stalin: provided by the Communist Party of India, a brilliant ex-communist, and a maverick communist turned anti-communist. With the hindsight provided by fifty years of reflection and research, we can see that it is the last verdict, that of Philip Spratt, which has endured the best. It certainly resonates with the views of the man who is regarded as the greatest living authority on Stalin and his times, namely Robert Conquest, whose works *The Great Terror* and *The Harvest of Sorrow* first conclusively established the human costs—running into tens of millions of deaths—of the dictator's policies of forced collectivization and the liquidation of political opponents. In 1991 Conquest published a biography of Stalin, which ended with these words:

> Stalin represented dogmatism, belief in millennarian theory, at its crudest level. Yet ordinary, coarse and limited though his personality may seem, the last thing that can be said about his career is that we can learn nothing from it, or that it was uninteresting. But it was interesting mainly for the extreme and massive scale of the physical, moral and intellectual destruction it inflicted. If we can now begin to write Stalin into the history of the past, it is in the hope that no one like him will appear again.

This will be dismissed as bourgeois propaganda by India's most powerful left grouping, the Communist Party of India (Marxist). For in the CPM's pantheon of heroes Stalin is still placed adjacent to Marx, Engels and Lenin. But the rest of us should take Conquest's verdict as a very close approximation of the truth. It is endorsed by all responsible and serious historians of Soviet Russia and, perhaps more significantly, by the Russian people themselves.

II

The scholarship on Stalin and the Russia of his day is dominated by Western writers. In the first part of this essay, we heard the voices of some representative Indian thinkers. Let me now turn to the writings on Stalin of a man neither Indian nor Western—the Yugoslav dissident Milovan Djilas.

Even by the standards of the twentieth century, Djilas led an un-usually interesting life. He spent his first eighteen years in Montenegro, a hilly land of peasants whose fierce sense of loyalty to family and clan also implied a readiness to engage in blood feuds. Djilas was raised a Christian but exchanged this religion for another—Communism—when he went to Belgrade University. Through the 1930s he was in and out of jail. By the time the Second World War broke out he was a member of the politburo of the Yugoslav Communist Party. When the Germans invaded his country, he became an active member of the Resistance. After the war and the coming to power of the commu-nists, he became a key member of the Yugoslav government.

Djilas was particularly close to the leader of the Yugoslav Commu-nist Party, Josep Broz Tito. He was sent on several important missions to Moscow, and stood by his boss when the latter broke with Stalin and the Russian Communists in 1948. His work was rewarded by the high office of vice-president. However, by the early 1950s, Djilas became disenchanted with communism. As he saw it, the dream of a classless society—in its Yugoslav as much as in its Soviet variant—had resulted instead in a stifling hierarchy in which the party commanded and the people obeyed. His criticisms were answered with criminal proceedings, and later, with incarceration. Eventually, this former inmate of a monarchist prison was to spend even more time in jails run by communists.

A publisher's blurb once described Milovan Djilas as having been 'at different times a revolutionary, a soldier, a political leader—and always a writer.' At least three of his books were translated into Eng-lish. These are *The New Class*, a devastating expose of the working of communist oligarchies; *Land Without Justice*, a wry evocation of his Montenegran boyhood; and the book we are to consider here, *Con-versations with Stalin*, a fascinating account of the Russian leader as seen through the eyes of a follower-turned-rebel.

Conversations with Stalin is divided into three parts, respectively entitled 'Raptures', 'Doubts' and 'Disappointments'. To the loyal young communist, Stalin was akin to a 'little old grandfather who, all his life, and still now, looked after the success and happiness of the whole Communist race.' When Djilas first met him, in 1944, Stalin and the Russians were just emerging, victorious, from a ferocious military struggle against the Nazis. But the Russian leader was 'something more than a leader in battle. He was the incarnation of an idea, transformed in Communist minds into pure idea, and thereby into something infallible and sinless. Stalin was the victorious battle of today and the brotherhood of man of tomorrow.'

Between 1944 and 1948 Djilas met Stalin several times. On each visit to Moscow he was asked to dinner, each meal providing a long introduction to the leader's mind and personality. The Yugoslav provides a vivid account of Russian gluttony.

> The variety of food and drink was enormous—with meats and hard liquor predominating . . . Everyone ate what he pleased and as much as he wanted; only there was rather too much urging and daring us to drink and there were too many toasts. . . . Stalin ate food in quantities that would have been enormous even for a much larger man. He usually chose meat, which was a sign of his mountain origins . . . He drank moderately, usually mixing red wine and vodka in little glasses. I never noticed any signs of drunkenness in him, whereas I could not say the same for Molotov, let alone for Beria, who was practically a drunkard. As all to a man over-ate at these dinners, the Soviet leaders ate very little and irregularly during the day, and many of them dieted on fruit and juices one day in each week, for the sake of *razgruzhenie* (unloading).

Over the years, the scales fell away from the follower's eyes, and the disenchantment grew. Djilas came to see the integral link between Stalin's domestic and foreign policies. Having in his own country 'subjected all activities to his views and to his personality', Stalin 'could not act in foreign affairs other than as a dictator.' Thus, outside Russia, he 'helped revolutions only up to a certain point—as long as he could control them—but he was always ready to leave them in the lurch whenever they slipped out of his grasp.' At crucial moments, Stalin refrained from supporting the Spanish, Chinese and Yugoslav struggles, fearing that success would lead to 'the creation of revolutionary centres outside Moscow [which] could endanger its supremacy in world communism.'

Djilas's first reservations about Stalin stemmed from his own Yugoslav nationalism. He would not abide his country being dominated by another in the name of 'communist internationalism'. Later, to national pride was added the cause of democracy. Djilas began to see that however powerful and monstrous Stalin's personality may have been, his interests were congruent with those of the party. For the ruling political bureaucracy 'needed just such a man— one who was reckless in his determination and extremely practical in his fanaticism', to exercise its control over society as a whole. By the 1950s, the rule of the party had exacted a horrific human cost in Russia. Millions had died in state-led drives against peasants, ethnic minorities, and political dissidents. Russians who were not killed or jailed were denied basic freedoms; unable to say what they thought, go where they wished, and meet whom they wanted to. Meanwhile, the rigidities of centralized planning had destroyed Russian agriculture and put back all-round economic progress by several decades.

After Stalin's death his 'excesses' were criticized by his successors. But the basic structure of the one-party state remained. As Djilas put it in 1961, 'despite the curses against his name, Stalin still lives in the social and spiritual foundations of Soviet society.' De-Stalinization could come only with the end of communism, with the end of the 'ideological and political monopoly' of a single party.

Djilas's final verdict on his former leader and hero was unambiguous. 'Every crime was possible for Stalin', he writes,

> and there was not one he had not committed. Whatever standards we use to take his measure, he has the glory of being the greatest criminal in history—and, let us hope, for all time to come. For in him was joined the criminal senselessness of a Caligula with the refinement of a Borgia and the brutality of a Tsar Ivan the Terrible . . . If we take the point of view of humanity and freedom, history does not know a despot as brutal and as cynical as Stalin was. He was methodical, all-embracing, and total as a criminal. He was one of those rare and terrible dogmatists capable of destroying nine-tenths of the human race to 'make happy' the remaining tenth.

Djilas would have regarded Nehru's Rajya Sabha eulogy of 1953 as the work of, at best, a well-meaning innocent. Oddly enough, when Djilas was in jail it was none other than Nehru who chastised Tito for imprisoning his former comrade. Although he could not get him released, Nehru's intercession did result in Djilas being removed from solitary confinement. This was not accidental, for despite his naïveté about Soviet Russia, the Indian was a confirmed democrat. And, at least by the time Djilas fell foul of the authorities, he had made his own reassessments about Stalin and what he stood for.

In July 1955 Nehru visited Russia, to return (in the words of Frank Moraes) 'with no illusions but some ideas.' Asked about his impressions, the prime minister said that 'the thing you've got to remember about the Russians is that they have never known democracy. When the Bolsheviks came to power nearly forty years ago the Russians jumped from one autocracy to another . . .' Asked his opinion about Stalin, Nehru said that he was 'a dictator, and gave Russia yet another taste of dictatorship. . . . When it was a question of preserving his country's existence, he was prepared . . . to shake hands with the devil. He even shook hands with Hitler.'

Thus, in the end, Nehru concurred with what intelligent and sensitive people everywhere thought, and still think, about Joseph Stalin: that he was a Russian nationalist—some would say chauvinist; and that he was a dictator—some would say the most brutal in human history. To this straightforward conclusion let me append some final and perhaps more complicated thoughts about Stalin. These appeared in an essay called 'What Made Stalin Great', which also was published in the issue of *MysIndia* dated 15 March 1953. This essay placed Stalin in the history of industrial society. Industrialism had shown its destructive side in the two World Wars, yet 'just as dangerous is its influence in peace: the mechanisation and dehumanisation of life, the impetus to expansion of the state, the enormous power it gives to the state.' With centralisation and a growth in state power also came 'the urge to uniformity of belief and expression and behaviour.'

And it was Stalin, 'a politically gifted but uncultured man, from a technologically backward country', who,

> caught up by the drive to 'modernise', came to express in its most highly developed form the negative, dangerous side of industrialism. Far more than Hitler, who remained aloof in spirit from industrialism and merely exploited it for the purposes of a primitive ideology, Stalin identified himself with industrialism. He committed his crimes in the name of steel, of turbines, of tractors . . .
>
> If we have anything to thank Stalin for it is this, that he showed us the horror of modern life in its full development; he showed us a mighty nation made over in the likeness of a machine.

The author of these words used that ancient subterfuge, 'Anon.' From this distance in time we have no way of knowing his identity. He may have been Philip Spratt, who wrote most of *MysIndia* in weeks good or bad, and who may have wanted more than one crack at Stalin. On the other hand, he may not have been Spratt. Anyway, the thesis he put forward was a striking one: that Stalin was not merely a tyrannical ruler, but the pre-eminent symbol and symptom of all that had gone wrong with modernity.

The Last Liberal:
Dharma Kumar

My copy of the second volume of the *Cambridge Economic History of India* bears the following inscription: 'To Ram, from a fellow radical'. It is dated 18 November 1983, and the handwriting is that of the volume's editor, Dharma Kumar.

At the time of the gift I was twenty-five, Dharma fifty-five. We were closely related by blood: too closely, some might say. She was at once my first, second and third cousin, and also my grandmother's first cousin. Beyond the genes we shared a friendship that in 1983 was already two decades old. When I was five, she bought me chocolates and chewing gum and we talked about cricket. When I was ten, I was identified by her father, the chemist K. Venkataraman, as the last PhD student he would have work under him at the National Chemical Laboratory—a laboratory of which he had been the first Indian director. But when I turned fifteen I abandoned the study of science, having been warned that practicals in the afternoon would not allow me to play cricket at university. My uncle then decided that if I would not be his last student, I might at least do a PhD with his daughter.

So I took a first degree in economics and, in 1977, joined the Delhi School of Economics, where Dharma Kumar was a professor. During the first terminal exams she was told by a colleague that I was sitting in the room looking out of the window, an empty page on the table in front of me. When I did poorly in the finals, the same colleague told her: 'I would advise your cousin to seek a change of career. It would be good for him, and better for economics.'

With Dharma's consent I proceeded to Calcutta to begin a doctorate in sociology. I became a Marxist, seeking to sublimate my failure in Delhi via a theory that promised individual as well as collective salvation. That choice of faith was not as surprising as it might now sound. For the Soviet Union was alive and well, the crimes of China's Chairman were not known to the outside world, and brave little Vietnam had recently vanquished imperialist America. If History Would End, we thought in 1980, it would be with our party as the victor.

These, at any rate, were the beliefs I carried with me on my visits to Delhi. Over lunch, and while walking in the Lodi Gardens, Dharma would engage me in furious polemic. I stood for equality and justice, these to be brought about by class war and revolutionary violence; she for democracy and freedom, these to be achieved through reason, persuasion, and constitutional change. If I wanted to become a social historian, she said, I must learn from varieties of historical method other than Marxism. And if I thought of myself as a patriotic Indian, I should seek to deepen and build upon the democratic foundations laid by Gandhi and Nehru, not ally with those who wished to destroy them.

One day, walking in the Lodi Gardens, we came face to face with a dapper little man in a goatee. He ignored me but greeted my companion by name, and with a certain effusion. Dharma smiled in turn, but as we walked on remarked: 'I've forgotten that man's name. A pleasant fellow, though fashionably left wing. Not left wing enough for you, of course, but too left for me. He used to be close to Indira Gandhi, but then fell foul of Sanjay.'

To this crisp summation of somebody else's c.v. I had only to supply the name: Inder Kumar Gujral, a former union minister and ambassador to the Soviet Union and—not that one knew it then— a future prime minister of India. It was characteristic of Dharma not to remember his name, and characteristic too that he not only knew hers but—judging by the spontaneous warmth with which he uttered it—rather cherished his slight acquaintance with a lady who had the reputation of being Delhi's most brilliant conversationalist.

II

Dharma Kumar was born in March 1928 into a family of unusual distinction and character. The achievements lay chiefly on the father's side. He, the famous chemist, had two scarcely less gifted brothers: one, K. S. Sanjivi, Professor at Madras Medical College and founder of the Voluntary Health Services, was a doctor of great vision, skill, and goodness; the other, K. Swaminathan, was first a legendary teacher of English at Presidency College and then the even more legendary editor of *The Collected Works of Mahatma Gandhi*. All three brothers were to be awarded free India's third highest civilian honour, the Padma Bhushan.

Dharma admired and respected her father's family but warmed more to her mother's. Her mother was one of six sisters who, growing up in Bangalore, could be 'forward' in ways that Brahmin girls in Madras could not. They spoke English and spoke their minds, rode on the pillions of their brothers' motorbikes and, in time, encouraged their children to marry outside the bounds of caste and community. On this, her mother's side, Dharma was the oldest of twenty-one first cousins; and not merely the oldest but by common consent the most beautiful, the most intelligent, and the most interesting.

Dharma spent her childhood in Lahore and Bombay, two once-polyglot cities where her father taught. She studied at J.B. Petit High School, where she did brilliantly in the matriculation exam. Her mother promptly bought her a new sari, which her father commanded her to return—for 'learning should be its own reward'. Dharma now joined Bombay's Elphinstone College, then at the height of its reputation. After she had been admitted the office clerk gave her a 'personal particulars' form to fill up. In the 'religion' column, Dharma—a precocious free-thinker and rebel—wrote: 'athe-ist'. When the babu objected, she changed this to 'nil'. This was not acceptable either. So Dharma now described her faith, in the desig-nated space, as 'Neo-Malthusian'. The clerk passed this: it seemed plausible enough, in a city that had all kinds of odd creeds, from Theosophy to Christian Science.

At Elphinstone, Dharma's closest friends were a Goan Catholic, Angela Soares, and a Parsi, Mani Vasunia. The ecumenism was typi-cal of the girl and of the city, or at least of certain sections within it. Once, this threesome was accompanied for a movie by a Miss Wand-rekar. The new member of the gang was later scolded by the daughter of Professor G.S. Ghurye, a renowned scholar and Sanskritist. 'Do you not know', she was told, 'that only one of the three is a Hindu, and even she is not Maharashtrian.'

In the summer of 1946, having just turned eighteen, Dharma took a slow boat to Cambridge. It was, in fact, a troop ship, and she was one of a handful of civilians among hundreds of war-weary soldiers. In Cambridge, as I heard from an aunt of ours later, almost every Indian college boy in England fell in love with her. The aunt men-tioned names which I cannot repeat, for they include some reputable and happily married scholars and civil servants. There were also Eng-lish admirers. Being chased and courted was one reason why Dharma got only a second class in her Economics Tripos. It was an upper second, a 'II:I', but a second nonetheless. A Tamil friend of her father told him, in disgust and triumph: 'You spent all this money and she spoilt her record by getting a second. You should have bought her a good husband instead.'

Dharma returned to an India in the first flush of freedom and joined the government—something Oxbridge graduates did then as naturally as they would now by staying on in the West and joining Goldman Sachs. Her job in the Reserve Bank of India (RBI) was dreary, but outside office hours she participated vigorously in the social and intellectual life of Bombay. She ran an art circle, wrote about dance (especially about Shanta Rao), contributed to the fledgling *Economic Weekly*, and ran rings around the young men of the city: intellectually speaking, that is, for she had now met and married Lovraj Kumar, India's first Rhodes Scholar, an individual of equal intelligence and charm, if somewhat less combative by temperament.

In or about 1960 the couple moved to Delhi. Lovraj had also joined the government, but Dharma was bored by fiscal policy. She took leave of absence and proceeded to Cambridge, enrolling for a PhD in economic history. Her thesis was awarded the Ellen MacArthur Prize for the best dissertation of the year, and later published by Cambridge University Press under the title *Land and Caste in South India*. On the methodological front, the book broke new ground by analysing the relationship between caste and class. Its principal conclusion was that a large class of agricultural labourers and serfs was not a creation of the British, but had been part of the social structure of pre-colonial India.

Land and Caste in South India demolished the myth, then prevalent among nationalist and Marxist alike, that British rule had destroyed the organic village community of pre-colonial India and created a polarized society of landowners and labourers. As Dharma demonstrated, 'agricultural servitude was obviously deep-rooted in South Indian society.' Her data showed that agricultural labour constituted a high proportion (in some parts, as much as 20 per cent) of the rural population in 1800, that is, when the British had barely begun to consolidate their empire in South India. During the course of the nineteenth century, this proportion does not seem to have altered very much.

On both counts Dharma's work became controversial—among nationalists who believed colonialism was a synonym of evil, and among Marxists who saw caste as a mere 'epiphenomenon' of class. *Land and Caste in South India* was a brilliant exercise in historical revisionism which, had it been published three decades later, would have been politically respectable, instead of suspect, which it was in 1965. For, Dalit intellectuals today recognize—following Phule and

Ambedkar—that pre-colonial Indian society was sometimes as brutally oppressive as British rule. And it is now a sociological common-
place that while caste sometimes operates in conjunction with class,
these domains cannot simply be collapsed into each other.

Land and Caste in South India allowed Dharma to move on from
her dreary bank job. She left the RBI and held short-term fellowships
at the Indian Council for World Affairs and the Institute for Economic Growth before moving to the Delhi School of Economics in
1966, as Reader in Economic History. Seven years later she was appointed Professor. She taught at the Delhi School until her retirement
in 1993. While she came to regard her years at the RBI as wasted, her
time at the Delhi School was unquestionably the happiest of her life.
There she remained for nearly thirty years, a vital member of a teaching institution that was world class as well as genuinely liberal and
collegial: *un*-Indian in both respects.

One would like to say of Dharma what she herself once said of her
Elphinstone College English teacher Kamal Wood: 'Her beauty lit up
the drab classrooms.' In truth, she did not much like addressing the
very large classes at the Delhi School. In turn, exam-minded students
did not approve of her discursive and sometimes rambling style. She
was more effective with smaller groups, and as a research supervisor.

Still, Dharma drew enormous sustenance from the Delhi School;
as she needed to, for outside was a range of hostile forces. With the
publication of her first book there commenced a long-drawn-out
battle between Dharma Kumar and the Marxists who then dominated the profession of economic history in India.

The debate between Dharma and the Marxists was, for the most
part, the story of a solitary woman pitted against a phalanx of angry
men. (There were other non-Marxist historians around, but they
lacked Dharma's intellectual feistiness and willingness to engage in
debate.) The Marxists differed from Dharma on questions of politics:
they thought the Soviet Union a progressive worker's state while she
regarded it as an abomination, with its brutal suppression of human
freedoms and its liking for concentration camps. The Marxists differed with Dharma on questions of methodology: her suggestion that

status and law sometimes operated independently of economics was anathema to their determinism. And, most immediately, they differed with her view of the consequences of colonial rule.

Twenty and thirty years down the line, it is difficult to convey the intensity of the debates between Dharma and the Marxists. Revisiting them now, I am compelled to outline five caveats. First, the resentment of Dharma's critics was based as much on being bested by her in conversation as by what she might have written in print. In person, Dharma was articulate and opinionated, often devastatingly so. To argue with her at a party or in a seminar room was to be reminded of what the historian and biographer Noel Annan said of Betty Behrens— another economic historian from Cambridge: 'No one denied that she was clever and, if they were generous, that she was a fine historian, superior to quite a number of staid middle-stump performers in the faculty. But she irritated her colleagues. She corrected errors so vehemently and did not acquire in her profession friends, let alone allies . . .' It was difficult to disengage the sometimes arrogant personality from the scholarship, to remind oneself that while she could be dismissive in conversation, in print Dharma was a careful and cautious historian with an abhorrence for certitude.

Second, there was sometimes a confusion, in Dharma's mind as well as the minds of her intellectual opponents, between Marxism as a historical theory and Marxism as a concrete application of politics. The Marxists who demonized British colonialism also happened to think the world of Soviet Russia and Communist China; whereas Dharma was clear that those countries were totalitarian. During the Cold War, Dharma and the Marxists found themselves on opposite sides. Such political differences of the day willy-nilly influenced at least the rhetoric, if not the substance, of intellectual debates about the past.

Third, it is a curious irony of the Indian left that all it deemed politically incorrect in the 1960s and 1970s has become resoundingly correct now. Thus, Dharma's demonstration of how deep-rooted was the practice of agrestic servitude has endeared her to some Dalit thinkers as confirmation that pre-British regimes were often more exploitative of the lowest castes: notably, it was a Dalit group that organized a memorial meeting for Dharma in Chennai in December 2001.

Fourth, as André Béteille has observed, in her assessment of British colonialism Dharma was (albeit unconsciously) closer to Karl Marx than were his Indian followers. 'Like Marx', Béteille jokingly points out, 'I too believed that British rule was, on balance, good for India, but unlike Dharma I did not have the courage to say so.' While recognizing the exploitative and self-serving aspects of colonial rule, Dharma, like Marx, compared it to pre-colonial regimes as well as other European powers before concluding that, as a vehicle for India's entry into the modern world, British rule was rather better than the alternatives. (She was delighted with a comment of Ho Chi Minh that I passed on to her: the Vietnamese leader had remarked that if Mahatma Gandhi had been fighting the Dutch or the French, he would have given up non-violence within a week.) Still, this admiration for things British was, like so much else that Dharma did, both brave as well as unfashionable. As she once wrote, 'my Anglophilia struck leftists in India as yet more proof that I was the running dog of imperialism.'

Fifth, despite these differences Dharma counted several Marxists among her close friends. Among historians, she had great respect for Amalendu Guha and Neeladri Bhattacharya, whom she saw as 'honest Marxists' who placed empirical research above political dogma. Among activists, she had much affection for the ex-Naxalites C.V. Subba Rao and Dilip Simeon, whose tireless work for, respectively, civil liberties and communal harmony, she greatly admired. Through her daughter Radha Kumar—herself a gifted social historian—Dharma also met and befriended many younger Marxist scholars associated, as Radha was, with that radical stronghold, Jawaharlal Nehru University.

Nationalism, remarked the Oxford philosopher Isaiah Berlin, was 'responsible for magnificent achievements and appalling crimes'. Dharma thought that the achievements of colonialism were modest, and its crimes modest too. Pre-colonial regimes had often treated their subjects more unfairly. Her own work on landlessness had been conducted with an open mind. It was *evidence* which showed that agricultural labourers were, as a proportion of the population, as large at the beginning of colonial rule as a hundred years later. This evidence clashed with received dogma; as the daughter of a scientist, Dharma could not but prefer facts to prejudice.

The hatred of Marxist historians for Dharma was long lasting. When the second volume of the *Cambridge Economic History of India* was published, there was an orchestrated campaign against it. To write a sneering review steeped in personal innuendo became almost a badge of loyalty to the Marxist cause. Indeed, the reception of Dharma's entire scholarly oeuvre was blighted by the long shadow cast by the Marxist/anti-Marxist debate. *Land and Caste in South India*, the *Cambridge Economic History*, and her substantial essay collection of 1998 titled *Colonialism, Property and the State*—all these were read and reviewed against the backdrop of that larger controversy rather than for what they were, original contributions to scholarship conceived and written with no agenda except historical truth.

Fortunately, the literature has since moved on, beyond sterile debates on whether colonialism was good or bad. Younger historians have opened up new areas of enquiry, found new forms of evidence, and discovered new ways of interpreting old evidence. Much of this work has been published in the *Indian Economic and Social History Review*, a quarterly of outstanding quality that Dharma Kumar edited from 1971 to 1998. This journal has featured high-class work in women's history, environmental history, the history of law and governance, of ideology and popular protest, of land and landlessness, and of science and technology. The scholars who have published in its pages include Indians and Pakistanis, Europeans, Americans, and Australians—young and old, famous and obscure. Among them have been plenty of Marxists, for its liberal-minded editor did not care to categorize or judge historians by doctrine but by method, empirical evidence, logic of argument, and coherence of presentation.

As for myself, it is only now, almost twenty years later, that I can truly understand the inscription in my copy of the *Cambridge Economic History of India*. For 'radical' means 'going to the root': and doing so fearlessly, regardless of fashion, conventional wisdom, and the likely reaction of your peers. In this regard Dharma Kumar was far more radical than self-advertised leftists and feminists whose positions are often founded on self-righteousness rather than logic or evidence.

III

Dharma Kumar was impatient with intellectuals who did not think for themselves, who thought in a herd or followed the party line. She abhorred the drawing of rigid boundaries according to ideology. She believed that individuals should be able to disagree on specific issues while coming together on others. But the tendency of Indian intellectuals has always been to stereotype and pigeonhole. If someone thinks, for instance, that the free market has certain virtues, the man is certain to be labelled an agent of the World Bank and multinational companies, and perhaps also as a persecutor of minorities and supporter of child labour.

Dharma herself suffered grievously from such labelling. But she refused to answer in kind. She never imputed motive or questioned an opponent's character. She merely contested their ideas. For her, an individual's caste, religion and social background were completely irrelevant. That is the moral and intellectual world in which she was raised. That world has now been replaced by the crude and morbidly vicious certainties of identity politics: by the identity politics of the left, which divides India into good and bad according to caste: Brahmins always bad, Dalits and Backwards always good; and by the identity politics of the right, where the distribution of virtues perfectly matches divisions by religion: Hindus always honest and patriotic, Muslims and Christians always secret agents of foreign powers.

Dharma's dedication to secular values was unwavering. After the demolition of the Babri Masjid she organized and in part paid for a newspaper advertisement in which leading industrialists, scholars and public figures deplored the demolition and urged a return to the values and principles of the Indian Constitution.

One liberal cause Dharma always upheld was freedom of speech. During the Emergency she made her opposition known, this despite being married to a senior government official whose position was endangered by her outspokenness. In an essay published in February 1976, she poked gentle fun at the doublespeak of the Indira Gandhi regime. Referring to claims that bonded labour had 'disappeared' in district after district, she suggested that 'perhaps in a more sophisticated country the Government would take a little longer to announce its achievements . . .' After the Emergency ended she supported the new civil liberties groups founded to protect democratic rights. She was one of the first to publicly protest against the Government of India's ban on Salman Rushdie's novel, *The Satanic Verses.* The ban, she said, was 'a sign of the Government's weakness. In a secular state blasphemy should not in itself be a cognizable offence; the President of India is not the defender of any nor of all faiths.'

As a liberal, Dharma sought to limit the influence of caste and religion on public institutions. Like other scholars at the Delhi School, she was opposed to the implementation of the Mandal Commission report. She thought the extension of job quotas to OBCs would lead to similar demands from other groups, and pointed out that reservations once conceded can never be withdrawn. With characteristic incisiveness she drew attention to the parallels between the case for Mandal and the case for the demolition of the Babri Masjid in Ayodhya. Both rested on the desire for historical retribution. But, in a secular democracy, 'political issues [should] depend on current laws, not ancient history.' And if one insisted that Brahmins were responsible for the sins of their forefathers, there was no stopping radical Hindus from blaming Muslims today for the extremism of some Muslim rulers of the past.

Dharma used to say of the Sangh Parivar that it 'wished to build an Islamic State—for Hindus'. Her simultaneous opposition to the

Mandir campaign and the Mandal agenda was consistent with her liberalism, but it did make her new enemies. She wrote in her un-published memoirs that, in her last years of teaching at the Delhi School of Economics, she discovered from talking to her students that she 'was India's worst enemy—a westernized atheist'. She took it, as always, with dignity and not a little humour. She would, she said, publish her newspaper articles on Mandal and Ayodhya under the title 'Politically Incorrect Essays', while her memoirs she would call, 'Angry Old Woman'.

Perhaps Dharma's most effective (and certainly most eloquent) public intervention came in the wake of the anti-Sikh riots of November 1984. In some quarters the riots were explained—or explained away—as a response to the celebration by some Sikhs of the assassination of Mrs Indira Gandhi. One columnist in the *Times of India* had written of how the 'ambivalent reaction' of some Sikhs to the death of the prime minister had caused 'understandable resentment' among 'most other people in the country'; another had claimed that 'the initial upsurge of anger' was 'perhaps understandable' in view of 'the ghoulish glee exhibited by some Sikhs'. In a brilliant rejoinder published in the same newspaper, Dharma first took apart the evidence that 'sizeable sections' of the Sikhs had actually rejoiced at Mrs Gandhi's murder. These claims were based on hearsay and mis-interpretation: but (and here the historian gives way to the liberal), even 'if all the sweets in India had been distributed that would not have justified the burning of one single Sikh.' For if 'burning alive were the punishment for vulgarity and folly, there would be few people left in India.'

Dharma then asked her own community, the Hindus, to consider the consequences if they applied to themselves the logic of revenge and retribution. 'Is any Muslim in Delhi, gentle Hindu reader, "justified" in roasting you alive because of Bhiwandi or Ahmedabad?' She also took issue with the pressure put on leading Sikh intellectuals to denounce or 'apologize' for the assassination. As she said with devastating sarcasm: 'I do not feel that I have to rush into print and beat my breast in public when any Hindu does something dreadful (which is fortunate since I would then be doing nothing else).'

Isaiah Berlin once described the political tradition to which he belonged as being composed of a 'small, hesitant, self-critical, not always brave, band of men who occupy a position somewhere to the left of centre, and are morally repelled both by the hard faces to their right and the hysteria and mindless violence and demagoguery on their left...This is the notoriously unsatisfactory, at times, agonising, position of the modern heirs of the liberal tradition.'

Dharma was likewise repelled by the hard right and the loony left, but she was not hesitant, and always brave. Among the scholars she most respected were J.P. Naik and D.R. Gadgil, two Maharashtrian liberals who were influenced by Gandhi and Gokhale, and who stood resolutely against the hard Hindu chauvinism that has also had such a strong ideological presence in Bombay and thereabouts. Dharma admired but could not follow their personal austerity; she admired and emulated their intellectual integrity. Naik and Gadgil both died before Indian liberalism beat a hasty retreat when confronted by the forces of casteism and religious fundamentalism. But this redoutable Tamil woman, who lived on after them, carried on the battle. Indeed, Dharma Kumar was one of the last liberals in Indian intellectual life.

IV

Among the greatest of Dharma's gifts was her ability to befriend the young. Boys and girls of any social background or political orientation were welcome to be dined by her or walk with her. She asked only that they read widely and have views of their own. She fed them, she argued with them, she educated and inspired them—and if the need arose she raised money for them. For the students of her beloved Delhi School she began the Sri Ram Travelling Fellowship, which allowed MA students to do a research project in the summer break between their first and second years. Over a period of decades she fought with the boards of the Rhodes and Inlaks and Nehru and

Radhakrishnan scholarships, demanding that their awards for further studies in the United Kingdom be reserved for young Indians who had a genuine aptitude for research, regardless of their facility with English or the years they had spent in St Stephen's College.

Among Dharma's younger friends was Vikram Seth. When he came on holiday from Oxford they played Scrabble together—it was, I gather, a terrific and very even contest. Later, it was at Dharma's suggestion that Seth went to Stanford University to pursue a doctorate in demography. That project was abandoned, but the two stayed in touch and would meet on the novelist's visits to India. One character who makes a cameo appearance in *A Suitable Boy* is based on Dharma. She is called Ila Chattopadhyay, a professor of charm and eccentricity who refuses to rubber-stamp a selection committee's choice of a candidate she considers unqualified. Seth's portrait is not unflattering, for it emphasizes the qualities of courage and independence of mind for which Dharma was famous and, in the Indian context, so untypical. Dharma might have been pleased by the depiction had the novel not appeared just as she was retiring from the Delhi School of Economics, an involuntary severing of a connection with a place that had meant more to her than any individual. So she grumbled about the fact that in Seth's portrait her *sari* was crumpled.

Dharma took her retirement from the university very badly. Not long afterwards, her husband died. What kept her going now was the *Indian Economic and Social History Review*, and the creation of the literary journal now known as *Civil Lines*. It was in her mind that the idea first incubated, and in her house that the first, formative discussions about the journal took place. She had brought on board three younger friends: Rukun Advani, Mukul Kesavan and Ivan Hutnik. I was then living in the apartment below hers and thus became a mostly silent participant at their meetings. The allusions flew thick and fast, novels and novelists were summed up with devastating precision and insight. These were among Dharma's last happy days, spent in the company of young Indians who shared her love of literature and matched her, remark for witty remark.

In these—Dharma's last years—my wife and I attended most of the gatherings in her home. We participated in the preliminaries and the preparation too. Thus, on the morning of a dinner party Dharma would summon her Nepali cook to her study and, in execrable Hindi, dictate recipes from a Turkish or Moroccan cookbook. He would nod uncomprehendingly and later come downstairs to ask my wife what the memsaheb had meant. What he turned out in the end beggars description: this fare Dharma would offer around as 'a speciality of the house'. Not that it mattered: the food was drowned in the whisky, which was always premium; and in the conversation, which was always top drawer.

Dharma was a greatly gifted storyteller, but it is impossible to capture in print the spirit and content of her stories. The slightly quavering voice, the immaculate diction and the graceful phrase so effortlessly chosen, the chuckle aforehand and the burst of laughter at the end: all this in the backdrop of Dharma's drawing room, with her in a sofa at the centre, allowing her to take in with one glance all the others present. Tragically, the academic prose of this peerless conversationalist suffered too much from what her Cambridge friend Jack Gallagher called 'Tamil terseness'. Her few non-scholarly essays are better in this respect, as for instance the essay 'Scenes from Scholastic Life' that appeared in the second issue of *Civil Lines*.

There are some fine stories in Dharma's unpublished memoirs. She recalls a conversation with Nicholas Kaldor, an eminent Cambridge economist who advised the Government of India en route to a British peerage. After meeting a beautiful Indian girl named Lata Sen, Kaldor told Dharma: 'I have done some research on your country, and discovered that all women named Sens are gorgeous and all men named Sens brilliant.' 'But Nicky, you know only two Sens', Dharma protested. 'Yes', admitted Kaldor, 'but my other generalizations are based on even less evidence.'

Kaldor's daughter, Mary, in time became a kind of protégé of Dharma's. Herself now a distinguished scholar of disarmament, Mary Kaldor has written of how the older Indian woman told her never to feel that she was in any way disadvantaged because she was born, so to say, in the 'weaker' sex. 'We are actually much luckier than men', Dharma said. 'We can do all the things they do, such as hold jobs and write books, but we can buy lovely clothes and have babies too.'

Dharma retained a warm nostalgia for Cambridge. She went back there often and was delighted when her old college, Newnham, elected her an Honorary Fellow. She took a just pride in her old university's world-transforming contributions to modern biology, economics, and physics, indeed, to modern civilization itself. In his biography of John Maynard Keynes, Robert Skiddelsky recalls a conversation in a Cambridge seminar room about those two fundamental concepts, space and time. The last word was Dharma's: 'I don't know about time', she said, 'but space is a device intended to make sure that everything was not invented in Cambridge.'

Besides the economists, Dharma's Cambridge friends included the scholar of Japanese mysticism Carmen Blacker, and the Turkish anthropologist Nur Yalman. Yalman, who had once worked on the Tamils of Sri Lanka, and Dharma had been Fellows together in a Cambridge college, but then had lost touch for many years. In the late 1980s, Yalman was in Chicago attending the annual meeting of the Assocation of Asian Studies when, from the other end of a long hotel corridor he heard someone saying 'That is *not* the point.' That can only be Dharma, he thought. It was.

Soon afterwards, Yalman came to Delhi on holiday. He stayed at a suite in the Oberoi Hotel, but spent the days with Dharma and a fellow anthropologist, T.N. Madan. I remember a dinner-table conversation, where Yalman tried unsuccessfully to convince her that a sign of how civilized the ancient Tamils were was the number of terms they had coined for 'cousin'. The debate went on until Dharma played her trump card: 'Even the Tamils cannot find enough words to describe how Ram is related to me.'

Dharma's friends were drawn from a wide circle; they included artists, social workers, businessmen, and writers. She was sometimes called a 'snob'; not an unfair characterization, in that she naturally gravitated to the specially talented. Among Dharma's favourite people were gifted and capable civil servants. Her husband was one, of course; and so were two younger officers I came to know well. This pair had a mix of qualities designed to endear them to Dharma. They were urbane but also patriotic, superbly efficient in their work but also interested in the world outside government. (One is a writer and translator; the other a musician and musicologist.) Both spoke Tamil, thus reminding Dharma of her childhood; both also possessed a humour and cosmopolitanism generally absent in Tamils reared in the neighbourhood of Mylapore and Triplicane.

No single story could ever typify Dharma, but one told to me by these civil servants comes closer than others. She had gone to the India International Centre for a performance by the accomplished Bharatnatyam dancer Alarmel Valli. She reached on time, but the performance was delayed by a complicated explanation which the artiste felt she owed the North Indian audience. For over a quarter of an hour the dancer spoke of how in Bharatnatyam there was a thin line that divided spirituality from sensuousness. At last Dharma had had enough. '*Dance*', she commanded from the floor, stopping the artiste mid-sentence.

V

One day, browsing in Dharma's bookshelves, I found a first edition of a novel by Khushwant Singh. It is called *I Shall Not Hear the Nightingale* and is dedicated 'To Dharma—who aspires to know'. I took the book to her and she at once said with a smile, 'This was in his pre-Sanjay Gandhi days.' The remark has to be placed in context. This conversation took place in 1978, and the professors of the Delhi School, Dharma included, had opposed the Emergency. About fifteen years later, the Emergency and Sanjay Gandhi both almost forgotten, Dharma suggested that I go meet Khushwant Singh in connection with my research on the anthropologist Verrier Elwin.

The Sardar settled me into a chair and asked how I was related to Dharma. Then he said: 'It took me two hundred and fifty pages to make a pass at Dharma—and it got me nowhere.'

So the rejection was long remembered: indeed, when the book was republished a couple of years ago the dedication was unaccountably dropped. Still, this act was gentle compared with the treatment of Dharma by some others in her declining years. In the summer of 1998 she was diagnosed with a brain tumour. She was operated upon in London, but returned to India with her movements and speech gravely impaired. Her mind was, so far as one could tell, still clear, but she would speak only a few words and was confined to a wheelchair.

Till her death on the 19th of October 2001, Dharma was cared for by her mother-in-law, Mrs Sushila Sahai, a lady of extraordinary bravery and compassion. Friends visited Dharma off and on, but not many. The intellectual class of Delhi disgraced itself. Dozens of men and women who had known Dharma well, who had been helped by her, who had been happy enough to partake of her conversation and hospitality when she was in her pomp, simply discarded her. Among these people were many who in print and in public meetings proclaim their concern for and their identity with the suffering masses of humanity.

Worse still was the behaviour of a Calcutta Marxist of Dharma's age, who wrote a column about her in the *Economic and Political Weekly*. Here he expressed concern—the young, charming girl he had known in Bombay and Cambridge had now become, he said, a 'vegetable'. This, on three counts, was an exercise in bad taste: as an obituary of a living person, as an account of a distinguished scholar on the basis of her looks rather than her books (not one of which was mentioned), and for the use of that deeply offensive (and as it happens, inaccurate) term, 'vegetable'.

The treatment of Dharma Kumar in her last years by such people may perhaps be an indication of how, contrary to popular myth, India does not show any more compassion to the elderly and ailing than does the much maligned West. Or perhaps it is only a comment on the amorality and selfishness of a certain kind of 'intellectual' Indian. Dharma herself would have wanted me to recall the other side, to remember also friends who stayed true. Indeed, in a single year, 2000, three scholars separately and independently dedicated books to Dharma. These were a cousin, a colleague from the Delhi School, and a younger economic historian who had been encouraged by her.

I have memories of Dharma that go back almost forty years, but shall close with a more recent one. When I went to see her just before her final hospitalization, she was entertaining another visitor. This was Professor K.L. Krishna, a quiet, self-effacing yet celebrated teacher of econometrics at the Delhi School of Economics, a man who in character and intellect and institutional commitment exemplifies the best kind of university scholar. With some effort, but with visible pleasure she told her nurse, 'Professor Leela Krishna *aye hain*.' Professor Krishna was carrying a gift for Dharma, a recently published book based on a dissertation on national income finshed at the Delhi School in 1966. The author, S. Sivasubramonium, had disappeared into the bowels of the United Nations, but at Dharma's urgings had returned to his thesis after retiring. This, suitably updated and polished and published, was now in the invalid's hands. The nurse asked her to read out what Dr Sivasubramonium had written on the fly-leaf. She did: 'To Professor Dharma Kumar, for her encouragement and inspiration without which I would not have finished this work.' Unlike her inscription for me, this one contained no teasing wit. But what it lacked in mischief it made up in manifest sincerity. And it was every bit as true.

Literature and Life

The Vadhyar of Bangalore:
T.G. Vaidyanathan

T.G. Vaidyanathan played first-division cricket in Madras, taught film criticism at Pune, defended Hitler in the *Deccan Herald* and challenged Freud in the journal of the American Academy of Arts and Sciences. But his primary identification, if he would ever have allowed one, was that of a teacher, an English teacher. His degrees in the subject were from Madras University, although he never taught there. His first job was in Sibsagar in Assam, his second at Nizam's College, Hyderabad, his third at Central College, Bangalore. He taught at Central College for almost twenty years before moving to the newly created Bangalore University, from whose English department he retired in 1991.

Down the decades of the twentieth century, the best teachers of English in the best Indian colleges came to acquire a special halo. For literature embraces the whole of the human universe in a way that the more specialized social sciences do not. Poetry and works of fiction are celebrated in themselves, for how they say what they say, but they are cherished also as a window into the wider world, for their insights into the functioning of family and community, society and the state. One reads Milton and Dickens for the beauty of their language, but also to understand the compulsions that have led one set of humans to dominate or resist another.

The most inspirational college gurus have generally been teachers of English literature and its precursor, Classics. Consider thus the influence of—to name names for illustrative purposes only—Oscar Browning and Goldsworthy Lowes Dickinson in Cambridge, Maurice Bowra and Helen Gardner in Oxford, Amal Bhattacharji and Sukanta Chaudhuri in Calcutta, Kamal Wood and Homai Shroff in Bombay, Brijraj Singh and Meenakshi Mukherjee in Delhi, and K. Swaminathan in Madras. The celebrated teachers of economics were listened to only by students of economics, but these teachers of English counted as their *chelas* their own students as well as those from other disciplines. This was certainly the case with T.G. Vaidyanathan. Those who came to hear TGV lecture were students of English, of course, but also students of politics and law and business and chemistry. There were also plenty of those, like myself, who were never students of Bangalore University but had come to take a special delight in listening to TGV speak.

In his pomp—which was a rather extended one, running from the early 1970s to the early 1990s—TGV had an awesome reputation among all in Bangalore who had pretensions to learning. The widely travelled editor Suresh Menon tells the story of the first time he met TGV. Suresh, aged all of twenty-one then, had just joined the staff of the *Deccan Herald* newspaper. One day he saw TGV stride into the room and boot a colleague out of his cabin. The apprentice watched in silence and wonder as the master wrote out an essay by hand. After composing a few paragraphs he stopped and started tapping his thigh vigorously. Then he looked up and caught Suresh staring at him. 'I was testing for rhythm', said TGV: 'This essay is being composed in *adi taalam*.' To this day Menon does not know whether TGV meant what he said or was merely trying to impress him.

In his last years Vaidyanathan wrote mostly for *The Hindu*, a homecoming of sorts for a boy who grew up in Madras's Sait Colony. But at various times his criticism and reviews illuminated the *Sunday Observer, The Illustrated Weekly of India,* the *Deccan Herald* and *Outlook*. He used to describe himself as a sprinter who preferred the 1000-word article to the 100,000-word book, but at times he ran the longer distance too. He co-edited *An Indian Cricket Omnibus,* published by Oxford University Press in 1994; the same publisher brought out

Hours in the Dark, his collected essays on film, as well as *Vishnu on Freud's Desk*, his anthology of other peoples' writings on Hinduism and psychoanalysis. His last book, published posthumously by Penguin India under the title *Mr Naipaul's Round-Trip and Other Essays*, ranges widely over matters of culture, literature, film, and sport.

TGV's writings educated and entertained many, but like a good Indian guru he worked best in the oral tradition. When he was younger TGV held court in Bangalore's coffee houses; later, in his home in Rajaji Nagar. Especially on Sunday mornings, friends and admirers would flock to his little flat, squatting on the floor around him while his gracious and long-suffering wife, Indira, dispensed *idlis* and coffee.

I sometimes felt that TGV was a Bengali intellectual trapped in the body of a Tamil Brahmin. Where Tambrahms are highly security conscious, checking their bank balance once every other week, TGV lived for his ideas. And while his caste men tend to speak condescendingly of 'idle gossip', he had the *bhadralok's* love for the *adda*, especially the adda centred around himself. Even his particular enthusiasms were as often as not Bengali. He wrote with great insight about the films of Satyajit Ray. Six of TGV's essays on Ray are reprinted in *Hours in the Dark*. It is said that the master himself felt that this Tamil from Bangalore understood his craft better than many a Calcutta critic. Another of TGV's Bengali heroes was the pioneering psychoanalyst Girindrasekhar Bose, the dedicatee of *Vishnu on Freud's Desk*. He drew the line, however, at Bengali cricketers, vastly preferring Vijay Hazare and Vinoo Mankad to their eastern contemporaries.

One of the nicest things about TGV—again, something that is un-Tamil—was the absence of cynicism. He took as fresh and as robust an interest in contemporary films and novels as in the classics, on whose virtues he had preached when younger. This, as Bangalore changed and became software- and dollar-obsessed, made him something of an anachronism in the city he had chosen as his home. But it made him warmly nostalgic about his visits to a place he called Culkhut-aa, where (so he liked to believe) new ideas still generated more interest than new fashions and commodities.

TGV once told a student that he would want to be reborn in Calcutta. As if in preparation, a map of the city hung on his walls, displayed alongside portraits of Marilyn Monroe and Jayaprada. His native Madras he found oppressive; Bangalore was nice, but to live in Calcutta would be nicer still. He liked to tell the story of a journey he made in a crowded Madras train, where he was chastised by a sour fellow traveller for standing in the way of passengers coming in and out. 'All you have done is talk', grumbled the man. 'Had it been Culkhutaa', TGV would comment, 'the fellow would have joined in the conversation, rather than complain about it.'

Characteristic, too, is the story of TGV taking his daughter, an only child, to join Mount Carmel College. He was met at the gate by the principal, who said that the girl could have the subject of her choice. She chose Commerce, to her father's disgust. For weeks afterwards he would tell visitors of her betrayal, inviting them to consider the rows of Freud and Dickens and Pauline Kael and Neville Cardus on his shelves. 'She wants to study Commerce', he would say, 'and what will happen to this library?'

II

I first met TGV twenty years ago, at a seminar organized by the sociologist Shiv Visvanathan. From this distance in time I cannot recall the subject of his talk. I think he spoke of the stories of Jose Luis Borges. But he spoke well, at any rate, his opinions given greater character by his beautifully expressive hands. Afterwards, when I introduced myself, I said I had liked an essay he had written on the Australian fast bowler Ray Lindwall. He asked me home the following Sunday, to make the first of countless visits to what I came to know as Bangalore's most entertainingly enlightened durbar.

In writing a memoir of Arthur Koestler, the humorist George Mikes apologized in advance for being simply Koestler's 'Hungarian friend'. He knew nothing of socialism and science, the scholar's chosen subjects, while for his part Koestler had no time for wit or frivolity.

But in exile in London these radically dissimilar writers met to speak
their shared language and exchange memories of Hungarian food and
Hungarian music. By the same token I was TGV's 'cricketing friend'.
I had no interest in films or psychoanalysis, and—as regards my own
fields of study—Vaidyanathan thought the environment too trendy
and Gandhi too dreary. But we were brought together by a boyhood
spent playing cricket, and by talking and reading about it as well.

In the early 1980s, I was returning to cricket after a brief encounter
with Marxism. As for TGV, it had been years since he had spoken
seriously about the game to anyone: in Bangalore, it seems, he had
literary friends and film-loving friends, but no cricketing companions. Thus it was that our conversations generally began and ended
with cricket. True, we also discussed other things: in between the two
slices of sandwich the meat might be provided by politics or literature.
But here too the idioms were often taken from cricket. Thus, commenting on a promising scholar who had since lost his way, TGV
compared him to Vinod Kambli. As he put it, '*Ipdi adchaan, apdi
adchaan, apron out*'. (A fine stroke here and a fine stroke there, then
a slash to a wide ball resulting in a tame catch to the wicket-keeper.)

TGV and I would discuss matches as they came to us on the box,
but also cricketers of an older era: especially, his heroes Lala Amarnath,
Vinoo Mankad, Mushtaq Ali, and Vijay Hazare. He spoke with
warmth of foreign cricketers too: of Clyde Walcott's straight drive,
and of the leg-breaks and antics of the Australian Serviceman Cecil
Pepper. Sometimes he would pass on recollections of his own time
in the field. He had kept wickets for his college and his club, though,
like the rest of us, he remembered best his turns with the bat. He once
told me of how, as a sixteen-year-old schoolboy, he had faced C.R.
('Kurmi') Rangachari, a fearsome fast bowler who, in his time as an
Indian Test player, had clean bowled George Headley and troubled
Don Bradman. The first ball of the over was a short ball that hit the
boy on the chest. TGV said the pain went round and round: he felt
as if there were bees buzzing inside him. 'And the bugger did not even
say sorry. I managed to keep out the other five balls, but the shock had

unnerved me. The next over I tried to hit a slow-left-armer for six and was stumped.'

Alas, by this time TGV was too old to come with me to the Chinna-swamy Stadium. But he did once drag me to a cricket match, played with tennis balls in the dry bed of a temple tank behind his house. The instruments were modest, and the boys only of the locality, but their ambition was anything but small scale. This was the final of the Chee-tah Cup, no less, played under floodlights and with prize money collected from the Rajaji Nagar shopkeepers. There was also a run-ning commentary on the match, in confirmation of my friend's thesis that real cricket has first to be heard, not seen. To his delight the boys had taken the names of big-time players: Imran Khan's eleven was playing Tony Greig's eleven. TGV was further tickled when the com-mentary switched from Kannada to English, to the language of metropolitan power whose use helped dignify this otherwise hum-drum match.

Later that year the Indian cricket team toured Sri Lanka. In one of the Tests, Sanath Jayasuriya found himself 290 not out at close of play on the fourth day. The next morning my television went on the blink, shortly after he had crossed 300—as only a dozen batsmen had done before him. I asked TGV to keep me up-to-date. He would phone at the end of each over, speaking in that bastard-tongue, cricket-Tamil. 'Cowper *poche*', was the first message, Bob Cowper's score of 307 has been surpassed. Then, as Jayasuriya moved to 312, 'Simpson Edrich *rendon poche*.' An English and an Australian opening batsman had also slipped down one of the most select of sporting lists. The next two calls were routine, followed, however, by 'Sandham *poche*.' Ten minutes later it was 'Gooch *poche*,' and then, after Jayasuriya went from 334 to 338 in one stroke, 'Bradman, Hammond, Hanif *moonon poche*'. An obscure Sri Lankan had shoved aside three of the greatest batsmen in cricket history, the wonder carried in the voice of an Ind-ian just this side of seventy. He was much distressed when Jayasuriya got out for 340; he would not be consoled even when I told him that by getting out when he did, Jayasuriya and Mahanama had fallen one run short of the all-time record for a batting partnership, which was held in part by the hero of his own youth Vijay Hazare.

III

Vaidyanathan's essays, as well as his conversation, were marked by a wide range of reference. He told a student who asked him to get to the point: 'Learn that I will always be around the point.' In cricketing and other matters TGV was genuinely cosmopolitan. As he once wrote of Satyajit Ray, 'he has taught us the most elementary and yet most difficult of truths that to be a true Indian it is first necessary to be a citizen of the world.'

In this respect, Bangalore, with its catholicity of social life and its absence of puritan guardians of moral behaviour, suited TGV better than did his native Madras. Outside his own room the city had changed; fortunately, however, outside his notice. For Bangalore, to quote an artist friend of mine, has become 'Duba-lore', its cityscape of glass and concrete mimicking Dubai and marking a fundamental change in the aspirations of its residents. In the space of five years the city lost three of its most esteemed intellectuals: the journalist P.K. Srinivasan, the literary scholar D.R. Nagaraj, and Vaidyanathan. These men stood for the mobility (and nobility) of ideas; their epigones, for the mobility of money alone.

Vaidyanathan's death led to a flood of tributes in *The Hindu*, this provoking a sour comment in a rival paper by a distinguished Tamil writer. Not even R.K. Narayan, said the writer, had so many column inches devoted to his passing. It was as well that this critic did not attend the memorial meeting in Bangalore, where more tributes were read out or spontaneously spoken. One student recalled an argument with her boyfriend about the composer Sibelius: he liked his music, she didn't. Somehow, the matter reached TGV for adjudication. The verdict, rather definitive, came in the words of Neville Cardus as carried in TGV's voice: 'The world of Sibelius is unpeopled; there are no men and women in it, not a single living human being. The sedges are bare and no birds sing.'

Another student, now a teacher of thirty years standing himself, remembered conversations about film and cricket from long ago. He was taken repeatedly by TGV to see (and help translate) a Kannada film set in the Malnad countryside. The film had just won a major national award, but TGV thought there was something wrong with it. It was only that he could not quite put his finger on what it was. It was on the fifth or sixth viewing that the penny dropped. In one scene, the hero, in his cottage, was tenderly pulling a blanket over his sleeping wife. 'The gesture is too refined', exclaimed TGV, 'too sophisticated for the setting.' Teacher and disciple left the hall, while the incident that provoked their departure was made the centrepiece of TGV's essay on the film.

Why, despite his manifest angularities, TGV still attracted so many students and disciples was eloquently explained in a tribute published in the *New Indian Express* by Sreekumar Menon:

> He took generations of students undone by formal schooling by the hand and taught them to think and through thinking, the excitement of the life of the mind. 'Attention must be paid', he quoted Willy Loman; nothing was too trivial to deserve attention and, attended closely, objects and events became vital, lively, beautiful. He read to us Thomas Kuhn [the philosopher of science] with the same enthusiasm as he read from the autobiography of the great British racing driver Stirling Moss . . .
>
> Years later, when I met him in one of his low periods, he said poignantly: 'My friend, you know, it's only Azharuddin and Jayaprada who kept me going' . . . He created heroes with generous abandon . . . He loved Frank Capra and Bergman—both Ingrid and Ingmar—Keats and Eliot, Vijay Hazare and Lala Amarnath. And he loved books with a passion. They lay piled up in the rooms and houses where he lived, in heaps and stacks on chairs and had often to be moved to seat a visitor. He loved the feel of books, their beautiful jackets, their typeset, their smell and he infected his companions with his love . . .
>
> He had little patience with social and political causes. The life of the mind was his province; the Mind and the ways in which it apprehended the world was his only Cause.

IV

Jawaharlal Nehru once told a young admirer who asked him some advice about a personal matter: 'I do not function as a guru for anyone and my life is such that I cannot give personal guidance to anyone in the manner you suggest.' TGV would not have approved of this diffidence. He advised his students, sometimes unasked, on what career they should follow or what kind of marriage they should make. He encouraged their deference and was puzzled or angry when this turned, as it sometimes did, to defiance. And while he enjoyed intelligent conversation, he enjoyed it best of all when its flow was guided, orchestrated and dominated by himself.

His students called him 'Sir'; friends of his own generation, 'TGV' Behind his back he was known, by both chela and colleague alike, as 'vadhyar' (teacher/mentor)—this said with a unique mixture of appreciation and exasperation. For, few among those who knew him had not, at one stage or another, quarrelled with him.

I liked to claim that I was the only one of TGV's friends who had never fought with him. I had not been his student and had no opinion of any worth on films. And, having grown up (in an intellectual sense) in Calcutta, I had learnt how to give gurus and vadhyars a long rope. Cricketing conversation would not bring us to blows, but I was sometimes challenged by Vaidyanathan's outrageously provocative cultural theories. He insisted that my saying '*poite varren*' (I will come back) to his wife as I departed was a manifestation of an unsuccessfully suppressed Brahminism. I replied that it was plain courtesy and had no connotation of caste. And did he not know that I was an anti-Brahminical Hindu who wore no thread, nor would permit my son to wear one? Wait, he would respond, wait a few years more. You will come back to where you belong, as I have. (I shall wait, but this is one argument that I hope to posthumously win.)

Vaidyanathan himself was quick to love—the strokeplay of Jayasuriya or the films of Ray, for example—but also very quick to fight. Among the people whom he had at some time offended was the playwright and actor Girish Karnad. When I first met Karnad at his house, we argued about a critical review he had recently written of Vaidya-nathan's *Hours in the Dark*. I felt the review was excessively sharp and perhaps unnecessarily personal. At length, Karnad admitted an old grievance. Twenty years before this, he said, he had made a film in the north Kannada dialect and Vaidyanathan had rubbished it in print without knowing a word of the language.

The publication of *Hours in the Dark*, then, allowed Karnad a chance to suitably hit back. Oddly enough, the next week our friend D.R. Nagaraj had lunch with Karnad, and also complained about his review of TGV's book. It was but a few days after this lunch that Nagaraj died. At short notice a memorial meeting was arranged in the Senate Hall of Central College. The night before, Karnad rang up to ask me to tell Vaidyanathan. 'I can't abide the man', he said, 'and won't speak to him myself, but D.R. greatly liked him, and he should be informed.' It was a handsome gesture and I duly passed on the message. 'Karnad told you to tell me to come?' asked TGV suspi-ciously. 'Yes', I said. 'That's the first decent thing the fellow has done for me,' was the grumpy comment. Still, the next day TGV and Kar-nad both sat in the front row while honouring the memory of their common friend.

This penchant for disputation TGV carried until the last. Three months before he died, I asked him to come for a lunch in honour of T.S. Shanbhag, a Bangalore bookseller whom he much liked and had for years patronized. I added that I would also invite a student close to him, who would give him a ride. When I mentioned the name of the student, TGV said: 'Don't you know I have fought with him?' I was stunned, for this was an especially devoted disciple of a particu-larly gentle disposition who had not long before published a long essay on what he owed TGV. 'How come you have quarrelled with *him*', I asked. 'He praised the film *Hannibal*', answered TGV: 'I can't permit such a lapse of judgement on his part.' I let him know, as gently as I could, that he was being ridiculous if he broke off relations be-cause of a disagreement on a film.

A little later TGV was hospitalized. I went to see him after he came home, and as I entered he waved a book at me, Martin Amis's *Experience*. This had been gifted to him, as he lay in his hospital bed, by the student whom he had dumped for his views on the film *Hannibal*. 'You will be pleased', he said, 'that I have made up with P.' In time, the reconciled student was to take the lead in putting together a posthumous volume of TGV's essays.

In Noel Annan's wonderful collection of portraits, *The Dons*, there is a remark about the Cambridge literature teacher George 'Dadie' Reynolds that much reminded me of TGV. It was said of Reynolds, as it should also be said of Vaidyanathan, that to be friends with him was like being on an ocean liner: at any moment one could be flung into the sea for a misdemeanour (this being most often a careless remark); but, as one surfaced in the sea, one saw the heads of a dozen other friends bobbing up and down.

One of TGV's less endearing traits was his penchant for swallowing your books. It did not matter if one was a student, patron or mere friend: he exercised a prescriptive right over your printed possessions. When I was younger I did not complain. I felt I owed him enough not to mind his borrowing, and then keeping, my copy of Philip Spratt's *Hindu Culture and Personality* (a scarce book, which I bought at a second-hand store) or Clifford and Marcus's *Anthropology as Cultural Critique* (an expensive book, which an unwilling uncle had been persuaded to send me from America). But over the years, as the borrowings accumulated, and in each case turned to theft, I began to resent this. A week before he died he phoned to ask whether I owned David Remnick's biography of Muhammad Ali. When I said I did, he demanded that it be sent to him that day, by courier. Then he continued: 'Can you also send me Alan Ross's *Cape Summer*? I read it forty years ago, and would love to see it again.' From where I sat I could see the spine of Ross's book looking out at me. But it was very rare, and the old man had had enough for today anyway. 'Sorry, TGV', I lied, 'someone else has borrowed it already.'

V

Such then were the warts: to be spoken of behind his back or after his death. Still, when one views TGV's life and career in the round, one cannot but be struck by its integrity. I was never TGV's student, but I knew him long enough to appreciate how nobly he fulfilled the best traditions of his calling. One illustration of this was the lack of favouritism in how he treated or responded to those who had passed through his classroom. A former student had had a nervous breakdown after being deported from America: disowned by his family, he roamed the streets and cafés of Bangalore, living off the remains of his modest inheritance and from supplements provided by friends. Another student was a Rhodes Scholar who had gone on to work for the Ford Foundation and the United Nations. I happened to know both men, thus to know also that TGV always showed an equal concern for each, and was as delighted by a visit from the Rhodes Scholar as from the tramp.

Part of TGV's charm was the wonderful austerity of his personal life. He did not care for money or indeed for social recognition beyond what a grateful circle had already bestowed upon him. He never possessed a car or scooter and lived most of his life in a one-room apartment. Like no other Indian intellectual of my acquaintance he *completely* lived out his calling, dedicating his life to books and films, and to these alone.

When TGV first came to Bangalore, he lived in a cramped room in Ambika Lodge, a stone's throw from Kempegowda Road and its two dozen cinema houses. By the time I got to know him, fifteen years later, he had moved to a lower-middle-class neighbourhood in Rajaji Nagar. To get to his home one had to pass small shops with plastic balls hung outside them, *agarbatti* stalls with ugly hoardings, and little houses with rows upon rows of mopeds and scooters parked in front of them. His own house—or room—would have been singular anyway, but especially so in that locality. Books crowded rather than furnished it. One would be asked to sit on the mat while he fished out a book to read and explain it to you.

One Sunday, several years ago, the magazine section of *The Hindu* carried essays by TGV and me on the same page. Knowing that he sometimes read the papers only in the afternoon, I took my copy and drove over to his place. His wife said he had gone to his favourite eatery, two blocks away. I followed him there and found him focused attentively on a *dosa*. I showed him the articles side by side, his on Kipling, mine on a radical journalist who had just died. I joked that, in view of our respective political orientations and the subjects we had written about, *The Hindu* had wisely put my piece on the left of the page, and his on the right. He laughed, too, but it struck me later that what was perhaps more relevant was that the conservative intellectual had walked, while the leftist had come driving a very large car.

As I have said, TGV and I rarely talked about films. However, when the cricketing epic *Lagaan* did not win the Oscar, we discussed the failure on the phone. Naturally he had a theory—that it was too heroic, cast in an archaic mould, whereas its rivals had explored more contemporary themes. It was our last conversation, for the next morning he was dead. He was cremated, as per his wishes, with a hockey stick and a cricket bat placed beside him. I saw that the bat had the legend: POWER SHOT. I would have preferred a more comfortingly classical label: Gunn and Moore perhaps, or Symonds, or even, at a pinch, Hans Raj Mahajan.

What would TGV have said? I suspect he might not have protested, seeing it as emblematic of changes in a game he had so long and so evocatively loved.

The Kannada Tagore: Shivarama Karanth

In the summer of 1994 I was in the town of Ranibennur at the invitation of a local environmental group. They had just won a
major award and wished me to share in the celebrations. The road
to the meeting hall was lined with banners that read: 'To celebrate the
Indira Gandhi Paryavaran Puruskar and Dr Shivarama Karanth's
ninetieth birthday.' This was a happy juxtaposition, for Karanth had
been a pioneer of environmentalism in South India, and had even
been the first petitioner in a case the group in Ranibennur had filed
in the Supreme Court, against a notorious polluting firm of the town.

The meeting was entertaining, not least because Karanth spoke.
Afterwards we repaired to the travellers' bungalow. There I got chat-
ting with the great Kannada writer's chauffeur. With a historian's interest in dates, I asked him when precisely had his boss turned ninety.
'Actually, sir', he replied, 'he is almost ninety-two.' Then why are they
celebrating the birthday now, I wondered. 'Because they also need
their chance', he said.

'They' were the people of Ranibennur, and 'their chance' was the
opportunity to pay tribute to a man who was more than a legend in
his lifetime. It turned out that for the past two years the writer and his
driver had been on the road. The white Ambassador that brought
Karanth to Ranibennur had the previous fortnight taken him to

Tumkur, for a meeting to 'Celebrate the Kannada Sahitya Sammelana and Dr Karanth's ninetieth birthday.' In Mysore, the birthday was clubbed with the opening of a new girls' school in Gadag with the opening of a new science laboratory. Nowhere was the event celebrated by itself. That would have offended Karanth, and in any case it was easy enough to find an excuse provided by one of his many spheres of achievement. A new dance academy would do in one place, a film studio in another, a library in a third. One way or another, the people of every decent-sized hamlet in Karnataka found a way to honour their man.

A cat, it is said, has nine lives. Vishnu had ten avatars. But Shivarama Karanth had as many as sixteen careers. These were: nationalism, social reform, commerce, journalism, photography, acting, dance, painting, music, cinema, experiments in education, rural uplift, the popularization of science (through a multi-volume encyclopaedia designed and written wholly by himself), the writing of novels (as many as forty-five), the writing of plays (not less than ninety), and environmentalism. This list is not necessarily exhaustive, and the man did not necessarily follow only one career at a time.

Shivarama Karanth was born on the 10th of October, 1902, in the village of Kota in Dakshina Kannada district. His early life is described in his autobiography, *Ten Faces of a Crazy Mind*, skilfully translated into English by H.Y. Sharada Prasad. *Ten Faces* is as heterodox as the man himself: unstructured, occasionally meandering, yet plush with epigrams and witty asides and philosophical insights. It is that altogether rare thing, a work of literary merit which is also a work of social history. Like most other autobiographies, this was written to pre-empt a future biographer. As Karanth put it, 'I do not desire to be killed by others' pens. I shall take my own life.'

As a boy, Shivarama Karanth's 'attitude to studies was one of disinterest'. He dropped out of college without taking a degree. As he put it, 'I did not have to experience the indigestion of high marks.' Still, he was lucky in his teachers. A middle-school teacher taught him to do interesting things with his hands; to garden and to weave mats, for example. In high school, one teacher inculcated an appreciation of Yakshagana; another opened up the library of Kannada literature to him.

Growing up, Karanth was contemptuous of the 'vanity', the 'tyranny', and the 'narrowness' of his Brahmin upbringing. He was disenchanted by his visits to Kashi and Prayag, places he found crowded, dirty, and full of grasping priests and *pandas*. Notably, the one holy place which 'gave satisfaction and was not culturally jarring was Dakshineshwar . . . I went to the Panchavati garden. That was the field of the Paramhansa's spiritual exertions. My feelings for Nature and my reverence for the sage led me to find more peace there than I did at Brindavan.'

While turned off by faith and studies, Karanth was enchanted by the arts. He was gripped by the travelling theatre companies that came to his neck of rural Karnataka—these the southern equivalents of the Bengali *jatras*. It was under their inspiration that Karanth taught himself music. The process of self-training he later described with characteristic wryness:

> It was a fellow student who taught me to shriek, to shriek in some recognisable raga . . . There was an open space near our house called *naribena* (jackal field). I used to go there at dawn and late at night to do my screaming. . . . Once a jackal came within ten yards of me and looked at me as if to throw a challenge. I am not joking; it did happen. To this day I feel that music-learners should find a place beyond the town limits.

Eventually, Karanth became quite accomplished, not merely as a singer but also as a connoisseur and composer. His great work for Yakshagana, the traditional dance-drama of the west coast, was helped immeasurably by the musical skills and innovations he brought to it. Some of the most attractive and sensitively delineated characters in his fiction are musicians and music teachers.

In college Karanth also became a 'great consumer of political harangues'. The non-co-operation movement inspired him to leave his degree halfway and take to the promotion of spinning, this at a time when 'patriotism had not yet become a profitable industry'.

In his mid twenties, Karanth started a correspondence with Mahatma Gandhi. Sadly, we don't have his side of the exchange. From the letters printed in the *Collected Works of Mahatma Gandhi*, we get a bare idea of what was on Karanth's mind. The topics alluded to in Gandhi's letters include the therapeutic value of *asanas* and *pranayamas* (Gandhi seemed sceptical), the life and ideals of Ramakrishna Paramhansa, and the moral life of actors. Of this last Gandhi seemed most sceptical: 'I should draw a sharp distinction between *kirtans* and theatricals. The question of theatricals is very serious, and as you seem to know all about the lives of actors, it may be as well for you to avoid the profession.'

A topic that preoccupied Karanth at this time, as it did Gandhi, was sex and marriage. Gandhi offered the view, presumably in answer to a query of Karanth's, that wet dreams were 'undoubtedly harmful'; for they released seminal energy better 'husbanded and reserved for reproduction, when the latter is desired, or transmutation into spiritual energy.' In response to another question, Gandhi assured the young seeker that to promote widow marriage—as Karanth was then doing—was not inconsistent with *brahmacharya*. Still, he saw it as a concession to human frailty: 'when I advocate the marriage of child widows, I presume that they want the pleasure which all animals seek and some human beings only can restrain themselves from seeking.'

The insinuation that brahmacharya was somehow superior to married life, Karanth came to reject, even as he disregarded the Mahatma's advice to stay away from the theatre. But he continued to work in khadi and swadeshi for five years, till about 1927, by which time the 'Nationalist Movement in our region was cold like stale porridge.' Fortunately, Karanth had already started writing fiction—detective novels, to begin with—as well as plays.

While still in his twenties, Karanth acquired the taste for very long walks through the southern countryside. He would walk through forests and swim across rivers, carrying little, sleeping in disused temples or peasant homes. Some of these journeys were made for pleasure, others to educate himself about the culture, the ecology, and the artistic traditions of his land.

When he came to plan a children's encyclopaedia, in the 1930s, Karanth was dismayed by the 'intellectual thinness' of the Kannada country. There was a way out: he would research and write the thing himself. His *Bala Prapancha* was followed by his science encyclopaedia. Then, provoked by a badly produced government book, he researched and wrote an illustrated history of architecture. All these works were to have an enduring impact. There were also other, relatively minor literary productions, among them a translation into Kannada of *Hamlet*. His contributions to dance and fiction, by no means minor, I shall come to presently.

Shivarama Karanth married late, when he was well past thirty. In his memoirs he is reticent about telling us what first attracted his wife to him. All he tells us is that she was a gifted dancer, and from another caste. The lady was more forthright. Karanth, she recalled, was explaining to his troupe how to make costumes for the characters. As he began to cut colour paper in different shapes, Leela's eyes 'observed the movement of his fingers. What speed! What skill! I stood there, completely lost, looking at his hands. . . . At that moment, I felt an intense desire to be near those hands . . . What I yearned for, for the first time in my life, was to possess those artistic hands of Karanth'.

The critic C.N. Ramachandran, who quotes these words, also quotes an appreciation of Leela Karanth by her second son, Ulhas. 'It was our mother who shaped Karanth's life', remarks Ulhas: 'She was the backbone of all his endeavours. She was also quite well read, and she dedicated all of her talents to her husband. She took care of all household responsibilities. I remember now that mother also, like our father, was an atheist; and she used to read and explain Bertrand Russell for us.'

Karanth's standing was not hindered by his appearance. In his later years, especially, he made for a striking figure, dressed in spotless white dhoti and kurta, with an impressive face framed by a silver mane combed backwards. He was charismatic and, it must be admitted, at times intimidating. As his associate L.S. Seshagiri Rao has written, he 'could be brusque and withering', and, especially as he grew older, 'impatient of criticism, and dogmatic'.

Some admirers liked to call Karanth 'Kadala Tiratha Bhargava', the Lord of the Coastal Lands. This seems to be a mistaken title, not least because it was originally given to Parusarama, that fervent up-holder of the Brahmin way of life. I prefer what Sharada Prasad once called him: 'The King Elephant of the Southern Forests'. Like the king elephant Karanth dominated the landscape by the sheer bulk of his achievement. Like him, he roamed wherever his fancy took him. And like him, he could go sometimes into periods of well-directed rage.

II

In the 1970s Shivarama Karanth moved from Puttur—where he had lived for forty years—to the village of Saligrama. In September 1989 I visited Karanth at his now no-longer-new home. After the mon-soon, the countryside was at its greenest and most glorious. The great man's house was a contrast: a large and inelegant structure, painted white outside but with the rooms inside very dark. We spoke of his campaign against nuclear energy. Sadly, I have lost my notes of the meeting, but I do recall his concern for the 'integrity of life', for life natural as well as human.

Not long after I met Karanth, I was looking at some old microfilms in Delhi of the now-defunct nationalist paper, the *Bombay Chronicle*. Searching for an article by Verrier Elwin, this headline unexpected-ly popped up: 'Yakshgana Art, a Real Approach to Masses: Troupe Gives Demonstrations of Their Talent in Bombay'. The text below told of a performance by a Yakshagana group from South Kanara, followed by a talk by Karanth on the history of the art form. He had spoken of the dance's fusion of rural life with a mass audience, of its forms of dress and make-up, and of recent innovations in music and presentation.

This, then, was the island city's first exposure to Yakshagana, as reported in the *Bombay Chronicle* of 28 November 1936. Later, I came across a reference to the trip in Karanth's memoirs. 'I gave quite a pompous lecture in English. It was attended by people of Bombay's upper crust. A few ladies wore so much paint they could have gone on the stage.'

I remember reading that faded microfilm with an almost indescribable feeling of wonder. This was 1989, and I had just interviewed Karanth about his environmental campaigns. Now, I was learning of his pioneering work in the promotion of Yakshsagana, as described in a newspaper report fifty-three years ago. I have known many remarkable Indians, but this experience might help explain why for me Karanth commands a place all his own.

If one were forced to rank Karanth's multiple careers, one might—reluctantly—allow that Yakshagana and the writing of novels should share first place. He both revived and redefined the dance-form of the West Coast. He rediscovered many ragas that were traditionally part of the Yakshagana repertoire but had fallen into disuse. He did away with dialogue, making songs and dance do its work instead. He added new instruments, linked dance rhythms and music rhythms, and searched for and trained talented young artists. Most significantly, he brought down the average time of a performance from eight to three hours, thus allowing Yakshagana to make its peace with the rushed modern world.

In the field of fiction, Karanth was prodigiously active, in part because he did not bother unduly about theory or technique. 'If you have something of your own to say', he remarked, 'technique will come of its own accord. If you are true to your experience and the values that your own life has taught you, if they are not borrowed values, what you say will find the best form.'

The first of his novels to have a wider impact was *Choma's Drum* (translated into English by U.R. Kalkur) Its central character was an Untouchable whose dream, or fantasy, was to cultivate his own plot of land. Meanwhile, he worked in the fields of a landlord half his age, his children labouring with him. He drowned his sorrows in drink, and by playing his drum. Stick in hand, he 'coaxed out of the [drum] the monotonous sound, *damadhamma dakadhakka.* There was never a new rhythm, never a new timbre in the sound. But he played it with all the pride of a mridangam pandit.'

This early novel, like the ones to follow, is replete with descriptions and images of nature: of animals, trees, insects, and landscapes. There is a vivid account, drawn undoubtedly from personal experience, of a walk from the coast to a coffee plantation on the crest of the ghats. But the human world is described with a biting irony. Consider these samples: 'The hut was his own—when not claimed by rains and storms'. 'Their dinner would be before dark, for no lamp had ever been lit in Choma's hut. What precious thing did they have to do at night to need a lamp?' 'Plantation debts are like plantation malaria: once in their grip no release till death.'

Choma's Drum has been compared to Mulk Raj Anand's *Untouchable.* The novel it reminded me of, however, is Gopinath Mohanty's *Paraja,* which too was published in the 1930s. There a tribal has his land taken away; here a Dalit can never own land. Both look to the forest for sustenance but are thwarted by the state. Both are forced to seek consolation in drink, both forced to burden their young with their sorrows. One novel is set in Orissa, the other in coastal Karnataka. Separated by five hundred miles of territory, the novels are united by a mood, a moment, and a movement: the Gandhian struggle for social reform.

Another of Karanth's novels available in English is a story of courtesan life, translated by H.Y. Sharada Prasad under the title, *The Woman of Basrur.* The rendering is feminist, but without advertising itself as such: it is sensitive and subtle without ever descending into stridency. There is a noticeable empathy with the courtesan: with her desire for acclaim, her devotion to her art, the haphazard life she leads in roaming theatres. Karanth penetratingly probes her hopes, fantasies and suspicions. The fickleness and animal feelings of her patrons are described with dry wit.

The novel spans four generations. Its core is a memoir of the legendary courtesan Manjula, found in an attic by her grandniece: this, the serendipitous discovery of forgotten texts, is a literary device more recently made popular in English fiction by A.S. Byatt's *Possession*. The tale is told entirely from the woman's point of view. 'To earn a moment of joy, a woman had to undergo a hundred moments of suffering.' 'But can a courtesan's daughter buy, off the shelf, someone in whom money and virtue are combined?'

When a lover gifts Manjula a bracelet, she 'felt as if soaked in syrup'. At other times she yearned for human understanding: 'silk is soft to the touch, it is true, but can silk soothe the ache of the heart?' There is a brilliant description of her feeling let down by a patron who had but one thing on his mind.

> I thought I would be like a basket of bright and fragrant flowers offered in music. Instead I was the goat sacrificed to the demon. He was a hungry animal and I was only a lump of flesh. From the moment he set foot in my rooms he acted as if I was someone without a mind and feelings.

Manjula's last lover is the swami of a *mutt*, who would visit her under cover of darkness and in disguise. This is a characteristic comment on the hypocrisy of an enforced asceticism: Karanth had little time for the forms and pieties of his ancestral religion. The critic C.N. Ramachandran observes that Karanth's novels are invariably biased towards women and against holy men: these he saw as humbugs, or as having run away from home to escape their responsibilities. And yet, in a bitter paradox, when he died in December 1997, this great anti-ritualist and rationalist was cremated amidst the chanting of Vedic hymns.

As both Gopalakrishna Adiga and U.R. Anantha Murty have pointed out, the strengths of Karanth's fiction are also its limitations. 'What strikes us most', writes Adiga, 'is his sincerity and earnestness.' The characters, dialogues, situation and story are 'so authentic that [they] become a part of our own living experience.' However, there is in Karanth's writings 'throughout a lack of imagery. Only when a novelist's intellect, feelings, contemplation, values, dreams, memories at the conscious and unconscious levels—only when all these ingredients are cooked to a delicacy, does it create a new experience for the reader.' Likewise, Anantha Murty comments that in becoming his people's 'most authentic writer', Karanth had to rigorously exclude the aesthetic and poetic dimensions from his fiction. Since humans for him are the product of specific social relationships, he cannot write about the intensity of mystical experience or the agonies of the alienated individual. His novels are rich, readable, authentic; yet they 'do not contain invisible eddies that catch the reader and draw him into subliminal depths.'

<h1 style="text-align:center">III</h1>

The bravest act of my writing career was to suggest in the pages of a Calcutta newspaper that a Kannada writer bore comparison with Rabindranath Tagore. I made the claim in 1995, and took care not to visit Kolkata for some time thereafter. But let me make so bold now as to revive it. For Shivarama Karanth was the most influential Kannada novelist, a noted playwright, a dancer and choreographer, an encyclopaedist, social reformer, patriot and educationist. His myriad-mindedness inspired a proverb in Kannnada: *Aadu muttada soppilla, Karantharu maadada kelasavilla.* (There is vegetation that a goat doesn't eat, but there is no work that Karanth has not done.)

The range of Shivarama Karanth's achievements bears comparison with Tagore's. So, more intriguingly, does the pattern of his life, and the choice of his particular passions. Consider the following.

Like Tagore, Karanth wrote as much for the young as for adults. Generations of Kannada schoolchildren grew up on primers written by him. And he took care to have these well illustrated: the painter he chose for the purpose being K.K. Hebbar, in this respect the exact Kannada equivalent of Nandalal Bose. His children's encyclopaedias were also attractively produced: he took many of the photos himself, and even had the colour separations done in Germany.

Karanth was proud of his work for children. Apart from the books he wrote for them, for some years he ran an experimental school with its own kitchen, fields, and menagerie. The children were all boarders and paid no fees. Much time was spent outside the classroom, in the forests and on the river or sea, and in watching or participating in theatre and music. The great Kannada writers, singers and dancers would all come visiting. In the school Karanth himself was always accompanied by a huge red Malabar squirrel, its tail stylishly draped around his neck.

Like Tagore, again, Karanth was an environmentalist before the time of environmentalism. He, too, was made by the gorgeous landscapes in which he was reared. 'I am in love with my region, and dote on its landscape', he once wrote.

> I could not understand why such a green stretch of land was made so grey in books of geography . . . The beach at Karwar would enslave anyone. The crowning glory of Malnad are the Jog Falls. I have not kept count of the number of times I have visited it. The gorge and the precipice are unfailingly alluring. I have sat, soaked, eaten and slept on the banks of the Sharavati, and romped on the sand. I have loved the violet-coloured moss on the boulders there.

In the 1950s Karanth worked for the plantation and preservation of trees and forests. In the 1970s and 1980s he launched campaigns against polluting industries, destructive dams, and—the ultimate threat to human and natural life—the nuclear establishment. In 1979 Karanth inspired a popular movement against a hydroelectric project on the Bedthi River, in Uttara Kannada. The dam would have inundated much rich farmland, and also thousands of hectares of rich tropical forests. Characteristically, Karanth was not content with opposition; if they thought the dam harmful, he told the agitating farmers, they must reform their own wayward agricultural practices, must be more sparing in their use of chemicals and more conserving in their use of water and energy.

In 1982 he translated the first Citizens' Report on the Indian Environment. Then, after the Chernobyl disaster of 1986, he led a popular movement against the siting of a nuclear plant in northern Karnataka. Karanth even stood for a Lok Sabha election on an independent 'green' ticket: although he did not make a single campaign speech, and he had not the money or muscle power of the established political parties, he still got 60,000 votes.

Karanth's ecological sensibilities also found their way into his fiction. The first pages of *The Woman of Basrur* speak of the landscape and of how man has made and unmade it. The town of Basrur had 'reservoirs built by the pious of an earlier age. They are fed by the monsoon rains, but in summer they turn yellow—or green, when the moss shows through. And the stone steps around them are in disrepair, looking like the misshapen teeth of the aged.' The river that flowed down the hills and past the town had 'palms growing in profusion for miles together on both banks, like unmarried girls lined up to welcome a bridal couple, swaying in the winds, unconscious of their own comeliness.'

Once a thriving port, trading to Portuguese Goa and beyond, the town was now derelict.

> All the glory that remains in Basrur is the glory of green—the bright green of the tops of palms, the light green of paddy squares which stretch from the outskirts of the town up to the sea, the deep green of the patches of sweet-potato and chilli. . . . , and the still deeper green of the copal trees which stand stately, looking down upon bush and thorn.

The parallels between the lives continue. Like Tagore, Karanth experienced acute personal sorrow—the death of a beloved child, the suffering of his wife from depression. Karanth too accepted honours from the state and, in a moment of principled anger, returned them. Tagore gave back his knighthood after the massacre at Jallianawala Bagh. Fifty-six years later, Karanth returned his Padma Bhushan in protest against the imposition of the Emergency. As he wrote to the president of India,

> In 1922, I like many others, joined Gandhiji in the Non-Cooperation Movement in order to serve my motherland. I felt I was doing my bit in fighting for the freedom of India.
>
> We all felt happy when freedom came to India in 1947 and our land became a democracy. Its Constitution gave me joy. But it was not to last long. As years passed, the Fundamental Rights assured to the people were

removed bit by bit, through amendments, negating the assurance given by the very leaders who took oaths to maintain them . . .

Today, at the age of 74, I hang my head in shame at the turn of events. I don't believe that a single soul has a right to bypass human freedoms under any cloak.

Though for decades I have refrained from active politics, I feel impelled to protest against such indignities done to the people of India. As such, to calm my own conscience at least, I feel impelled to surrender the title to your Government.

May truth prevail over untruth.

Both Tagore and Karanth travelled widely abroad and wrote about their experiences. (One had family money and generous patrons, the other did what he could with a lean purse.) Both were always experimenting with new ideas, new careers. All their geese did not turn out swans. Where Tagore failed or exceeded himself is for the Bengalis to say. But of Karanth it can be safely said that he was a lousy painter and a worse film-maker. He made what is possibly the first Kannada feature film, in the 1930s—fortunately perhaps, the cans of film perished in a fire at the end of the shooting. Years later he made another feature. A young Kannada writer who otherwise reveres Karanth and his works told me simply that it was a 'horrible film—*horrible*'. Apparently, Karanth would shout 'action', and turn his eyes away from the shot. He would call 'stop' when he felt the dialogue had run its course.

When I first compared Tagore to Karanth, I thought I was being novel. But then H.Y. Sharada Prasad alerted me to the fact that another writer had long ago made the same claim. As it happens, this writer was a Bengali, and a rather learned one—Suniti Kumar Chatterji. However, as Sharada Prasad points out, while the two men were alike in the many-sidedness of their genius, they differed in one respect. 'There was a grandeur about both, but Tagore was the sage, a modern-day *rishi*, a man who gathered disciples around him and relished his title of Gurudev. Karanth remained a fierce individual, a lone tusker who sought no followers, built no sect or ism or institution, and spurned the role of a preceptor.'

Recalling his student years, Karanth wrote that his mind then was 'full of Swadeshi, social reform and Shantiniketan'. Where the prescribed texts in college were the works of Kipling, he chose to read Tagore instead. He wrote to C.F. Andrews, asking whether he should study in Santiniketan. Andrews encouraged him to go, but his father vetoed the idea, apparently on the grounds that Bengali Brahmins were so degraded that they even ate fish. A peculiar reason, but perhaps in the end we should be grateful that Karanth did not go to Santiniketan. For he might have fallen fatally under the spell of Tagore, to become a faithful disciple instead of what he became unaided: his own man.*

*I am grateful to my friend H. Jayadeva for his fascinating insights into Karanth's life, and for supplying me with some key quotes.

Black is Bountiful: C.L.R. James

I know a collector in Singapore who has two copies of every book he possesses. One copy is wrapped in polythene and sent down to his basement, where it lies in a sanitized and dust-free environment, away from the hand of man. The other copy is placed in his bookshelves, where it is accessible to him and to such of his friends as he can trust.

I have not this fellow's bank balance, nor the space in my home to follow a practice that is at once paranoid and practical. I keep a single copy of each book I own, except in one case, where I keep not two copies but three. One is the first edition, complete, with its original dust jacket. This I have placed on the highest shelf in my home, away from the reach of my children. I hardly get to touch it myself. The second is the first paperback printing, its soft covers concealed in the beautiful leather binding of a master craftsman from Old Delhi. This copy is for me alone; to be read, on average, once a year, every year since it first came into my hands during the World Book Fair of 1976.

The third of my copies is a recent paperback, with a lush cover designed to attract the illiterate American to its contents. This is the least valuable of the book's many editions; printed in New York, and with an introduction by a baseball critic. Still, except for the preliminary pages, the contents are as in the original, and so highly prized. This copy of mine is currently in the possession of a poet who lives in a forest clearing somewhere on the Tamil Nadu–Kerala border. When he returns it, the book shall be passed on to a scholar and cricket writer in Hyderabad who first asked me for it more than five years ago.

This most prized of my books is C.L.R. James's *Beyond a Boundary*. Born in 1901 in the Trinidadian village of Tunapuna, James was educated on the pitches of the Queens Park Oval in Port of Spain and, more formally, in the Queen's Royal College. After school he worked as a teacher and critic. In 1930 he travelled to England at the invitation of his friend Learie Constantine, then playing as a professional in the Lancashire Leagues. They lived in the little textile weaving town of Nelson; with the exception of a dustman, they were then the only black men in the place.

James had carried to England the manuscript of his first book, *The Case for West Indian Self-Government*. The book was published in 1932 by Leonard and Virginia Woolf at the Hogarth Press. The next year appeared Constantine's autobiography, *Cricket and I*, with an introduction by the prince of cricket writers, Neville Cardus.

James and Constantine forged a unique partnership, an alliance (to quote Paul Buhle) between 'the intellectual-minded athlete and the athletic intellectual'. It was Constantine who financed the printing and publication of *The Case for West Indian Self-Government*. And it was James who rewrote and put into proper shape *Cricket and I*, where Constantine explained to the British public how he became the first black cricketer to achieve a reputation outside his native land. The two books were united by a shared agenda. *The Case for West Indian Self-Government* was to have a notable impact on Caribbean nationalism, of which it was the first intellectual statement. And *Cricket and I* was, in James's words, 'the first book ever published in England by a world-famous West Indian, writing as a West Indian about people and events in the West Indies.'

In his foreword to *Cricket and I*, Neville Cardus presented a stereotypical view of cricket in the West Indies, echoes of which are still sometimes heard. He called Constantine's cricketing style 'a consequence of impulses born in the sun and influenced by an environment and way of life much more natural than ours ... His cricket is racial.' He went on to describe Constantine's strongest suit, his fielding, as 'almost primitive in [its] pouncing voracity and unconscious beauty'.

Notably, the tenor of the main text of *Cricket and I* is at odds with Cardus's preface. Constantine—or was it James?—is at pains to refute racial stereotypes. He contests the notion that blacks are 'temperamental', pointing out that they excel at boxing, a sport requiring steely nerves and great force of character. He stresses the training and thought that goes into fast bowling, a craft that blacks were to make their own. And he observes that the black Trinidadian, Joe Small, had a batting technique as orthodox as that of any English professional. Thirty years later, these themes were to be picked up and amplified by James in *Beyond a Boundary*, the first cricket book to appear under his own name.

At the time his and Constantine's first books were published, James also worked as a cricket correspondent for the *Manchester Guardian*. In the winters he studied history and Marxism. These endeavours resulted, in 1938, in the publication of *The Black Jacobins*, a brilliant analysis of a successful slave revolt that took place in Haiti at the turn of the nineteenth century. Based on years of research in the French archives, written with uncommon fluency of language, and centred around the compelling figure of the slave leader Toussaint L'Ouverture, the book became a classic of social history. The distinguished scholar of slavery Robin Blackburn has written that *The Black Jacobins* 'proved, long before the mature work of Isaac Deutscher, Christopher Hill or Edward Thompson, that a Marxist historian could make excellent use of the archives and ally biography to the understanding of wider social and political contexts.' To this judgement an Indian can only add: long before the work of the 'Subaltern Studies' historians as well. Indeed, so influential did James's book become that its title even became a separate entry in the *Penguin Dictionary of Religions*: denoting a black cult that combined political aspirations with spiritual values.

In the same year, 1938, that he published *The Black Jacobins*, James went to the United States. He spent fifteen years in that country, participating eagerly in left-wing politics of a sectarian variety, and attempting to organize the black underclass. He does not appear to have been a particularly successful organizer, while his political writings—though still quoted by some American radicals—seem to this reader to be dialectical hair-splitting of a rather unconstructive kind. Of the circles James then moved in, it was later said: one Trotskyist is a branch; two are a party; three are a split.

In 1953 James was deported from the United States for his views, but he appealed against the order. While the case was being heard he was in an internment camp on Ellis Island, working on a book on Hermann Melville, later published under the title *Mariners, Renegades, and Castaways.* James regarded Melville as 'the greatest [mind] since Shakespeare's that has ever concerned itself with literature'. The novel *Moby Dick* he read as a parable of the 'mechanization and destruction of human personality' under industrial capitalism. But he also noted Melville's celebration of the wit of ordinary sailors and renegades, whose 'unfailing humour is an assertion of life and sanity against the ever-present threat of destruction and a world in chaos'.

Although it was the middle of the Cold War, and although it was the government of the United States that had interned him, James clearly preferred America to the Soviet Union. Soviet Russia was for him the 'greatest example of barbarism that history has ever known'. While the treatment of blacks and workers in America was abysmal, the country had a faith in democracy which might one day be redeemed. That was his hope, but meanwhile James lost the case against his deportation and returned to England. Here he renewed his work in the Pan African movement, and became a mentor to the first president of Ghana, Kwame Nkrumah.

Back in England, James began watching and writing about cricket once more. He helped that other great West Indian cricketing pioneer, George Headley, put together his memoirs. In 1957 he watched the touring West Indians lose comprehensively to a strong English side. This did not excessively dishearten him. Of the West Indies batting he wrote in the Madras magazine, *Sport and Pastime*, that it

was potentially the best in the world. Of the twenty-one-year-old
Garfield Sobers he commented that he 'sees the ball earlier and plays
it later than any cricketer I have seen since Don Bradman'. The next
winter Sobers broke the world record for the most runs in a Test
innings.

II

In 1958, C.L.R. James was called back to Trinidad, to assume the
editorship of the *The Nation* newspaper. In the winter of 1959–60,
the West Indies hosted England in a five-match Test series. As the
teams went from island to island, they were followed around by a
burning controversy with regard to the home side's captaincy. The
man at the helm was F.C.M. ('Gerry') Alexander, a fine wicket-
keeper-batsman and Cambridge Blue who happened to be white-
skinned. Among the people playing under Alexander was Gary
Sobers, a better cricketer by far, and Frank Worrell, who was not only
more skilled at the game than the Cambridge man, but also possessed
a wider experience and a more subtle cricketing intelligence. The editor of *The Nation* thought this an abomination. 'The idea of Alexander
captaining a side on which Frank Worrell is playing', he wrote, 'is to
me quite revolting.' 'Man for man', insisted James, 'the West Indies
team is as good as or even better than the M.C.C. It is bad captaincy
that is causing us to be scrambling as we are doing.'

The next year the West Indies were to make a trip Down Under,
their first in ten years. Who would take them on this arduous tour?
James had no doubt that it should be Frank Worrell rather than
Alexander. 'I hereby give notice I shall not let this question rest until
it is corrected', he thundered: 'This fooling with West Indies' captaincy has gone on too long.'

The English writer Alan Ross, who was covering the tour for *The
Observer*, thought that these were the sentiments of a 'malicious xeno-
phobe'. He seems to have failed to understand the historical depth of
resentment that underlay them, the accumulated anger at people like

Constantine and Headley and Weekes having to play under cricketers who were manifestly inferior to them but had a lighter skin.

In the event, Worrell was appointed captain of the side to tour the West Indies. But James's joy was tempered somewhat by a letter he received from the respected cricket critic John Arlott. The letter, posted on 7 December 1960, gently informed James that the firm of British publishers whom Arlott advised could not see their way to publishing his book *Who Only Cricket Knows*. This—and I speak as one who has received many such—was a typical publisher's letter of rejection, poison delivered in sugar coating. It was a 'very good book indeed', wrote Arlott, but 'cricket book sales—apart from star reminiscences and the occasional Neville Cardus—are struggling nowadays . . .'. The letter ended with a piece of advice intended to console but designed only to hurt: 'I wonder if printed and published in the West Indies it might be a worthwhile proposition.'

James was by now, as he put it, 'hardened by rejection'. However, two days after John Arlott wrote to him the first Test began in Brisbane. This was marked by thrilling cricket and ended in a tie. The other matches were equally compelling, and the series is still regarded as perhaps the most exciting in cricket history. The veteran Australian writer Jack Fingleton, to whom James had sent a draft of his manuscript, wrote to him—'you will be able to now add a final chapter that I think will round it off—the classical success of Frank Worrell, not only as a captain and a team man, but as a diplomat.'

The chapter was added, the title changed, and in 1963 Hutchinson of London published C.L.R. James's *Beyond a Boundary*. An early reviewer, in *The Observer*, was Alan Ross, he who had not seen the point of James's campaign to have Worrell chosen cricket captain of the West Indies. Ross now generously remarked that *Beyond a Boundary*'s 'range exceeds that of most books on sport'. Here, for the first time, had a writer 'established cricket in its proper visual, as well as literary context.' Filled with 'incidental pleasures and fascinating insights', this was 'a remarkable book, though one marred here and there by a disfiguring militancy'.

The review in the *Sunday Times* was written by Ross's own mentor, R.C. Robertson-Glasgow. He too found the writer's left-wing views sometimes hard to stomach: 'as for Mr James's excursions into politics, I see his points; but I prefer his cricket.' Once it came to the game, these British liberals set aside ideological differences. Robertson-Glasgow thus speaks of James as 'a cricket writer of distinction and conscience', his work marked by 'strong observation, loving memory and a dignity that never swells into pomposity.' All in all, he wrote in conclusion, 'this book is as individual as some national drink; or as the batting of Constantine.'

Perhaps the most generous judgement, however, was that of John Arlott. When he first read it he thought it wouldn't sell; but when he read it again, after its publication, he wrote in *The Cricketer* that 'in the intellectual sense, it is quite the "biggest" book about cricket or, probably, any other game, ever written.' This would have pleased James, but not necessarily surprised him. For he knew all along the extent of his achievement. When, in 1957, some young colleagues asked to read an early draft, he answered: 'I defy [you] to read those first three chapters without at a certain stage being moved to tears.' Or, as he put it while presenting the published book to the American Marxist Martin Glaberman, 'I cannot prevent myself from saying that within these covers, there is *everything.*'

James had been working on *Beyond a Boundary* all his life, but it was good that its eventual publication was delayed. For it came out in the summer of 1963, and was thus read and discussed in England while Frank Worrell's team were consistently and stylishly outplaying the home side in the Tests of that year. As the English cricket writer Michael Parkinson wrote, 'there have been better teams (not many, and not much better) but there has been no more significant and influential a team in the recent history of the game than Worrell's West Indians.' In the winter of 1960–1 they 'gave a life-saving boost to Australian cricket'. Down Under, Worrell's team 'lost the series but started the renaissance.' Now, in England in 1963, 'they came like crusaders to the country to find the English game in a coma. It

was over-polite, over-coached, dying on its well-bred feet.' For English cricket, remarked Parkinson, 'the West Indians were a necessary
and long-overdue purgative. They gave a new dimension to the game,
put a bomb in the Long Room, peeled the skin from an audience long
blinded by boredom.'

Such was the quality of cricket played in the summer that *Beyond
a Boundary* was published. With justifiable pride, the author wrote
to the West Indian manager that 'as I see the book it is 12th-man on
your side.'

III

In 1963, the same year that *Beyond a Boundary* was published in
London, an American publisher reissued *The Black Jacobins*. The
author had added an epilogue entitled 'From Toussaint L'Ouverture
to Fidel Castro'. The Cuban Revolution was but four years old, and
its leader carried with him the energy and authenticity of youth. (In
1963 Castro was the boy who stood up to the Yankee bully; it would
be years before he would be revealed as just another Latin American
dictator.) James's own Trinidad had recently achieved independence,
and he saw Fidel's revolution and the emancipation of the British
colonies as harbingers of a coming age of freedom for the Caribbean.

In this hopeful future writers would walk alongside political leaders. The West Indian national identity, suggested James, was to be
found in the novels of Vic Reid, George Lamming, and Wilson Harris, in the poetry of Derek Walcott and Aime Césaire, and in the
multi-genred work of V.S. Naipaul. These writers 'have discovered
the West Indies and West Indians, a people of the middle of our dis-
turbed century, concerned with the discovery of themselves, determined to discover themselves, but without hatred and malice against
the foreigner, even the bitter imperialist past.' James remarked of
Naipaul's early masterpiece, *A House for Mr Biswas*, that in its pages
'the East Indian has become as West Indian as all the other expatri-
ates.'

As it happened, Naipaul was one of the early reviewers of *Beyond a Boundary*. Writing in *Encounter* magazine, he celebrated the 'originality and rightness of Mr James's book', its deft handling of social history and its suggestive linking of cricket with political developments. Like Nirad Chaudhuri's autobiography, James's work was 'part of the cultural boomerang from the former colonies, delayed and still imperfectly understood.' 'Let us rejoice over what he has given us', said Naipaul, for '*Beyond a Boundary* is one of the finest and most finished books to come out of the West Indies, important to England, important to the West Indies. It has a further value: it gives a base and solidity to West Indian literary endeavour.'

Twenty years later, the first American edition of *Beyond a Boundary* was reviewed in *The New York Times* by a man with whom Naipaul has sometimes been compared (and contrasted), Derek Walcott. (This, by the way, seems to be a double first for James: his book may be the only cricket book ever to be reviewed in America's pre-eminent newspaper, and also the only cricket book to be publicly praised by two future Nobel laureates.) One would like to reproduce the appreciation in its entirety but, like the others, one has to make do with meagre excerpts. Walcott called it 'a noble book about poor, beautifully built, but socially desperate men'. He particularly drew attention to the richness of the historical and cultural analysis. *Beyond the Boundary*, wrote the poet, is 'a book whose light is as clear as a summer's game.' It was a book 'every writer should read', for within it was 'the history of a colonial epoch: its rigours, its deprivations, and its pride.'

As I have suggested, *Beyond a Boundary* was splendidly timed, its publication coinciding with a successful tour of England by a West Indian cricket side led by Frank Worrell, the first black man appointed to the post. Notably, James and Naipaul watched the Edgbaston and Lord's Tests together. At the time, Naipaul was content to be counted as part of a *West* Indian community of writers, able to see himself with James and Harris and Walcott as constituting the 'cultural boomerang from the former colonies'.

Years later, James's devoted assistant, Anna Grimshaw, brought out a collection of his essays on cricket. This book also printed letters written by the sage to such well-known cricket writers as Jack Fingleton, John Arlott, and Rowland Bowen. Also published here are some letters from James to Naipaul. They deal, for the most part, with *Beyond a Boundary*. But one letter of September 1963 strays into the wider domain of cultural studies. James had been reading Naipaul's periodical essays on India, anticipations of what was to become *An Area of Darkness*. These essays, said the older man, are 'very fine'. But, he added, 'effective as we are in stripping the wrappings from the underdeveloped countries, we will be more effective if . . . we are ready to strip or have already stripped the wrappings from Western civilization itself.' 'I believe', insisted James, that 'we have an immense amount to say about Western civilization which we more than all other writers from the underdeveloped peoples can say. We not only open ourselves *but we open them up too.*'

James is here speaking, decades before such talk became fashionable, of the importance of a non-Western understanding of the West. Once, white people wrote with confidence of what brown and black people were all about. Later, a generation of brown and black scholars wrote about their own societies, in the process challenging or upturning analyses originating in the metropolis. But as early as 1963 James looked forward to a third stage, where writers from the former colonies would be able to speak with insight and authority about their former masters.

That is the general import of these remarks, but they also carry a specific charge, directed at the letter's recipient. You, says James to Naipaul, you with your special gifts of listening and interpretation, with your sophisticated understanding of culture and history: *you* must now turn your attention to a critical study of the West. This was a piece of advice that Naipaul chose to disregard. Having documented his distaste for India, he went on to write about Africa and Islam, in books marked by a close attention to detail and an immaculate prose style, but disfigured by a sometimes unreasoning prejudice towards their subjects. Meanwhile, the 'West' remains a part of the world that has escaped his sceptical and questioning eye.

In the early 1960s V.S. Naipaul and C.L.R. James were friendly acquaintances; they wrote to one another, and they watched cricket matches together. Later they drew apart, as one man stayed where he was, politically speaking, whereas the other man moved steadily towards the right. James died in 1989; five years later, he reappeared in fictional disguise as the character Lebrun in Naipaul's book *A Way in the World.* This is a profoundly unsympathetic portrait, a post-Cold War reviling of the left-wing thinker as an admirer of Stalin, a supporter of East Germany and, from his safe haven in the West, an amoral instigator of the guileless young. Naipaul has since admitted to Faroukh Dhondy that Lebrun was in part modelled on James. As Dhondy points out, James was actually a bitter opponent of Stalin and the regimes he created in Eastern Europe. Novelists are free, of course, to take characters out of the real world and embellish them any way they like. What I find unsettling is that Naipaul waited until James died before casting him in one of his books. This shows spite as well as a certain cowardice—to caricature a man only after making sure that he is not there to answer back.

A clue to the changing nature of Naipaul's relationship to James can be found in an essay by Derek Walcott written in 1987, before either Walcott or Naipaul had been dignified by the Nobel prize. Walcott remarks here that the 'myth of Naipaul as a phenomenon, as a singular contradictory genius who survived the cane fields and the bush at great cost, has long been a farce.' He provides a list of creative artists from the West Indies: historians like C.L.R. James, novelists like Lamming, Harris, Samuel Selvon, Jean Rhys, and Jamaica Kincaid, poets, short story writers and 'a few hundred calypsonians' of the quality of Bob Marley and Lord Kitchener. But Naipaul, says Walcott, must pretend these people never existed, for 'how weak [his] struggle would seem if it were communal; if his dedication was seen to be shared; if what he felt in his youth was held to be felt in common by thousands of young . . . writers from all the former provinces of the empire . . .'.

Till the early 1960s Naipaul saw himself as West Indian. The islands had provided the character and context for his first, marvellously evocative works of fiction. Nor, as his review of *Beyond a Boundary* demonstrates, did he feel uncomfortable with being seen as contributing to a general renaissance of Caribbean writing. But as time went on he recast himself as the lonely exception, the self-aware and superior man who alone saw through the horrors of life in the Third World. In this process of distancing he had necessarily to dump C.L.R. James, as a friend, and then dump upon C.L.R. James in his fiction. His treatment of James is of a piece with his treatment of the Caribbean, the homeland he chose not to mention in his statement accepting the Nobel prize—an unhappy manifestation of what Derek Walcott once called 'the peevish sixth-grader still contained in an almost great writer'.

IV

As a peripatetic revolutionary who worked on three continents, C.L.R. James can be compared only to Ho Chi Minh and our own M.N. Roy. His work and his life took in most of the twentieth century. His interests were staggeringly wide: from sport to literature, from the civil rights struggle to world revolution. Both Paul Robeson and E.P. Thompson, plus plenty of other leftist icons, were proud to be called his friends. Because of his writings on cricket he was sometimes called the 'Black Cardus' (although we might argue that Cardus should instead be called the 'White James'); because of his work in political theory and philosophy he was sometimes called the 'Black Plato'.

James was in many ways a classical Marxist who admired Western civilization while attacking its ugly manifestations in the colonies. He believed that the West Indies were luckier than, say, India, in that it

was unburdened by an ancient past. (Like Marx himself, James seemed to regard tradition as a dead weight on the brain of the living.) His
life's mission might be defined as the relocation, outside the West, of
all that is valuable in Western culture. In a moving address to the
people of the West Indies, James hailed them as 'a strange, a unique
combination of the greatest driving force in the world today, the
underdeveloped [and] formally colonial coloured peoples, and more
than any of them, by education, way of life and language . . . completely a part of Western civilization.'

However fierce and enduring his support for black nationalism,
James was a committed anti-racist. He would have deplored the claim
of the former West Indian captain, Viv Richards, that only men of
African descent had contributed to cricket in the Caribbean. James
handsomely acknowledged the contributions of white cricketers such
as George Challenor and H.B.G. Austin, and of players of Indian extraction such as Sonny Ramadhin and Rohan Kanhai. Kanhai's in-
ventive strokeplay he saw as a magnificent example of the West Indian
quest for national significance. As he wrote, the little Guyanese's bats-
manship had even 'found its way into regions Bradman never knew.'

James spent his last days in a tiny flat in Brixton, still listened to
by men and women of the left. By all accounts he was a compelling
speaker, whether to an audience of one or a hundred. Speaking as a
fellow cricket writer, John Arlott said that as 'a conversationalist he
was a delight, his long, sensitive fingers combining with the restful
tone of his voice to produce an almost hypnotic effect'. Speaking as
a fellow Marxist historian, Robin Blackburn remembered that 'James
was an enthralling conversationalist and lecturer. Standing 6ft 2in he
was a commanding figure, with his white hair, slender build and lilt-
ing voice. Wagging his finger he would gently reprove the younger
generation for 'whoring after fashionable enthusiasms or forgetting
the importance of culture to the class struggle.' A third obituarist,
Clayton Goodwin, suggested that James's 'soft voice and manner of
bringing his tapering fingers together [was] reminiscent in some ways
of Mahatma Gandhi . . .'.

This last is an intriguing comparison. I guess in courtesy of manner and gentleness of disposition James was akin to the Indian Mahatma. Both liked playing the role of guru. Both were unswerving in their opposition to all forms of colonialism and imperialism. Still, their philosophical outlooks were fundamentally different. As a good Marxist, James believed in an always imminent millennium (in 1988–9, as he lay dying in Brixton, he thought he saw capitalism collapsing all around him). His utopianism and disregard for tradition is at odds with Gandhism. Again, unlike classical Marxism, Gandhism is painfully aware of human fallibility, and sceptical of utopias built in the name of science or socialism.

Perhaps James's political life will come to be seen, like Marxism itself, as a failure. What then of his work as a writer? He wrote a great deal, not all of it of lasting value. He wasted much time, and ink, on Marxist polemics, writing essays with titles such as 'Dialectical Materialism and the Future of Humanity' and 'The Revolution Abandoned': essays that few people read when they first appeared and no one reads anymore. But he did publish three works of lasting importance: *The Black Jacobins*, that massively researched and groundbreaking work of social history; *Mariners, Castaways and Renegades*, his powerful and original work of literary criticism; and *Beyond a Boundary*, which, forty years after its first publication, still is what John Arlott claimed it to be, 'the "biggest" book about cricket or, probably, any other game, ever written.'

Beyond a Boundary is a work of history, a magisterial analysis of the role played by sport in the making of the modern world. It is also anthropology, a suggestive exploration of the impact of colour and class on the cricket field. It is comparative sociology, a framing of the West Indian experience in the light of Victorian England and the ancient Greeks. It is autobiography, an account of one man's lifelong engagement with the game of cricket. And it is literature, a piece of writing crafted with care and love, a work that captures with subtlety all the moods of the human experience: happiness, humour, triumph, despair and tragedy.

Like no other work I know, *Beyond a Boundary* beautifully brings together these different genres of literature and scholarship. I have read and re-read it for its evocative portraits of West Indian cricketers, the immortals such as Headley and Constantine and the now-forgotten local heroes such as George John and Wilton St Hill. I have read it for its account of colonial cricket clubs obsessed with shades of white and black, for its analysis (still unequalled by any British writer) of what W.G. Grace meant to his age, for its account of the Worrell campaign, and—not least—for its fine technical understanding of the game, its perfectly executed cameos of strokeful innings and hostile bowling spells.

Despite its periodic reprinting in the West, *Beyond a Boundary* remains a book difficult to get hold of. Not many copies, for good reason, get into the second-hand shops Who, having got one, would ever want to dispose of it? The reader in search of a copy to own might try his luck on the net. As for the reader who simply wants to *read* the book, my third copy is on offer: except that the first available slot on the waiting list is number one hundred and fifty-five.

The Gentleman Scholar:
Sujit Mukherjee

S ujit Mukherjee was learned without being showy, good without being sanctimonious, witty without being malicious, and a patriot without being xenophobic. Among his contributions to literature are the finest books ever written on cricket by an Indian, some pioneering translations, and an authoritative study of novels by Englishmen which took India as their theme. Other contributions were less direct: through the generations of students he taught at Patna and Poona universities, and the many interesting and unusual books he brought to birth while working as chief publisher at Orient Longman.

I used to say of Sujit Mukherjee that he was the only Bengali I knew who could laugh at Bengalis. Like many others of his ilk, he read *Desh* regularly and with attention. Yet he was always amused by the magazine's obsession with Bengal's alleged victimization by the rest of India, and especially by Delhi. He claimed that once every year *Desh* ran a cover story or at least a major article with the title: '*Aar koto din ei anyayi . . .*' (For how much longer this injustice . . .) The headline was portentous; but the contents of the article usually rather trivial, complaining that a Bengali cricketer had not been chosen for the Indian test team or that a Bengali writer had been overlooked (yet again!) for some literary award.

Sujit Mukherjee had numerous friends and admirers but, so far as I know, no disciples. He inspired affection and respect rather than deference. He befriended the young and, more unusually, would listen to them. (Despite the nearly thirty years that separated us I never felt obliged to call him 'Sujit-da'.) In a culture riven by hierarchies of all kinds, Sujit scarcely cared about the age, gender, class or status of the individual he happened to be speaking to. Nor of his place of origin, either. I have hardly met a less parochial Bengali, or a Bengali more curious about or more widely travelled in other parts of India, or a Bengali whose best friends were more likely to be from Cuttack or Bangalore rather than from Calcutta.

Sujit also spoke Hindi better than any other Bengali of my acquaintance. This came from being born and raised in Patna, and from intensive exposure to its fields and streets. Meanwhile, at home, he had learnt and refined the use of his native tongue. This youthful multilingualism nurtured a lifelong interest in translation: in rendering novels and stories from one language to another (as he did with Tagore), and in the theory and practice of translation (as in *Translation as Discovery*, a precocious collection of essays he published on a now fashionable subject). While at Orient Longman, Sujit also presided over a programme of translations of novels and stories from Indian languages. Among the works he helped commission were a translation of Moti Nandy's *Striker/Stopper*, and *Poisoned Bread*, a wide-ranging and still unequalled anthology of Marathi Dalit literature.

Sujit Mukherjee's first book was based on his doctoral dissertation. Called *A Passage to America*, this is an elegantly written account of Tagore's reception in the land of hope and glory. Using local newspapers, Sujit tracked the poet's journeys through small- and big-town America, chronicling with care and wit the mixed reactions Tagore evoked: from open wonder to sheer disgust. *A Passage to America* is an exemplary work of literary history, as is a later book, *Forster and Further*, which treats giants like Kipling and Orwell as well as long forgotten novelists with equal felicity. A literary scholar I respect once

told me that *Forster and Further* was worth a whole shelf of trendy
works of poststructuralist criticism.

Nowadays, professors of English are among those who most abuse
the language. The turgidity of their prose is notorious. As one critic
sardonically put it, their dollar salaries rise in proportion with the
obscurity of their work. Sujit Mukherjee's first language was Bangla,
but he wrote English like a master. To sample his style, consider this
first sentence of a chapter on shikar literature called 'Slouching from
Kumaon':

> Those of us who are old enough to have seen that Stewart Granger film
> entitled 'Harry Black and the Tiger' were treated to all the essential in-
> gredients of a typical tiger-shoot in Anglo-India—blazing sun and tall
> grass, sunburned Englishman and his trusty rifle, a beautiful but unsat-
> isfied woman somewhere in the background, the 'native' tracker and his
> mysterious intention (a role played to perfection by I.S. Johar), finally the
> great black-and-yellow beast leaping.

One literary critic wrote of Sujit Mukherjee that he was 'a sure
contender for the best Indian cricket-writer slot.' As a young man
Mukherjee represented Bihar in the Ranji Trophy, batting doggedly
down the middle order and bowling a handy medium pace besides.
From an early age he also read extensively in the literature of cricket.
This mix of learning and experience informs the five books he wrote
about the game. The best of these are the first, *The Romance of Indian
Cricket* (1968), and the last, *Autobiography of an Unknown Cricketer* (1994). *Romance* was a loving evocation of the players he had
grown up watching and revering: Mankad, Merchant, Amarnath,
C.K. Nayudu and the like. *Autobiography* presented sepia-toned
memories of cricket in places as far apart—spatially as well as culturally—as Bihar and the East Coast of North America. Yet, as M.J.
Akbar observed, Sujit's autobiography was not about cricket alone: 'it
is about an education, a lifestyle, a state of mind, a moment of history
and, since the years bridge the transfer of power, a shift of mood.'

A selection of Sujit Mukherjee's writings on the game is contained in the recently published *An Indian Cricket Century*. This includes, among much else, superb portraits of Amar Singh and Nissar, Sunil Gavaskar and Gundappa Viswanath, and Imran Khan. Also included is an essay called 'Cricket in the Mother Tongue', on the linguistic indigenization of the game in India. This speculates that soon there might be a flourishing new field of scholarship on 'The Teaching of Cricket in a Foreign Language', with solemn professors churning out theses with titles like, 'The effect of non-aspirated consonants on the off-drive of left-handed batsmen'. In the same essay, he also pointed out that the fact that the Indian Test team was not monolingual was richly productive of dissension:

> Thus, it was hypothetically possible during our last (1974) tour of England for Bedi and Madan Lal to say uncomplimentary things about Vishwanath's batting form to his face without poor Vishy understanding a word of what the other two were saying. Such a situation would not be possible in unilingual sides like the Australian or the English or the West Indies.

II

I first met Sujit Mukherjee more than twenty years ago, in a large, airy hall in New Delhi's Pragati Maidan. The Third World Book Fair was on, and he was presiding over the Orient Longman exhibition. I was introduced to him by his daughter, who went to the same college as I, and knew of my passion for cricket. I had already read—and re-read—Mukherjee's books. So I listened as he spoke, of the curious fact that the two best books on Indian cricket had been written by Australians—E.L. Docker's *History of Indian Cricket* and Richard Cashman's *Patrons, Players and the Crowd*. (These are indeed good books, but so were his own. His modesty would not permit him from mentioning, either, that he was instrumental in the publication of Cashman's work.)

Later that winter we watched, together, a day or two of an absorbing Ranji Trophy semi-final. Delhi were playing Karnataka, at the Ferozeshah Kotla. After the home side were dismissed for a score in the region of 300, the match really depended on how many G.R. Viswanath would get. Delhi's hopes rested on the great Bishan Bedi getting him out early. This did not happen, but when Vishy had proceeded in silken fashion to 70 not out Bedi took the new ball, in a last, desperate throw of the dice. In Mohinder Amarnath's first over, Vishy played his trademark square cut, for four. Mohinder now bowled an inswinger fuller in length, but the batsman pivoted, opened up and stroked the ball past mid on. 'Hazare!', exulted Sujit Mukherjee, 'only Hazare could play the on drive like that.'

While a student in Delhi, I cultivated Mukherjee for his range of cricketing reference and his ability to link the past with the present. As I have said, he had other work outside cricket, so when he was asked to revise and update *Playing for India* he suggested that I help him. I agreed, but shortly thereafter went away to Calcutta to do a PhD. In that city I became, inevitably, a Marxist, and gave up my interest in cricket. A decade later I returned to a job in Delhi. Mukherjee lived in the same town, but I was too ashamed to get in touch. He heard of this and sent a message through a mutual friend, the writer Mukul Kesavan. 'Tell him I have revised the book myself', ran the message. 'He has no further reason to feel guilty. Give him a kick on the butt, and ask him to come and see me.'

I called, and went over. By now I had been abandoned by the Marxists, and returned to cricket. I now lived just a sharp cover point's throw away from Sujit' house, and thus partook of many *addas* hosted by him and his wife Meenakshi. Meenakshi is a well-known teacher and scholar herself, a pioneer in the study of the Indian novel and an authority on Jane Austen. Like her husband, she has much charm and no malice. In those *addas* at Hauz Khas we spoke, of course, of cricket, but also of literature, history, and Marxism. In the Mukherjees' home I met a range of unusual people, including Sujit's own regular whisky buddies, the Hindi novelist Rajendra Yadav and the Oriya playwright J.P. Das.

One evening, when I went over to Hauz Khas, Sujit was alone. Meenakshi was out of town, and so were J.P. Das and Rajendra Yadav. We talked while Sujit poured himself a drink—I am a tetotaller—and then another. Suddenly, in the middle of his third whisky he asked me, in Hindi, '*Kya tum off-spinner thé?*' Yes, I answered, I did indeed bowl off-breaks. '*Tab ham tumko aisé*'—this said with a flick of the wrists and with a long stress on the first syllable, in the Bihari style— '*hum tumko aiii-se mid-wicket ke upar sé uttha deté*'—this is how I would have lofted you for six over mid-wicket. This, I think, might have been the only boastful remark I ever heard him make.

III

Sujit Mukherjee's conversation, like his prose, conveyed much learning with a lightness of touch. Our *addas*, alas, ended with my move to Bangalore from Delhi in 1995. Shortly thereafter Sujit and Meenakshi also shifted home, to Hyderabad. In these, the last years of his life, he wrote often, sometimes a teasing postcard, sometimes an expository letter six pages long. I valued all, not least those that commented on stuff that I had published in *The Hindu*. An essay on the old I.C.S. officer C.S. Venkatachar provoked this reflection: 'What a tricky time bureaucrats of his vintage must have had in passing from one set of masters to another.' Still, they 'must have found it much too easy to serve the British. It was far more difficult for Bankim [Chandra Chatterjee] and Bhudev [Mukhopadhyay] to serve the East India Company. What a pity you can't read Bangla, otherwise you could have seen their lifelong dilemma.'

As he grew older, Sujit Mukherjee was depressed by the quality of Indian cricket and more so by the quality of Indian crowds. A letter of 4 March 1999 says it all:

> India are already three down, not even 50 on the board, and somebody has thrown a plastic bottle at Wasim Akram. Why didn't the man sitting next to the thrower stop him and quickly strangle him? I see no other cure for this crowd behaviour which, alas, has travelled from Calcutta to Bangalore.

His sense of humour, however, stayed intact. When I wrote something on Chandu Borde, he recalled how, after one of Borde's hundreds against the West Indies, 'some resolutely Hindu organization in

Pune wanted to felicitate him at a public function. But on the day of the function it transpired that Borde was Christian—consequently, somebody quickly fell ill and the function was cancelled. Cancelled, not just postponed!' An essay on the election rhetoric of Narendra Modi elicited this helpful advice: 'I think you should do a series chasing the Sangh Parivar all around the country.'

Sujit Mukherjee's last letter to me was written on 6 January 2003. It was, as ever, elegantly worded as well as wise. He recalled hearing Parveen Sultana sing in Patna in 1955, this probably her first public recital. She was then a slip of a girl

> practically hiding behind other performers . . . Thereafter she put on weight, diamonds, and voice as the years went by. I heard her two or three times again in Delhi. She ended up with 'Bhawani dayani . . .'. When at the end of the first line she let go on all cylinders with 'sakala budhi giani' I used to shiver through every part of my body. I think that is what classical Indian music does—obliterates all your other perceptions for the time being. That is why it doesn't matter whether the performer is Hindu or Muslim.

When Sujit Mukherjee turned seventy, Orient Longman organized a public felicitation in Hyderabad. Among the speakers were a fellow cricket writer, a fellow translator, a fellow publisher, and a couple of old students. Also paying tribute was an old teacher, the distinguished Shakespearean scholar S. Nagarajan. Professor Nagarajan suggested that Sujit's character was best summed up by the definition of a gentleman in Cardinal Newman's *Idea of a University*. He then read out a relevant excerpt. I wish I could reproduce the excerpt here; but, since I do not have Newman's book at hand, I must make do with an anecdote that says much the same thing. It relates to Sujit's translation of *Gora*, which was commissioned for the Sahitya Akademi by its then president, U.R. Anantha Murthy. This was the first translation into English in sixty years; moreover, the translator was known to be a wise and experienced hand. When word got around of the project, other and more reputable publishers began queueing at Sujit's door. Penguin approached him; as did Oxford University Press, who were keen to use his work in their new series of Tagore translations.

Anyone with an ounce of common sense would have deserted the Sahitya Akademi. I certainly would have, had I been in his position. Indeed, I was deputed by one of these other publishers to persuade Sujit to come round. I told him the obvious: that his work would sell more, get more reviews, endure longer, and be better produced if he abandoned a dodgy and insular *sarkari* publisher for an efficient and globally oriented private one. To all my arguments and reasons Sujit said, simply, 'I have given my word to Anantha Murthy.'

In literature, as in life, success comes more easily to those willing to seize the main chance and cut the necessary corners. Those were not the ways of Sujit Mukherjee. Yet he was highly regarded in each of his chosen fields in any case. His life demonstrates that old world values are not necessarily incompatible with distinction and achievement.

Journals of Opinion

'I want the cultures of all the lands to be blown about my house as freely as possible. But I refuse to be blown off my feet by any.' These lines, attributed to Gandhi, are engraven in school and college buildings across the land. Emblematic of a once dominant (and now threatened) strand of Indian nationalism, they have recently acquired a fresh lease of life outside this country. Thus Gandhi's words have been cited in the debates on curriculum reform in the divided campuses of élite American universities. They are, it appears, an argument-clinching mantra for our multicultural times.

How many of those who quote these words here or there know how they came to be uttered? In truth, they were squeezed out of a reluctant Mahatma by Rabindranath Tagore. For Gandhi had started this particular argument as a cultural nationalist, as one who insinuated that Raja Rammohun Roy and Lokmanya Tilak were mere 'pigmies' for thinking and writing in English; and also as a political authoritarian who commanded all patriots to take up non-cooperation and a daily round at the *charkha*. Where countless others signed up, unthinkingly, Tagore opposed both the project and the ideals behind it. Underlying non-cooperation and its presumed cultural superiority, he said in the first months of 1921, was a self-destroying isolationism that, in setting India above, also set it apart from the rest of the world.

Today, at this critical moment of the world's history, cannot India rise above her limitations and offer the great ideal to the world that will work towards harmony in co-operation between the different people of the earth? . . . The idea of India is against the intense consciousness of the separateness of one's own people from others, and which inevitably leads to ceaseless conflicts. . . . Let us be rid of all false pride and rejoice at any lamp being lit at any corner of the world, knowing that it is a part of the common illumination of our house . . .'

A wounded Gandhi thereupon pointed out that

Non-co-operators worship Andrews, honour Stokes, and gave a most respectful hearing to Messrs. Wedgwood, Ben Spoor and Holford Knight at Nagpur, that Maulana Mahomed Ali accepted the invitation to tea of an English official when he invited him as a friend, that Hakim Ajmal Khan, a staunch Non-co-operator, had the portraits of Lord and Lady Hardinge unveiled in his Tibbi College and had invited his many English friends to witness the ceremony.

Personal friendship with white men and women was one defence offered by Gandhi; a second was openness to their ideas.

I hope I am as great a believer in free air as the great Poet. I do not want my house to be walled in on all sides and my windows to be stuffed. I want the cultures of all the lands to be blown about my house as freely as possible. But I refuse to be blown off my feet by any.

Of these four sentences, the last two are the ones most often cited. Occasionally, the second sentence is included to preface the third and fourth. But I cannot recall, in the dozens of times I have had the words thrown at me, a single occasion on which the critical first sentence has also been included: '*I hope I am as great a believer in free air as the great Poet.*'

Now the Gandhi–Tagore debate has the same kind of resonance and contemporaneity as the Gandhi–Ambedkar and Gandhi–Nehru debates. It was to continue through the 1920s and 1930s, kept alive by the poet's resolute opposition to the cult of the charkha and his horror at the Mahatma's characterisation of the 1934 Bihar earthquake as divine retribution for the practice of Untouchability. One telling detail about these exchanges is that while Gandhi's contributions were published in his own journal, *Young India*, Tagore's were generally printed in that sturdily non-party magazine, *Modern Review*.

Begun in 1907 by Ramananda Chatterjee, the *Modern Review* quickly emerged as a vital forum for the nationalist intelligentsia. It carried essays on politics, economics and society, but also, being run by a Bengali, poems, stories, travelogues and sketches. It was in the *Modern Review* that Radhakamal Mukerjee published his early, pioneering essays on environmental degradation in India; and it was to the *Modern Review* that Verrier Elwin sent his first reports from the Gond country. A more certain indication of the journal's stature was the publication, within its pages, of Jawaharlal Nehru's pseudonymous auto-critique ('Rashtrapati', by 'Chanakya', November 1937).

Modern Review was the stable-mate of *Prabasi*, which was published in Bengali and catered exclusively to one linguistic group. As a vehicle for bilinguals from all parts of the subcontinent *Modern Review* appeared, naturally, in English. While being broadly nationalistic it did not hold a brief for any particular political party. The first feature meant that it could act as a genuinely all-India forum; the second that it stood apart from party journals concurrently run by the Congress, the Communists, the Muslim League, the Hindu Mahasabha and the Scheduled Castes Federation. In both respects it had only one real competitor, the *Indian Social Reformer*.

The *Indian Social Reformer* was founded in Madras in 1890 by Kamakashi Natarajan, an associate of that great campaigning journalist and founder of *The Hindu*, G. Subramaniam Iyer. Natarajan quickly realized that his home town was too provincial for a paper of his kind. In 1897 he moved the journal to Bombay, a culturally catholic city and also an epicentre of social reform and political action. Unlike the *Modern Review*, the *Indian Social Reformer* was a weekly. But it shared with its eastern counterpart a willingness to create and catalyse controversy. On the burning social issues of the day (such as the Age of Consent bill) it pressed the wavering nationalist to take a progressive stance. One of its early campaigns, interestingly enough, was inspired by developments on the cricket field.

In February 1906, a representative side of the Hindus challenged the Europeans of the Bombay Presidency to a three-day match and, against all odds, defeated them. The Hindu victory owed itself in the main to the all-round performances of two brothers of the *chamaar* caste, Palwankar Baloo and Palwankar Shivram.

Born in Poona, the Palwankar brothers fought a long battle with Hindu orthodoxy. Alerted to their prodigious playing skills, the Poona Hindus included them in their team to play the annual grudge match against the all-white Poona Gymkhana. At first the Brahmins played with them but would not dine with them. Slowly, interdining was also allowed, a practice which continued when the brothers moved to Bombay to play for the representative Hindu side. They were the undoubted stars of that epic victory over the Europeans. In a low scoring match (Hindus 242 and 160 beat Europeans 194 and 102 by 106 runs) Shivram scored 34 and 16 not out and his brother 25 and 11. Baloo, bowling left-arm spin, also took eight wickets in the match.

While Ambedkar was still in school and Gandhi still in South Africa, the *Indian Social Reformer* had fought the good fight for the abolition of Untouchability. Now it opportunistically used the cricketing triumph to push forward its agenda of caste reform. 'The history of the admission of these chamar brothers in the Hindu Gymkhana', it remarked, 'is a credit to all and has done far more to liberalize the minds of thousands of young Hindus than all other attempts in other spheres'. The Hindu cricketers' admittance of the Palwankar brothers, it claimed, was a

> a landmark in the nation's emancipation from the old disuniting and de-nationalizing customs. This is a conscious voluntary change, a manly moral regulated liberty, not, as in [the] railways [where members of different castes had willy-nilly to sit with each other], a compulsory change . . . Hindu sportsmen of Poona and Bombay have shown in different degrees that, where national interest required, equal opportunity must be given to all of any caste, even though the offer of such opportunity involved the trampling of some old prejudices . . . Let the lesson learnt in sport be repeated in political, social and educational walks of life. Let all disuniting and denationalizing customs in all high, low or lowest Hindus disappear and let India cease to be the laughing-stock of the whole world.

II

I came to these journals through a personal interest in those two vast if generally incompatible subjects, Gandhi and cricket. But, of course, both the *Modern Review* and the *Indian Social Reformer* took up and publicized a wide array of issues—widow remarriage, adivasi rights, conservation of nature and natural resources, land reform. They played a stupendous part in the process of national self-awakening—more's the pity that they have not (yet) attracted their chroniclers. Significantly, the coming of political independence dealt a body blow to the two journals. For their perspective was forward-looking, the nurturing of reforming sensibilities among the men and women who would one day come to rule India. When the former freedom fighters slipped comfortably into the chairs in the secretariat, both magazines seem to have lost their bearings. It didn't help either that their founder-editors, Chatterjee and Natarajan, had died before 1947. *The Indian Social Reformer* finally ran aground in 1953, the *Modern Review* carried on twelve years longer, unread.[1]

Into the breach stepped the *Economic Weekly*, begun in 1949 by a *bhadralok* gentleman of more-than-modest means and plenty of leisure. This was Sachin Chaudhuri, who with his money and the money of his friends founded the Sameeksha Trust, which in turn floated the *Economic Weekly*. Within months the new journal had become the leading edge of critical discussion on what India should do with its hard-won independence. Its list of contributors was a veritable who's who of thinking Indians. It included socialists like Asoka Mehta, Gandhians like J.C. Kumarappa, old economists (V.K.R.V. Rao), young economists (Amartya Sen), coming sociologists (André Béteille). The topics they discussed took in the whole sweep of social life in independent India: planning, technology choice, rural development, federalism, caste, elections. If you were articulate and

[1] Honourable mention is also owed to the *Indian Review*, published by G. Natesan from Madras, and the *Hindustan Review*, which appeared from Patna. These journals also carried interesting essays and commentaries on political debates in the inter-war period, without, however, commanding the authority or influence of the *Modern Review* and the *Indian Social Reformer*.

patriotic, there was no better place than the *Economic Weekly* to subject your ideas to the cold scrutiny of the reading public. You were sure to be read, and to be disputed. For the historian of independent India, those faded pages still remain an invaluable source of the ideas and individuals that shaped the career of the nation.

In or about 1960 Krishna Raj joined the *Economic Weekly* as an assistant editor. He had been recommended to Sachin Chaudhuri by K.N. Raj, no relation, but a teacher of his at the Delhi School of Economics. When the Bengali grandee died a few years later, the editorship was briefly assumed by the economist R.K. Hazari. In 1966, however, the journal was renamed the *Economic and Political Weekly* (*EPW*) and Krishna Raj moved into the editorial chair. He stays there thirty-some years later, an outstanding and selflessly serving editor of a journal whose real worth is reflected not in its balance sheet but in the affection and love it inspires among its readers, and, beyond that, in the privileged position it commands in Indian intellectual life.

The *EPW* is a unique, threefold mix of political prejudice, dispassionate reportage, and scholarly analysis. The weekly begins with a few pages of unsigned editorial commentary, arch and acid reflections on the events of the past few days. The second part of the journal is taken up with signed reports from around the country. Here we find the 'news behind the news', so to say, stories of conflict between landlords and labourers in Bihar or of ethnic and seccesionist movements in north-east India. These reports are generally longer than what a newspaper would allow, and (but not for that reason alone) also more informative. The journal's back pages are filled each week with book reviews and two or three academic papers, soberly presented and massively footnoted. As in the 1950s, it is here that one finds the most authoritative accounts of the key debates in contemporary India. A student of the Mandal and Masjid controversies, or a future chronicler of the environmental and feminist movements, could do much worse than begin with files of the *EPW.*

For much of its existence the *EW* and the *EPW* have had as their contemporaries three other journals of opinion. *Seminar* was founded in 1959 by that public-spirited and variously talented couple, Raj and

Romesh Thapar. It is a monthly, like the old *Modern Review*, but published in the city that, after 1911, took over from Calcutta as the political capital of India. Each issue takes up a single theme, this investigated by contributors of different backgrounds and political orientations. A year after *Seminar*'s founding there appeared, for the first time, the weekly *Opinion*, printed in Bombay, edited, owned, and mostly written by the indefatigable A.D. Gorwalla, a liberal-minded scholar and ex-civil servant: above all, a steadfast servant of the people of India. Gorwalla was a man of much courage and independence of mind—he dared disagree publicly with Mahatma Gandhi and, thirty years later, with Indira Gandhi—qualities that were richly reflected in his journal. In the late 1960s, the company of exalted journals was enriched by *Frontier*, a weekly edited out of Calcutta by Samar Sen, a man of character and whimsy; and a legendary figure of the Bengali left.

These other journals were also published in English, and they all contributed worthily to the life of the nation. But it is no disrespect to their editors and contributors to say that they could not command the intellectual influence or political salience of the product of the Sameeksha Trust. There is nothing like the *EPW* in India or, indeed, anywhere else in the world. To be sure, there are other independent weeklies of opinion such as the *Nation* of New York and the *New Statesman* of London. Their pages glow with ideas and polemic, but they do not carry the *EPW*'s academic authority. Nor are they as consistently non-partisan. In fact, both have been loosely associated with political parties, the Labour Party in the case of the *New Statesman* and the Democrats in the case of the *Nation*. Other journals that come to mind are Washington's *I.F. Stone's Weekly* and *Viewpoint*, once edited by Mazhar Ali Khan from Lahore. Sadly, both are now extinct. While they lived both shared the *EPW*'s crusading spirit without matching its range of contributors or depth of analysis.

It must be admitted, however, that the anti-establishmentarianism of the *EPW* has, at times, a weary air about it. Among the journal's regular columnists are some Maoists who should have been put to grass long ago. Their idea of utopia on earth is the one proposed (and brutally implemented) by the Red Guards in China during the Cultural Revolution. In general, the *EPW* tends to give excessive space to doctrinal disputes within the left, a misallocation of scarce resources that could more fruitfully be used by the publication of additional research essays.

A German friend of mine once described the *EPW* as 'sometimes impossible, but always indispensable'. There is an austere integrity about the journal and its editor that shines out in an epoch when the business of most journalists has become business. A recent and half-hearted 're-design' has left it looking much the same as before. The type remains small, the paper is still faded, the covers wearily similar—but the contents as astonishingly diverse and unpredictable as ever.

For twenty years now the *EPW* has been the item in the post I most look forward to. I feel extraordinarily proprietorial about it—and I am not alone. Some years back the economist Dharma Kumar—a reader of and writer for the journal since its inception—wrote in annoyance that a once-liberal church was now dominated by arcane leftist jargon. This provoked a furious correspondence, pro and anti. More recently, a bunch of scholars from that last redoubt of intellectual Marxism—New Delhi's Jawaharlal Nehru University—have written in to complain that the *EPW* is getting to be dangerously liberal. These anguished and emotional letters bespeak a readership that cares, of a commitment and engagement that must be the desperate (but usually unfulfilled) desire of every journal's editor.

III

Let me, in conclusion, compare the low-circulation journals I have paid tribute to here with periodicals more widely read and more handsomely paying. Browsing through some old issues of the *Bombay Chronicle*, I came across an interesting and still relevant comment by one journalist on another. In October 1944 Frank Moraes of the *Times of India* was due to speak at the Tata Institute of Social Service on 'Journalism as a Social Service'. In his widely read 'Half-Column', carried in the *Bombay Chronicle*, D.F. Karaka remarked that 'friend Moraes is always inclined to take a kind view of things in life. I suggest, however, that to give a balanced view of journalism there should be a sequel to this lecture: "Journalism as a Racket".'

The tension between racketeering and social service exists in a good many professions that pretend to a higher calling. A politician, a lawyer, a university professor: all claim to dedicate their life to the public weal. In some cases this claim might be justified, but in other cases it serves merely as a fig leaf for personal advancement or monetary gain. There are lawyers who are moved by the call of justice, and there are lawyers whose talent lies in greasing the system. There are professors who live to seek knowledge and serve students, and there are professors whose energies are directed to building a political base, to becoming vice-chancellor, or, better still, member of the Planning Commission when their party comes to power. And there are journalists who are racketeers, and journalists who are not.

One would be hard pressed to find someone now employed in the *Times of India* qualified to speak (as Frank Moraes undoubtedly was) on journalism as a social service. While that newspaper—and others too—have succumbed to the pressures of finance and fashion, the ideals of the profession are still upheld by the odd fellow here and the odd journal there. *Opinion* passed away with A.D. Gorwalla, but *Seminar* has survived the death of the Thapars and *Frontier* the death of Samar Sen. And, still published week after week is Krishna Raj's *EPW*.

This is a role that cannot be played by newspapers. Even before Rupert Murdoch came to cast his baleful shadow over Bahadur Shah Zafar Marg, the 'premier' newspapers of India were seriously constrained by the bottomline. That is to say, they could not *afford* to print essays that are too long or too contentious. They would never carry 10,000 word accounts of the genesis of agrarian class conflict, or 5,000-word analyses of what is wrong with Indian foreign policy.

Journals like the *EPW* have acted as a moral conscience for independent India. They have consistently exposed wrongdoing, whether by the state or political parties or landlords or industrial houses; explored, in refreshing detail, the patterns and processes of social change in city and countryside; and highlighted critical issues (environmentalism, for instance) ignored by the formal political system as well as by the Establishment press. They constitute a vast and continually enriched archive of the history of independent India, an archive raided by generations of students and scholars. There will, I trust, be a history, one day, of the *Economic Weekly* and the *Economic and Political Weekly,* as indeed of their distinguished if insufficiently acknowledged predecessors, the *Modern Review* and the *Indian Social Reformer.*

Why South Asians
Don't Write Good Biographies,
and Why They Should

In contrast with the art of the novel, the art of biography remains undeveloped in South Asia. We know how to burn our dead with reverence and bury them by neglect but not how to honour or judge them. There is no obituary page in the best of our newspapers. In other cultures, the passing of a great or unusual individual is the occasion for a reflective assessment of his life and work. In India the death will be noticed as a 'news report', and left at that. Thus it was a British weekly, *The Economist*, which carried the only decent obituary of C. Subramaniam, the remarkable politician who was the architect of the Green Revolution. As for the book-length lives that do exist, these are for the most part exercises in deference, recitations of achievement with little reference to context. Indian biographers tend to be excessively respectful towards their subjects.

The Calcutta historian Rudrangshu Mukherjee points out that whereas in the West 'the second half of the twentieth century has been an era of great biographies', this has 'left Indian writers and scholars unaffected. Biography is not an art that flourishes in India despite the nation's obsession with individuals.' The record in the countries that neighbour India is not much better. The standard, or at any rate most accessible, lives of Mohammed Ali Jinnah, Zulfiqar Ali Bhutto and S.W.R.D. Bandarnaike have all been authored by Western scholars. It should be admitted that there are two outstanding exceptions: S. Gopal's life of the philosopher Sarvepalli Radhakrishnan, published in 1989 to mark the centenary of its subject's birth; and Amrit Rai's life of the novelist Munshi Prem Chand, first published in Hindi in 1962 and, twenty years later, deftly translated into English by Harish Trivedi. Both are son's books, not at all uncritical, but helped by the intimacy that comes from shared genes and the luck to have all the subject's papers in one's own attic. Both pay proper attention to the lived life but also set it in historical context. (Honourable mention is due to B.R. Nanda's political biographies of Mahatma Gandhi and Gopalkrishna Gokhale, and to Rajmohan Gandhi's books on the nationalist stalwarts C. Rajagopalachari and Vallabhbhai Patel.)

There would, however, be at most a dozen biographies written by South Asians that are both well researched as well as moderately well written. This is a meagre harvest, if one considers that biography lies at the intersection of history and literature, fields where the region has made handsome contributions. Social and economic historians from South Asia have acquired increasing visibility outside the region, particularly in the United States. And the works of South Asian novelists have been widely appreciated. Having excelled with history and fiction, why have South Asians been so laggard with biography?

To answer this question we might look no further than the region's dominant religion, Hinduism, and its dominant intellectual tradition, Marxism. Both grossly undervalue the role and status of the singular human being. For Hindus, a man just dead has already been reborn as something or someone else: why bother to recall or document the life? For Marxists, the individual life is reflective of wider historical forces: of the clash of classes or the progress of technology. Why unduly dignify the solitary man by writing about him rather than about the social changes that his life mirrors?

Admittedly, while Hindus have not written biographies as *Hindus*, there have been professedly Marxist lives of individuals. These have generally been written to advance a particular historical thesis. Isaac Deutscher's three-volume life of Trotsky was an extended essay in sectarian vindication which sought to prove that if, instead of Stalin, his hero had succeeded Lenin, the Russian Revolution would have been faithful to its original aims. E.P. Thompson's large life of William Morris was written to prove that *his* hero was a scientific socialist who believed in dialectical materialism, rather than a romantic radical with a sentimental attachment to justice and community.

Deutscher's books on Trotsky were once much praised in revolutionary circles, but no one reads them any more. And Thompson is now remembered for his books on the working class and on the history of English law, rather than for his life of Morris. When that book was first published, in 1955, its author was a card-holding member of the Communist Party of Great Britain. But when it appeared in a revised edition, twenty-two years later, Thompson had long since left the party and most of its tenets. In the foreword to the revised edition he admitted that in the original work he had 'intruded far too often upon the text with moralistic comments and pat political sentiments.' That, indeed, shall always be the case with avowedly Marxist biographies: they shall be strongly coloured by the party-political beliefs of their author.

As it happens, within South Asia Marxists have not ventured into biography at all. They have felt more comfortable writing about social aggregates: about peasants, workers, and the state, rather than about individuals. Take West Bengal, the epicentre of contemporary Marxism, and home to India's most highly regarded historians and political scientists. Bengali scholars have written insightfully about such topics as peasant protest, industrial evolution, literary history, and street culture, but not about their exemplary individuals. The most readable biographies of the icons of modern Bengal—of Rammohun Roy, of Vivekananda, of Subhas Chandra Bose, even of Tagore and Satyajit Ray—have been written by foreigners.

Whether Marxist or otherwise, Indian scholars tend to work with what the sociologist Dennis Wrong once called an 'over-socialized conception of man'. Doctoral dissertations almost never approach a problem through an individual, even when he had a fundamental influence in its articulation or resolution. Students and professors alike would choose to write on 'The Dissolution of the Princely Order' rather than on 'Vallabhbhai Patel and the Dissolution of the Princely Order'. It is striking how some of the most influential figures in modern India have yet to find their biographers. There are no books, good or bad, that one can turn to for the basic facts about such men as Sheikh Abdullah of Kashmir, Master Tara Singh of Punjab, A.N. Phizo of Nagaland and C.N. Annadurai of Tamil Nadu: men whose legacies continue to shape the politics of the land.

To religious prejudice and scholarly dogma one must add a third reason for the paucity of good biography, namely, that it is the most challenging of literary forms. As André Maurois observed many years ago, biography

> will always be a difficult form of art. We demand of it the scrupulousness of science and the enchantments of art, the perceptible truth of the novel and the learned falsehoods of history. Much prudence and tact are required to concoct this unstable mixture . . . A well-written life is a much rarer thing than a well-spent one.

The biographer must possess the instincts of a sleuth, a nose for smelling out hidden documents and a flair for persuading people to part with them. He must have the staying power of the historian, the willingness to read and take notes from millions of words written in shaky and indistinct hands and lodged in dark and distant archives. Last, but certainly not least, he must display the imaginative insights of the novelist, the ability to turn those years of source-finding and note-taking into a compelling and credible narrative.

In his 'Questions for a Biographer', the Bombay poet Ranjit Hoskote nicely captures the essence of the enterprise:

> How to phrase what must be told,
> how force the seals, twist back the locks,
> burgle the cabinet of the soul?
> How to riffle his cupboard of masks
> and then to squeeze into the damp
> between costume and true colours?

The biographer is an artist, but, as Desmond MacCarthy long ago pointed out, he is an artist *under oath*. He stays close to his sources, and while he may plausibly speculate on his subject's thoughts and moods, he cannot invent. The novelist-turned-historian is thus most likely to write good biography, as is the case with A.N. Wilson, who has written a riveting life of Tolstoy as well as biographies of C.S. Lewis and Hilaire Belloc; and more recently of Jesus and St Paul.

Wilson is British, as is my own favourite biographer, David Gilmour. Gilmour is a historian who trained at Balliol College, Oxford, under the great Richard Cobb. He is also a published novelist. Besides, he is no Little Englander. He is a cosmopolitan scholar who has worked in the Middle East and travelled extensively in Asia and southern Europe.

Gilmour has written lives of three rather dissimilar characters. He began with Giuseppe di Lampedusa, the Sicilian aristocrat who lived a life of complete obscurity, spending his days reading and, towards the end, writing. A couple of years before he died Lampedusa completed the manuscript of a novel. He couldn't find a publisher in his lifetime, but his book, *The Leopard*, posthumously won recognition as among the finest novels of the twentieth century. Based on a hoard of previously undiscovered letters and papers, Gilmour skilfully reconstructs the life of his subject, writ small against the social and political context of twentieth-century Sicily.

From Lampedusa Gilmour moved on to a man who, by contrast, always sought to live a very public life. Very early, this man acquired a reputation for insolence. As the Balliol rhyme went, 'My name is George Nathaniel Curzon/I am a most superior person/My cheek is pink, my hair is sleek/I dine at Blenheim once a week.' He seemed destined for high office and served as viceroy of India as well as a cabinet minister in several Conservative British governments. Like his close contemporary Winston Churchill, he was a prolific and best-selling author and, like Churchill again, closely connected to America (both his wives came from there). But unlike him he never became prime minister, an office that his contemporaries had always thought would be his. Curzon's was a life rich in incident and achievement as well as controversy, these captured with elegance and understanding by his biographer.

Gilmour's most recent book is *The Long Recessional*, subtitled 'The Imperial Life of Rudyard Kipling'. This looks at the poet's complicated views on empire and the encounter of races. This biography is in some ways revisionist, seeking to show that Kipling was not always the gung-ho cheerleader of imperial expansion that leftist scholars have portrayed him to be, that he had an abiding love for India and, at least, for some Indians. The 'poet of empire' was often sharply critical of British policies, while this admirer of generals and rulers refused always to accept any favours from them. His artistic integrity was uncompromising. In this, as in Gilmour's other books, the industry is massive but carried lightly. Judgement is nicely balanced with exposition, the poems and letters quoted to effect but not to excess.

My own enthusiasm for Gilmour stems perhaps from his being more than a narrowly 'literary' biographer. He probes his subject's emotions, as he must, but also displays a sharp awareness of his place and time. When writing about Curzon he can grasp the complex structure of colonial administration in British India, when writing about Kipling suggestively explore the ideologies of empire and the rivalries between European powers. His books combine scholarship with style, the analysis of politics and policy with the delineation of personality.

Gilmour's biographies have won many awards, but, as much as those prizes, he might cherish a line in Jan Morris's review of his Kipling book. This wise writer (and sometime biographer) termed *The Long Recessional* a 'fine, fair and generous work', where, 'in hundreds of pages of dense narrative, there is never a flaccid line, and never a hasty judgement.' Gilmour's other works are marked likewise by solid research and a fine style, but also by balance and proportion. He knows what to say and how to say it, but also what to leave out. This sense of balance is indirectly manifest in the length of his various works. The life of Lampedusa, a fascinating but ultimately marginal figure, extends to 223 pages: the life of Curzon, a more important man by far, runs to 684 pages, including notes and index. Kipling is perhaps as or more important than Curzon, but unlike him has already been much biographized. So Gilmour's book on the poet sought not to be definitive, but, rather, to focus on a particular if contentious aspect of his life and legacy. From this perspective its length, 351 pages, seems about right.

'You have to be a genius to sustain a biography of 900 pages', wrote A.J.P. Taylor once. I would add: to justify that length either the biographer or his subject have to be geniuses, and preferably both. Some Indians have not heeded Taylor's warning: nor have many Americans. In the USA there is in fact a long tradition of the multi-volumed life, going back at least to Carl Sandburg's six-volume study of Abraham Lincoln. American biographers tend to throw everything into their books. The urge for comprehensiveness keeps historical judgement in abeyance. Their books are often too long and sometimes too solemn. Paradigmatic here is Robert Caro's life of Lyndon Johnson; three published volumes thus far, all of two thousand pages, and we still haven't got to Johnson's presidential years.

There is no question in my mind that the British make the best biographers. One could add, to the names of A.N. Wilson and David Gilmour, those of Richard Holmes (biographer of Shelley and Coleridge, and also a superb essayist on the art and technique of biography); Michael Holroyd (biographer of Lytton Strachey and George Bernard Shaw); Victoria Glendenning (biographer of Anthony Trollope and Vita Sackville-West); Claire Tomalin (whose subjects have included Samuel Pepys and Jane Austen); Francis Wheen (author of a wonderfully entertaining life of Karl Marx); Hilary Spurling (author of lives of Matisse and Paul Scott), Ray Monk (biographer of Wittgenstein and Bertrand Russell); and Andrew Motion (biographer of Keats and Philip Larkin). Intriguingly, most of these biographers are freelance scholars without a university position. This may not be an accident: it might have helped them escape the tyranny of academic fashion, which typically scorns biography and, where it deigns to allow it, subjects it to the canon of political correctness—

the lives ultimately judged with regard to how they retard or further the biographer's own chosen cause.

Now, fifty-six years after the British departed these shores, South Asian scholars look to the universities of North America for inspiration. Anglophilism is *passé*. Young Indians and Pakistanis are hardly likely to read the British writers I have here praised, their ignorance of these biographers and this biographical tradition constituting another hurdle to the writing of good biography. And there are other hurdles, too. For one thing, if the USA is going to be the main area of inspiration, biographies will tend towards unreadable jargon if written by academics and towards a verbose length if by journalists or writers. For another, South Asians are very careless about keeping letters, records, and historical memorabilia in general. For a third, they are absurdly oversensitive about their heroes. In this age of identity politics, which non-Dalit would dare write a dispassionate study of the extraordinary Dalit leader B.R. Ambedkar? And which Delhi-based publisher, dependent like others of his ilk on government patronage, would willingly publish a critical biography of the leading 'Hindutva' ideologue M.S. Golwalkar? Lives of political icons, be they of the left or of the right, risk being suppressed or burnt if they are too candid or too argumentative.

When they do venture into biography, South Asians are generally too genteel and fastidious to attempt burgling the souls of their subjects. We somehow don't know how to deal with tension and contradiction, with our subjects saying one thing or meaning another, with them showing a healthy regard for their self-interest, or (especially) with their falling in love or failing in their careers. In most cases, reverence and respect comfortably supersede analysis and understanding.

Hinduism, Marxism, Anglophobia, the indifference to record keeping, the fear of giving offence: to these impediments add the complexity of the craft, its unique combination of art, industry, scholarship, and literature. Still, the poverty of biographical writing in South Asia must be reckoned a pity. For the region is hardly lacking in men and women of character and interest. In a collection of his essays Edward Said has written feelingly of how his friend Eqbal Ahmed took him to meet the legendary Urdu poet Faiz Ahmed Faiz. In a Beirut café, Eqbal and Said listened as Faiz spoke, mournfully at first—he was in enforced exile—but then with passion, as he moved from politics to poetry. Not long after I read Said's piece I came across a lovely essay published many years ago by the veteran human rights activist of Delhi, R.M. Pal. This was a tribute to the social worker Akhtar Hameed Khan, at that time (the 1980s) being persecuted by the Pakistan government. Pal wrote of his own early encounters with Khan, in Comilla (in present-day Bangladesh), where he was pioneering a new approach to rural development. This was the second of Khan's careers: the first had been in the Indian Civil Service and the third in the slums of Karachi, where he inspired the admirable experiment in community living known as the Orangi Project.

In an intellectually alert and sensitive world, Edward Said's cameo on Faiz Ahmad Faiz and R.M. Pal's on Akhtar Hameed Khan would inspire younger scholars to research and write full-fledged biographies. Certainly, both Faiz and Khan figure at the top of my personal wish-list of South Asians whose lives need to be more fully documented. This list of mine does not include figures of high political authority—the Nehrus and the Bhuttos—who have been and will be written about anyway. Nor does it include the truly 'subaltern'—the workers and peasants who do not usually leave a trail of personal papers and thus, regrettably, have to be usually written about in the aggregate. Rather, my list privileges the fascinating intermediary figures: the men and women in the middle, the scholars and activists whose lives are noteworthy in themselves *and* who provide a window into the great social and political issues of our time.

Thus, a writer interested in the tortured history of Tamil–Sinhala relations in contemporary Sri Lanka might take as his theme the life and endeavours of the Colombo lawyer, scholar and statesman Neelan Tiruchelvam, killed by a Tamil suicide bomber for seeking to make peace with the 'enemy'. A historian of Indian science and conservation could do worse than approach the topic through the remarkable self-trained ornithologist Sálim Ali. A feminist might choose as her subject Mira Behn (Madeline Slade), the daughter of an English admiral who went to jail with Gandhi, fell in and out of love with a Sikh revolutionary, did pioneering environmental work in the Himalaya and ended her days in the Vienna woods listening to Beethoven. A like-minded Bengali could tell the tale of Nirad C. Chaudhuri, the unknown Indian who became a well-known Englishman. A young and radical scholar might write in some depth of Gadar, the folk poet and singer whose career has been so deeply interwoven with the bloody politics of his native Andhra Pradesh. In each case the life would be richly illuminative of the times. In any case the best days of South Asian biography lie ahead of us.

Postscript: After the first publication of this essay, a friend sent me the script of a talk on All India Radio in 1963 by M.M. Bhalla, then head of the English department at St Stephen's College, Delhi. The talk was titled 'This Barren Field' and it lamented the poverty of biographical writing in India. Professor Bhalla felt that this was due in part to a lack of curiosity about the individual person, about 'his private self rather than his formal public conduct'. He also related the absence of good biography to the absence of a historical sensibility among the mass of Indians. As he put it, 'our anti-historical consciousness has produced a vagueness of outlook, a divorce from life as it is lived, a certain kind of woolliness, a scepticism about the individual's place in society, and an uncritical mind where facts are concerned.'

This atmosphere, felt Professor Bhalla, was inhospitable both to historical learning and to biographichal writing. But he hoped that Indians would, nonetheless, 'break through our apathy to history'. 'Perhaps a philosophy of history', he wrote, 'may create the conditions for biographical writing. What we need is not a meticulous chronicle of facts but the recognition that history is a process which shapes men and which in its turn is shaped by men. Till such a time the field of biography may remain a barren field.'

In the forty years since these words were written, historical scholarship in South Asia has achieved a great deal of depth and sophistication. Yet it might, on present reckoning, perhaps take another forty years for there to be a comparable flowering of biographical writing in the subcontinent.

The Arts of Autobiography

Indo-Anglian autobiography is dominated by the triumvirate of Mohandas Gandhi, Jawaharlal Nehru, and Nirad Chaudhuri. The second was inspired by the first, the last provoked by the other two. Gandhi's experiments were first narrated in Gujarati, but it is the English version (translated by Mahadev Desai, and published almost simultaneously) that has made its mark down the ages. Nehru's autobiography was written as confirmation of his status as the likely successor to Gandhi as leader of the Indian freedom movement. Chaudhuri's autobiography was, among other things, a statement of defiance, its title a means to an ironic distancing from the books of those manifestly public and globally famous Indians.

All three works were written in middle age. Gandhi's appeared in book form when he was 59, Nehru's when he was 47, Chaudhuri's when he was 54. The autobiographer had a substantial reservoir of experience to draw upon, and more to look forward to. The books are also united by a shared tone: a curious if characteristically Indian combination of the reflective and the pedagogic. In the memoirs of both Gandhi and Nehru the reader is introduced to the making of a historically determined yet socially conscious individual. Gandhi's book is aimed in the first instance at the uncertainly patriotic Indian, whereas Nehru's reach is more international. (*My Experiments with Truth* was originally serialized in the Mahatma's own journal, *Young*

India, while *An Autobiography* was first published in London in 1936, to be read by the European torn between fascism and democratic socialism.) Gandhi's meditations are biased inwards, Nehru's outwards. Yet consider how in both works the career of the individual is so inseparably interwoven with the career of Indian nationalism.

Nirad Chaudhuri has never acknowledged that his own book was written in the shadow of those by Gandhi and Nehru. His admirers will probably reject the suggestion on the grounds that his autobiography is intensely personal (politics enters more centrally in its long delayed sequel, *Thy Hand, Great Anarch!*). But the connections are not hard to make, or to sustain. A thinker detested by Chaudhuri, Karl Marx, once wrote that 'men make their own history, but not in the circumstances of their choosing.' This could well have served as an epitaph for *The Autobiography of an Unknown Indian*, a book which shows how an individual is shaped by history yet able to (partially) transcend it. In Chaudhuri, as indeed in Gandhi and Nehru, the hope is that the reader will be inspired and educated by the experiences, errors, judgements, and actions of the autobiographer. But the teachings are addressed also to oneself. The autobiographer knows that he is not done with life yet. Might he not, in the years that remain, implement with more certainty the credo that he has so strenuously worked out?

Three books do not make a 'tradition'. One might, however, contrast these works with what I shall with more authority call the Western tradition of autobiography. The Western autobiographer rarely waits till middle age to take up his pen. *A Precocious Autobiography* is the title of a book written in the 1960s by the Russian poet Yevgeny Yevtushenko. A few years later Dom Moraes (always European by sensibility and, at the time, also British by nationality) published his memoirs, *A Son's Father*. He too was less than thirty. Long before Yevtushenko and Moraes, Robert Graves had emerged from the trenches of the First World War to write his *Goodbye to All That*.

The arrogance of these accounts is affecting. Poets, it seems, know all about life as soon as they have fought their first war or divorced their first wife. At the other pole of the Western tradition are the memoirs written in the evening of life. These latecomers are more likely to be scientific men who turn to autobiography when their real work is done. Among the great works of this type are those written by Charles Darwin, Bertrand Russell, and Benjamin Franklin.

Western autobiographies, whether precocious or ripe, tend to more closely scrutinize the self. They can be self-absorbed and simultaneously self-deprecatory. Society is generally kept at a safe distance. There is little effort to hand out lessons. By contrast, the Indian autobiographer is solemn. For all their worth, one cannot recall a witty remark or a joke well told in the autobiographies of Gandhi, Nehru and (it must be said) Chaudhuri.

II

Let me now consider a lesser trinity of Indo-Anglian autobiographies. Lesser, but not necessarily less readable.

Let me take them in order of appearance. Jim Corbett's *My India* was published in 1952, when its author was seventy-seven. The book is not so much a conventional autobiography as a collection of incidents in the life of the great hunter, and portraits of men and women he knew. It was written as Corbett prepared to migrate to Kenya which, unlike India, was then still under British rule. Before he went he left behind, in print, fragments of the land he knew and loved. Beyond its literary purpose the book aims also to pre-empt the imminent nationalist erasure of all that the white man did in, and especially for, India. Of course *My India* has many heroes, and not all of them are white. But the presentation compels one to seek out, among them, the policeman Freddie Young, for his courage, humour, and devotion to duty.

The Tribal World of Verrier Elwin: An Autobiography appeared twelve years later. When he began to write the book Elwin was sixty, and the victim already of two heart attacks. He knew he had not long to live (in fact the book was published three months after his death).

Elwin deliberately set about recording the details of his life before a biographer could. There is thus a satisfying completeness about the narrative, which runs from the cradle almost to the pyre. The focus is on his work for the tribal communities of India, among whom he lived for thirty years and of whose culture he became the foremost interpreter. People, incidents, campaigns, books and landscapes are all described with care and detail. There remains in his book a political purpose, which is very nearly the reverse of Corbett's. The shikari had sought, albeit indirectly, to memorialize the empire. The anthropologist, on the other hand, shows how it is possible to subordinate one's Englishness to the claims of Gandhian nationalism. He had even wished to call his book *Autobiography of a British-born Indian.*

Sálim Ali's *The Fall of a Sparrow* was published in 1985. He was then eighty-seven. As a 'last' work it shares some of the characteristics of the Western scientific memoir. The ornithologist knew that his days of original research had passed, much as Russell recognized, when he wrote his autobiography, that he had nothing more to offer to philosophy or social theory. The scientist could, however, recount with affection how the experiments had been conducted and the books written. *The Fall of a Sparrow* is remarkable for the absence of even a whiff of politics. Sálim Ali had lived fifty years as the subject of an alien empire and nearly forty as a citizen of a free nation. But unlike Corbett or Elwin he sought neither to apologize for the British nor to justify the Indians. His background may explain this silence. He came from one of the most distinguished of Bombay families, which had produced an early president of the Indian National Congress as well as one of the first 'native' members of the Indian Civil Service. Sálim Ali could partake without any fuss both of Indian nationalism and Western culture. Why bother to declare a preference for one or the other?

The work of Corbett, Elwin, and Ali is notable for its spotlight on aspects of Indian life otherwise neglected by historians, journalists, anthropologists, and autobiographers. For the classic opposition of literature and politics in India, as elsewhere in the modern world, is between city and village. Gandhi wished to reground Indian political life in the countryside, Nehru to bring the best of urban civilization (science, rationality, industry) to the peasant, Chaudhuri to move beyond the village to the world of ideas contained in the city. Their preoccupation with this polarity was completely reproduced by their contemporaries. One might write of the clash between the two domains, or of the exploitation of one by the other, or how each is marked by a certain set of morals, attitudes, and lifestyles. One might loudly declare a preference for one over the other. But, as with Gandhi, Nehru or Chaudhuri, one could not escape the basic opposition of city and village.

Our latter three authors, by contrast, wrote of a third India which lay beyond the first two. Thus, in his ethnographies Elwin brought to wider attention the poetry and ways of life of people separated from a Hindu civilization which noticed them only to patronize. Sálim Ali wrote more than twenty books about non-human residents of the forest landscape, birds in particular. This thematic obsession, with tribals in one case and birds in the other, also dominates their respective autobiographies. In this respect Jim Corbett's *My India* is at a slight angle to his other works. In books such as *Man-Eaters of Kumaon* and *Jungle Lore* he had written with rich insight and deep intimacy about the wild animals of the Indian forest. In the memoir the balance between man and animal is roughly even. But taking his oeuvre as a whole, one sees humans making a late and even apologetic entry.

The three works by Ali, Elwin and Corbett were all written very late in the lives of their authors. That alone distinguishes them from the holy trinity of Indo-Anglian autobiography. So, more decisively, does their style. These are works of enchantment and discovery, not personal victories disguised as political testaments. There is always an innocent wonder about these accounts. Unlike Gandhi or Chaudhuri, these men did not turn prematurely grey. One does not read their autobiographies for insights into Indian nationalism or Western civilization. The India of their books is more appealing, if sometimes slightly less worthy than the India of Gandhi and Nehru. What shines through is a love of natural beauty and cultural diversity. Also, a completely unselfconscious humility. One could read these three books and still not know for certain that Verrier Elwin was a great pioneering anthropologist, that Sálim Ali was (with the exception only of C.V. Raman) the finest scientist produced by India, that Jim Corbett was the most accurate marksman this side of the Suez.

I am fairly certain that Corbett never knew either Sálim Ali or Elwin. The latter two were closer in age, and both were connected with the cultural world of Bombay. But there is no record of their meeting. However, there was one person who had close dealings with all three—who, in fact, helped make each of them. He was their editor, R.E. Hawkins. Hawkins is explicitly acknowledged in *The Fall of a Sparrow*, as its dedicatee. He peeps in and out of *The Tribal World*, once as a caring host, again as a conscientious proof-reader. He is mentioned not at all in *My India*, although he contributed a great deal to that book as well.

After graduating from Oxford, Hawkins came to India in 1930 to teach. But the college he was to join was closed in sympathy with Gandhi's non-cooperation movement, so Hawkins went to Oxford University Press instead. For thirty years he ran OUP's India operations. As one of his successors has written, 'although the OUP had been established here in 1912, much of the credit for strengthening its foundations and making it into an enduring first-rate publishing house goes to Hawkins.'

Himself a keen naturalist, Hawkins must have met Sálim Ali through the Bombay Natural History Society. At a time when Indian ornithology was the exclusive preserve of European officials, Sálim Ali had written a new, updated account of the birds of the subcontinent. He was not white; worse, he did not even have a college degree. But his *Book of Indian Birds*, first published by the BNHS in 1941, was recognized early on as a classic. Hawkins persuaded him to shift to the OUP for his other books, which appeared at regular intervals over the next four decades. By the time Sálim Ali's last work was published,

Hawkins had retired. But its dedication acknowledged that without
him there might never have been a first.

Hawkins also had a formative role in the rise to literary stardom of
Jim Corbett. In 1943 Corbett wrote to OUP from the Kumaon hills,
offering some shikar stories for publication. The covering letter indicated that he hoped they would be read by army officers and other
outdoorsmen. The publisher had higher or, shall we say, more material ambitions. When the stories, considerably revised, were published
as *Man Eaters of Kumaon* they were read in places other than the
Saharanpur Infantry Officers Mess. The book became a worldwide
bestseller, was translated legally into a dozen languages, and illegally
into another dozen (these behind the Iron Curtain). It was even dis-
torted into a Hollywood film. Prodded by Hawkins, Corbett wrote
a very successful series of such books and, finally, the memoir *My
India*. All his books are making the OUP money still.

Hawkins and Elwin were friends long before they became publisher and author. Both lived on the margins of white society in India.
The sahibs never knew quite what to make of them. Were they, or
were they not, paid-up members of the Club? Both were attracted by
Gandhi's spiritualism but repelled sometimes by his sanctimonious-
ness. They wore khadi but also liked their whisky. Both experimented, unsuccessfully, with *brahmacharya*.

In the mid 1930s, Elwin had published four books with John Mur-
ray in London. Then came the war, and paper shortages in England.
In 1940 Hawkins adroitly asked Elwin to switch allegiance to the
OUP. For the next twenty-five years the relationship continued, to
great mutual profit. OUP was to publish all but one of Elwin's major
ethnographies and folklore collections. The bonds, both personal and
professional, were deep and lasting. Although Jonathan Cape in the
U.K. and Alfred Knopf in the U.S. both expressed an interest in publishing his autobiography, Elwin chose finally to put friendship above
pecuniary gain, staying with the OUP for his last book.

As I have said, the name of R.E. Hawkins does not appear in *My
India*. It is casually mentioned in *The Tribal World*, although one

must have access to the OUP archives in Mumbai to appreciate how much the editor contributed to the printed book. And one can be certain that if Hawkins had still been general manager of OUP, *The Fall of a Sparrow* would have been dedicated to somebody else. How different are the times we live in. No autobiography, it seems, can now go out into the world without extended and equal acknowledgement of the role played by the author's agent, partner, editor, and dog.

The Street Where You Read

Scholarly essays generally end with a solemn list of names to be thanked: teachers who showed the way, colleagues who corrected the errors, foundations who paid the bills. Altogether the loveliest acknowledgement I ever saw appeared in an essay by the anthropologist Shiv Visvanathan. This analysed the Cold War through the novels of John Le Carré and ended by thanking 'the pavement sellers of Delhi, on whose wares my article is based.'

Like Visvanathan, I have a lifelong and countrywide experience of sellers of old books. I studied in Delhi and Calcutta, visit Bombay frequently, and call Bangalore my home-town. The chaps I know best in these cities are those who sell old books. I go to them for business and for pleasure, to buy light stuff for night-time reading and to search out research materials that our libraries do not stock.

The market I have known longest is the Sunday book bazaar in Delhi. This starts from Delhi Gate, and extends on the left side of the pavement almost all the way to Jama Masjid. It begins unpromisingly, with science and medical textbooks, but as one goes along the novels and biographies make their appearance. Experience has taught me what to pass over and where to linger. There is a shop just short of Golcha Cinema which has a fine collection of old history and anthropology books. A little further, beyond the Moti Mahal restaurant, is a sour fellow who stocks illustrated works on art and nature. At the end of the street, just before the overbridge, is a stall that specializes in the spillover from the capital's libraries.

In twenty years as a workaday writer, I have published several million words, of which only about a thousand have actually helped anyone other than myself. These were contained in an article I published in a Delhi newspaper in 1992 after the city's police commissioner summarily evicted the pavement bookstalls in Daryaganj, holding them to be an encroachment on public space. Allow me to quote excerpts from what I wrote in response:

> Without holding a brief for other forms of encroachment on government land, one can only say that the Daryaganj bookshops are episodic, not permanent; that a weekly bazaar is one of the most charming and widely prevalent features of Indian life; and that in furthering the sale of old books the Daryaganj shops are a public service, rather than a nuisance . . . Should the commissioner prevail, an institution as vital to the capital's cultural life as the Siri Fort or Kamani auditoriums, will be lost forever. I shall feel the loss more keenly than most; since I was a schoolboy, a good proportion of my time, and most of my money, has been spent in second-hand book stalls.
>
> . . . [F]or many of us, the prospect of Delhi without the Daryaganj bazaar will be too painful to contemplate. As a petty and philistine exercise of power, the police commissioner's campaign can only be compared to Mrs Maneka Gandhi's equally mindless drive against performing animals and their owners. That drive was undone by the ballot box, but it is unfortunately the case that bureaucratic ordinances are usually more permanent than ministerial fiats. Perhaps the only course is to remove oneself to Bombay, Calcutta or Ahmedabad.

My essay sparked a wider campaign to save the market, into which were drawn a former cabinet secretary who wrote novels and a high policeman who wrote poems. Thankfully, the order was rescinded, and the market returned. And thankfully, too, police commissioners in other cities of India have not sought to emulate that act of (luckily withdrawn) vandalism.

The pavement sellers in Bombay's Flora Fountain know their books better than their Delhi counterparts, and charge more. I shall always associate these stalls with one of the city's more gifted writers: Dom Moraes, whose *Green is the Grass*, written when the author was thirteen, I have picked up on two separate occasions, the second copy a replacement for the first—this borrowed by a friend and never returned. (I have since learnt that Mr Moraes himself does not own a copy.) Some shops specialize in old Penguins; others in pirated books, one (behind the High Court) even in art and architecture. A short distance away, near Metro Cinema, lies the New and Second-hand Bookshop, with its two floors of old stuff stacked from floor to ceiling.

Calcutta, it must be said, has a grossly inflated reputation as a city of book lovers. Certainly, the stalls at College Street, once so renowned for their stocks, now sell nothing but college texts. Indeed, the only worthwhile shop is not on the pavement but in a building just off the street. This is Subarnarekha, run by an occasional publisher of left literature who is not above stocking cricket books for the more bourgeois members of his clientele. Of more worth, till their recent eviction, were the shops located on the pavement between Gariahat and Gole Park in south Calcutta, in a smoky, dimly lit stretch finely described in the opening pages of Amitav Ghosh's novel *The Shadow Lines*. These stalls would keep a range of history, fiction, and social science books, a surprisingly low proportion of which were of Marxist provenance.

Here and there on the street in the city one might still buy old novels. But it is more or less clear that the used-book market in Calcutta is dying. In Madras, alas, it is dead, extinguished fifteen years ago by the arsonist who, at the behest of the property mafia, burnt down the Moore Market, within whose red walls lay at least forty bookshops. Moore Market was lucky in its location—right next to the Madras Central Railway Station. The broad verandahs of the rectangular red building were lined with bookstores, some spilling over into the interior. While most stalls had eccentrically mixed collections, some were more focused in their choice of what to stock: one shop was even known for its collection of books on, and magazines about, the game of bridge. The fire that devastated Moore Market was widely believed to be sabotage. In any case, it was to the Madras book trade what the demolition of the Babri Masjid was to

Indian secularism: a single, definitive and comprehensively destructive act of annihilation.

It is curious how particular bazaars call to mind particular books. The used-book trade in Ahmedabad finds expression, as in Delhi, in a colourful market that unfolds itself once a week, on Sundays, under Ellis Bridge. Here, bookstalls run cheek by jowl with sellers of pots and pans, nuts and bolts, and steel almirahs. On half a dozen visits, I never failed to pick up a copy of *The God that Failed*, a collection of essays by writers disenchanted by communism, such as Arthur Koestler and Ignazio Silone. The book was the perfect present to take back to the Calcutta intellectuals in whose midst I then lived.

Pavement bookstalls are in some respects quite different from stores housed in more permanent structures. These latter are usually run by men who are keenly aware of the nature and value of what they stock. By contrast, a visit to the pavement is rich in the unexpected, for one never knows what one will find, and at what price. It can also be a test of character. For example, if you sight a Verrier Elwin first edition, it takes an effort of will to keep the thrill out of your limbs and out of your voice. The trick is to casually hold the book between two fingers, pretend to look elsewhere in the pile, while casually asking the owner the price. But more often than not, he has noticed the way your eyes lit up when they chanced upon the book. This, indeed, is psychological warfare of a high order. There is, however, one situation when you are assured of victory; when rain clouds gather overhead, book prices come tumbling down as fast as the mercury. Faced with the end of the day's business, the man will sell you the Elwin for half the price he would ask when unthreatened by nimbus.

Also on Ellis Bridge, if in a very permanent old stone building, is the New Order Book Company, established as far back as 1939. I first visited the place in the early 1980s, but was intimidated by the learning of its founder and owner, Dinkar *bhai*, and the prices of his books. He was very superior with me, as he needed to be, for he was accustomed to dealing with the Tatas and the Sarabhais. Feeling for my

pride and—perhaps more crucially—for my wallet, I chose to patronize the Sunday Market the other side of the bridge.

Last year I was back in Ahmedabad and, a working man now, walked into New Order. Dinkar *bhai* was dead, but his work was carried
on by his wife, Saroj *behn*, and her assistant, Leela *behn*. Judging by
the dust and cobwebs I might have been the only visitor there in
months. I was allowed to potter around. When I enquired about stuff
on Gandhi, I was asked to come home to look at the books there:
lunch was also offered. The two ladies gave me a lift, in an ancient Fiat
driven by a more ancient driver. En route we made several stops, to
allow Saroj *behn* to buy the *roti* and *sabzi* she needed for the unexpected guest.

The house, when we got to it, was out of Charles Dickens's *Great
Expectations* and *Bleak House*, combined. No outsider had been in it
for years. A bra lay carelessly draped over a sofa: it could have belonged
to Miss Havisham. The grime on the bathroom mirror was a couple
of inches thick. Still, what stood out was the old lady's devotion to her
husband's work (they had no children). She was very pleased when I
told her I owned a copy of New Order's very good and very scarce reprint of the set of Gandhi's journal, *Young India*; Dinkar *bhai*, she
said, had planned also to reprint its successor, *Harijan*. In fact, some
old issues of *Harijan* lay around the house. I demanded to see them
and, when they came, bought them. The prices the lady charged made
me deeply ashamed of what I had once felt about her husband.

My own favourite of all India's second-hand bookshops is Bangalore's Select, run by K.K.S. Murthy from an unprepossessing white
building situated in a quiet lane off Brigade Road. Murthy's father,
K.B.K. Rao, was a local legend, both for his charm, a part of which
lay in his ability to consistently undervalue his books. The son, who
has inherited the charm, has acquired a national reputation through
his biannual appearances at the World Book Fair in Delhi.

Some years ago, a friend who knows my passion for used-book-
stores visited Hay-on-Wye, the village on the Welsh border where
there are some fifty such stores. There he picked up, for me, a limited
edition of this John Arlott poem:

A Second-hand Bookshop

The sunlight filters through the panes
Of book-shop windows, pockmarked grey
By years of grimy city rains,
And falls in mild, dust-laden ray
Across the stock, in shelf and stack,
Of this old bookshop-man who brought,
To a shabby shop in a cul-de-sac,
Three hundred years of print and thought.

Like a cloak hangs the bookshop smell,
Soothing, unique and reminding:
The book-collector knows its spell,
Subtle hints of books and binding—
In the fine, black bookshop dust
Paper, printer's-ink and leather,
Binder's-glue and paper-rust
And time, all mixed together.

'Blake's Poems, Sir—ah, yes, I know,
Bohn did it in the old black binding,
In '83.' Then shuffles slow
To scan his shelves, intent on finding
This book of songs he has not heard,
With that deaf searcher's hopeful frown
Who knows the nightingale, a bird
With feathers grey and reddish-brown.

This was written about a bookshop in a small Sussex or Hampshire town, but the spirit certainly applies to other such shops elsewhere in the world, and three lines seem to have been written for the Select Bookshop of K.B.K. Rao and K.K.S. Murthy: 'This old bookshop-man who brought/ To a shabby shop in a cul-de-sac/ Three hundred years of print and thought.'

II

What kinds of books might one pick up in these places? Once, in Select, my eyes seized upon a pamphlet exquisitely bound in green and gold cloth. From its size and appearance I thought it might be a rare nationalist tract, a first edition of a Tagore lecture perhaps. When I opened it I found that the first few pages were written over in hand. 'This is the horoscope of my daughter Janaki, born on March 22, 1910', the text began. Three or four pages of astrological calculations followed. These were then bound up with the Tamil calendar, or *panchangam,* for 1910–11. Although Mr Murthy charged an excessive price (fifty rupees) I brought the pamphlet home and showed it to my grandmother, who is named Janaki, and who, as it happens, was born on March 22, 1910. She confirmed that it was indeed her horoscope. 'After your grandfather died', she told me, 'our possessions were scattered here and there, and I lost many things.'

My collection includes many books that have passed through the hands of the rich or famous. On the road in Daryaganj I bought *Duleep: His Man and His Game,* a rare, privately printed volume of tributes in memory of the great cricketer K.S. Duleepsinhji. It was a presentation copy, given to the former owner by the dashing left-handed Test batsman, K.M. (Khandu) Rangnekar. Behind the High Court in Bombay I once bought a massive book on Berlin by Giles McDonough. After I reached home I saw that the prelim pages had been carefully pasted together; cutting them open, I discovered that the author had previously presented the book to that column of Bombay society, Camelia Panjabi. Then, in Mr Jayavelu's still-mourned shop in Moore Market, I happened upon a first edition of Verrier Elwin's *Maria Murder and Suicide.* This was inscribed 'To Violet, with love from Joachim.' These were Joachim and Violet Alva, Congress politicians who read and appreciated books that their heirs (also Congress politicians) evidently had no place for.

The last time I was in Bombay, I had arranged to meet an old friend for lunch in Churchgate. I spent the hour before our meeting on the pavement. Here I saw a collection of science fiction stories edited by Kingsley Amis, dating to the 1960s. When we were in college my friend had liked this kind of stuff. Since our lunch was, among other things, a nostalgia trip, I bought the Amis to gift him. When I handed it over he looked inside—which I had omitted to do—and found from the fly-leaf that this was the very copy which he and his wife had gifted one of *their* friends twenty years before.

But the most curious of all my purchases was a little biography of Gandhi I bought at the New and Second-hand Bookshop. This was written by a priest, Joseph Doke, and first published in 1907. Although my copy was a later reprint, I was glad to have it, for the author had been a close associate of Gandhi's. I asked the shop to post it to me in Delhi, where I then lived. When the book arrived and I opened it again I noticed that the one-time owner's name was written on the fly-leaf: 'Gopalkrishna Gandhi, July 1957.' I knew this man well, and in fact his hand had scarcely changed in thirty-five years. I immediately went over to his place with the book. He had forgotten that he once owned it. But he remembered that in the summer of 1957 he was in Bombay, for his father was critically ill. He supposed that after his father died the book had got lost in the turmoil. I suggested that the book was rightly his. 'No, you keep it', he said generously. He then pulled out a volume from his shelf, and said: 'I have this, anyway.' 'This' was the first edition of the Doke book, laminated and bound for the owner by the National Archives. On the book's fly-leaf Devadas Gandhi—Gopal's father and the Mahatma's son— had written: 'This is the finest biography of Bapu.' Gopal, naturally, is well pleased with his copy of Doke. And I am more than moderately satisfied with mine.

Half-Marx

My feelings about *Das Kapital* are the same as my feelings about the *Koran*. I know it is historically important and I know that many people, not all of whom are idiots, find it a sort of Rock of Ages and containing inspiration. Yet when I look into it, it is to me inexplicable that it can have this effect. Its dreary, out-of-date academic theorising seems so extraordinarily unsuitable as material for the purpose. . . . Will you promise to read it again, if I do?

—John Maynard Keynes to George Bernard Shaw,
December 1934

When Karl Marx published *Das Kapital* in 1868, he thought he was doing for economics what Charles Darwin had already done for biology with *The Origin of Species* (which had appeared nine years before). So did his friend Engels, who wrote eight reviews puffing his friend's book, in four languages, and under at least three pseudonyms. However, subsequent history has brutally distinguished between *Capital* and *Origin*. Where biology textbooks always begin and often end with Darwin, the posthumous status within economics of the German revolutionary is best captured in Paul Samuelson's remark that Marx was a 'minor post-Ricardian'.

That remark—buried somewhere in the middle of Samuelson's bestselling textbook, *Economics*—so enraged two Swedish Marxists that they wrote a two-volume 'alternative' textbook, entitled *Anti-Samuelson*. The publisher has long since pulped the unsold copies of this book, although I am told it still circulates in xeroxes in the hostels of the Jawaharlal Nehru University in New Delhi.

In JNU they believe that *Das Kapital* is the first and certainly the last word in economic theory, but one tends to agree with Samuelson. There is a problem with Marx's main assumption—that labour was the source of all value, and another with his main prediction—that there would be a progressive impoverishment of the Western working class. But *Capital* is unreadable as well as wrong. When Mahatma Gandhi was interned at the Aga Khan Palace in the early 1940s, he was persuaded by one of his socialist colleagues to take up *Capital.* He guiltily gave up after the first chapter on commodities and 'commodity fetishism'; so did I, forty years later and fifty years younger, when ordered to study the book as a student in Calcutta.

Gandhi's difficulties, and mine, can be better appreciated by considering the table of contents, not of the book as a whole, but only of that remarkable first chapter:

CHAPTER I: COMMODITIES

1. The two Factors of a Commodity: Use–Value and Value (Substance of Value, Magnitude of Value)
2. Twofold Character of the Labour Embodied in Commodities
3. The Form of Value, or Exchange–Value
   A.   Elementary, Isolated, or Accidental Form of Value
      a. The two Poles of the Expression of Value: Relative Value Form and Equivalent Form
      b. Relative Value Form
         (i) Nature and Meaning of Relative Value Form
         (ii) Quantitative Determination of Relative Value Form
      c. Equivalent Form
      d. Elementary Form of Value considered as a Whole
   B.   Total or Extended Form of Value
      a. Extended Relative Form of Value
      b. Particular Equivalent Form

        c. Defects of the Total or Extended Form of Value

    C.   Generalized Form of Value
        a. The Changed Character of this Form of Value
        b. Developmental Relation between the Relative Form
           of Value and the Equivalent Form
        c. Transition from the Generalised Form of Value to the
           Money Form

    D.   Money Form of Value

    4. The Mystery of the Fetishistic Character of Commodities

This is taken from an early English edition; I cannot imagine how it must read in the original German. For all this, *Capital* was issued in the Everyman's Library, a decision based (one supposes) on other than literary grounds. Asked to introduce the book was the Oxford economist G.D.H. Cole, of whom A.J.P. Taylor once wrote—'he was as close to a saint as any man I have ever known.' The good don Cole had to struggle while deviating, as decently as possible, from the principle that one must only introduce books one can or should recommend. He allows that '*Capital* is not an easy book to read; and it is a safe guess that only a small minority of those who regard themselves as Marxists have read it all.' He concedes that 'for the modern reader who approaches Marx in any spirit save that of blind acceptance, these [first] chapters are extraordinarily hard to understand.' He admits that the labour theory of value is all wrong, but thinks that it is not Marx but his predecessors who must take the blame: for 'it is important to observe that not one single idea in this theory of value was invented by Marx, or would have been regarded by him as an original contribution of his own to economic science. Marx merely took over this conception of value from the classical economists . . .'

Capital is definitely not a book for every man, as witness its reception in the Soviet Union, where the exchange value of the book was accurately measured in the literary black market. A Western Sovietologist visiting Moscow in the 1970s found that for seventeen volumes of Brezhnev you could get ten volumes of Lenin, for Lenin unexpurgated the first volume of *Capital* (the only one published in Marx's lifetime); and for the latter, considered by some the most influential book since the Bible, you could get, if you wished, the Nobel Prize acceptance speech of Alexander Solzhenitsyn.

II

Karl Marx was trained as a philosopher, made a living as a commentator on social and political issues and ended life as a self-trained economist. Marx himself believed that his career path reflected the importance of economics in intellectual work, and beyond that, in human life in general. In *Reading Capital*—a book once much cited by leftists in College Street as well as JNU—the French philosopher Louis Althusser gravely announced that there had occurred, sometime around 1855 or 1856, an 'epistemological break' in Marx's thought. Before the break, Marx had been a bleeding-heart idealist, pained by human suffering; after it, a firmly grounded materialist, whose diagnosis of capitalism bore the stamp of a coldly clinical and revolutionary science. Althusser, a former schoolmaster, was in effect awarding Marx fifty per cent, zero for the first half of his intellectual life and full marks for the second.

My Marx marks card also adds up to fifty per cent, but it distributes the zeros and hundreds rather differently. With the near-simultaneous death of Althusser and the command economies of Eastern Europe, it is safe once more to study (and celebrate) the eloquent and immensely powerful works of the early, so to say 'pre-scientific', Marx. I think, for instance, of the 'Economic and Philosophical Manuscripts', written in 1843–4, which Marx modestly left 'to the gnawing criticism of the mice'; disinterred and published only in the 1930s, these present a moving and soulful analysis of how modern society alienates men from each other and from nature. I think also of the *Communist Manifesto*, a work (to quote Edmund Wilson) which combines 'the terseness and trenchancy of Marx with the candour and humanity of Engels, compress[ing] with terrific vigour into forty or fifty pages a general theory of history, an analysis of European society and a programme for revolutionary action.' I think, last, of his marvellous reports on contemporary French politics, *Class Struggles in France* and the *Eighteenth Brumaire of Louis Bonaparte*, both illuminated by the author's sharp sociological insight and his unforgiving portraits of effete rulers and failed revolutionaries.

Economics was to easily absorb the shock of *Das Kapital*, but well before that work was conceived Marx had already transformed, for ever, the terrain of the 'other' social sciences: history, sociology, anthropology, and political science. It was Marx who taught us that inequality was not natural but rooted in institutions created by men; it was Marx who told us to look out always for the resistance to authority by those at the bottom of the heap. Respectable economists might think that Marx added but a footnote or two to the work of David Ricardo; but I honour him as *the* 'major pre-Weberian', the forerunner and inspirer of the greatest social theorist of them all, Max Weber.

The Mahatma's Marksheets

Once, while I was in college, I picked up the autobiography of a man who, at various points in his career, had served as vice-chancellor of the University of Delhi, governor of the Reserve Bank, and finance minister of the Government of India. Curiously, his memoirs had as many pages on his achievements in school and college as on his experiences running central banks and devising union budgets. He first reproduced his matriculation results: the marks listed by subject, never less than 96 per cent. We then learnt of how, in his intermediate examination, he set a record that stood for years in the Bombay Presidency. As if this was not enough, a statistical proof of his gold medals in the B.A. and M.A. followed.

Later, as I read more such works, I came to regard this as characteristic rather than curious. When they came to write their memoirs, famous professors of sociology and high officials of the Indian Civil Service alike seemed to single out, above all other high-water marks, success in school examinations. Then I came across an exception: the autobiography of Mohandas K. Gandhi. The Mahatma claimed: 'I was not regarded as a dunce in high school', before—in the spirit of truth with which the work was conceived—speaking of the difficulty he once had with Sanskrit and, for a time, with Euclidean geometry.

Gandhi spoke in general terms, but his somewhat vague recollections of life at school were to be given a devastating specificity in a book published in 1965. It is called *Mahatma Gandhi as a Student*, and its author, J.M. Upadhyaya, had been principal at the high school in Rajkot where the Mahatma had spent seven years.

Upadhyaya's book packs a great deal into its seventy-four pages. The boy Gandhi, we learn, changed several schools before he reached the age of ten. At times his attendance was noticeably lax: a mere 110 days out of 238 in standard III, for example. His marks at the annual examinations normally averaged between 45 per cent and 55 per cent. In junior school he was always comfortably beaten by one Tribhuvan Bhatt, who in the manner of 'toppers' of the time ended as a babu, albeit an elevated one. (His last job was as chief minister of Rajkot state.) The one early sign of the young Mohandas's superiority to his fellows was that his elder brother Karsandas was a less distinguished student still. Karsandas lost two years, and ended up in the same class as his sibling, where he usually logged lower marks.

Things turned worse in middle school. Mohandas's attendance slipped again, as he attended on a sick father and a newly wedded wife. Asked to repeat a year, he bucked up and for once 'grew quite serious in studies'. He achieved 8th rank in class, with a (for him) remarkably high overall score of 66.5 per cent. The momentum carried over into high school. Outside the classroom, his life was rich in incident—he played the 'lustful husband', experimented with meat, and tried unsuccessfully to sell some of the family gold to pay off a debt incurred by brother Karsandas. Yet, despite this, his attendance at school was 125 days out of 125, and he came fourth in class, with an average in excess of 60 per cent. In Upadhyaya's words, 'he could no longer be described as a mediocre student.'

This judgement was put sternly to the test in the third week of November 1887, when Gandhi travelled by train to Ahmedabad to take the matriculation examination of Bombay University. This was his first visit to a city he was to later make his own. In a lovely detail, Upadhyaya notes that Gandhi's examination number was 2275. There were 3067 candidates in all. Of these, 799 were successful. Gandhi's rank was 404th, and his marksheet was as follows:

English   89/200
Gujarati   45.5/100
Mathematics   59/175
General Knowledge   54/150

The total, 247.5 marks out of 625, comes to an average of about 40 per cent. Mohandas K. Gandhi could once again be described as a mediocre student.

Mahatma Gandhi as a Student is a work that bears testimony both to the author's industry and to the Gujarati respect for old records. And it contains much more than marksheets. We learn here that despite his rather ordinary peformance in examinations, Gandhi's middle-school teacher marked his conduct as 'very good', whereas the best any other student achieved was 'good'. Upadhyaya's reproduction of the English paper that Gandhi answered in his matric exam seems to give certain clues to his later development. For 45 marks, he was asked to 'write an essay of about forty lines on the advantages of a cheerful disposition.' Could not this answer have helped encourage him to become that *rara avis*, a politician who was never known to have lost his temper? For 25 marks, he was asked to paraphrase a poem which described how Jesus would reveal himself only to the poor peasant, not to the rich men whose chariots went contemptuously 'whirling past'. Might not this exercise have stoked a precocious awareness of exploitation and injustice?

We must also consider the significance of the sociological snippets that Upadhyaya so casually throws our way. Consider this: Mohandas's best friend in high school was a Muslim, while their headmaster was a Parsi. The school building was constructed with a gift of Rs 63, 000 from the Nawab of Junagadh. In his last years in school, as Mohandas's marks percentage climbed into the upper fifties, he was given a scholarship of Rs 10 per month, this award being in the names of two Kathiawari nobles, one Hindu, one Muslim. Should we not consider this as part of an early training in multiculturalism, as essential preparation for the making of the interreligious Mahatma?

But, the cynic will say, we can't finally get away from the marksheets. By way of apology and, indeed, justification, let me then remind the reader of the career of one Albert Einstein. Nothing, writes one biographer, '*nothing* in Einstein's early history suggests dormant genius'. The boy was able to speak fluently only at the age of nine. When Albert's father asked the headmaster of his elementary school what profession he thought his son should prepare himself for, he got the answer: 'It doesn't matter; he'll never make a success of anything.' Later, at the Luitpold Gymnasium in Munich, Einstein was 'still slightly backward' and failed to complete his diploma. Later still, after he had moved to Zurich, Einstein failed the entrance examination to the university. 'The accepted reason for his failure is that although his knowledge of mathematics was exceptional he did not reach the necessary standard in modern languages or in zoology and botany.'

Such, in summary, were the academic records of the two men commonly regarded as the best, the wisest, and the most influential individuals of the twentieth century. Long ago, in the 1930s, the Bombay journalist D.F. Karaka wrote a biography of Gandhi entitled *Out of Dust, He Made Us into Men*. The reference was to the countless nationalists whose heroism and self-sacrifice was a direct consequence of the Mahatma's influence. Without him, these Indians would have been content being ordinary lawyers, teachers, brokers, and clerks or, perhaps, even black-marketeers. One knows what Karaka meant. So did J.M. Upadhyaya, except that he added a meaningful caveat: 'Gandhiji, it has been well said, could fashion heroes out of common clay. *His first, and, undoubtedly, his most successful experiment was with himself.*'